A Manual for the Modern Mystic

How to Practice Being in the Presence of God

Rio Olesky

iUniverse, Inc.
Bloomington

Copyright © 2011 by Rio Olesky

All rights reserved. No part of this book may be used or reproduced by any means, graphic, electronic, or mechanical, including photocopying, recording, taping or by any information storage retrieval system without the written permission of the publisher except in the case of brief quotations embodied in critical articles and reviews.

iUniverse books may be ordered through booksellers or by contacting:

iUniverse
1663 Liberty Drive
Bloomington, IN 47403
www.iuniverse.com
1-800-Authors (1-800-288-4677)

Because of the dynamic nature of the Internet, any web addresses or links contained in this book may have changed since publication and may no longer be valid. The views expressed in this work are solely those of the author and do not necessarily reflect the views of the publisher, and the publisher hereby disclaims any responsibility for them.

Any people depicted in stock imagery provided by Thinkstock are models, and such images are being used for illustrative purposes only.

Certain stock imagery © Thinkstock.

ISBN: 978-1-4502-9403-4 (sc)
ISBN: 978-1-4502-9405-8 (hc)
ISBN: 978-1-4502-9404-1 (ebook)

Printed in the United States of America

iUniverse rev. date: 03/14/2011

Dedication:

To my wife Arrow and my children, Heidi, Jeremy, Avra, Josh, and Tai, who collectively have brought me more challenges to keep me on track then anyone or anything else. You have also provided me with the love, inspiration, joy and support that made the work worth doing

Contents

Acknowledgments — ix

Preface — xi

Introduction — xv

Chapter 1: The Law of Creativity — 1

Chapter 2: The Law of Survival — 29

Chapter 3: The Law of Both/And — 55

Chapter 4: The Law of the Eternal Present — 79

Chapter 5: The Law of Love — 105

Chapter 6: The Law of Service — 128

Chapter 7: The Law of Harmony — 150

Chapter 8: The Law of Eternal Life — 179

Chapter 9: The Law of Abundance — 205

Chapter 10: The Law of Karma — 234

Chapter 11: The Law of Impermanence — 260

Chapter 12: The Law of Transcendence — 283

Chapter 13: The Universe Wants Us to Be Happy — 313

Bibliography — 331

Acknowledgments

To all the people who have been students in Tuesday Nite Class. You have consistently kept me growing as an astrologer and mystic in order to keep up with your own growth and to satisfy your curiosity about the nature of life as I perceive it to be.

I would also like to acknowledge three outstanding editors -- Susan O'Terra Foster, Diana Badger and Arrow Olesky. You helped teach me how to write and held my feet to the fire to make this book as good as it can be.

Preface

In 1967 I was a student at the University of California at Berkeley. This was a time of awakening. Radical political shifts, behavioral transformations, and consciousness development were pervasive. It was a confusing time but also a liberating one. I felt constantly challenged to be aware of everything, have an opinion on everything, and be ready to change it or fight for it at a moment's notice. In school I was confronted with intellectual challenges common to all students—read this, memorize that, write, speak, or analyze what other people found important. But my real education came outside the classroom because my questions rarely coincided with the curriculum. I was consumed with the meaning of life. Why are we here? Where is here? Who is the "I" who is asking these questions? Who and what have made me as I am? My major was interdisciplinary humanities, and I took classes in history, philosophy, literature, art, and music history. Regardless of the breadth of the course of study, I did not find satisfactory answers to my questions. I was confronted with the enormity of life, yet felt I had no tools to help me unravel the meaning in the mystery.

One day, while visiting a friend, I happened upon an astrology book. It was simplistic and superficial, and as a "college-educated intellectual" I had a bias against the superstition inherent in this mystical mumbo jumbo. But something about the content of this book appealed to me in a riveting way. I felt compelled to buy the same book, go into my room, close and lock the door (so none of my friends could see I was reading this garbage), and read. Good astrology books were hard to find at that time. Most of the really good ones written to that point were out of print. What excited me wasn't the quality of the book that I picked up but that astrology addressed so many of the issues that had consumed my mind for years and that I had found no one and nothing that had provided reasonable answers. A lifetime love affair had begun. I realized that astrology is a system that provides a conceptual framework that enables me to pose my many questions, as well as to find plausible answers to them. Eventually, I became a professional astrologer and continue in private practice to the time of this writing.

In my years of study, I discovered that astrology is a language through which to develop an understanding of the nature of life. It is a concept of universal order based on the harmony of the celestial bodies of our solar system. Astrology is one of the most ancient mystical methods that correlates planetary bodies to the experiences of people and earth-based events. It is a system that enables a person to see who he is and what is his place in the universal scheme of things. Learning to work within the astrological system enabled me to become more aware of the totality of life without feeling alienated or intimidated. I learned that the signs of the zodiac and the planets of our solar system provide a symbolic system that is a reflection of the laws of the universe. A personal horoscope is a structure that interfaces the individual soul, the universe, and the soul's past and current emotional, psychological, familial, spiritual, and physical reality. It is a language that provides a matrix for understanding the individual incarnation of an eternal spiritual being, which is what you and I are. Astrology is a way to understand that we are all from the same point of origin but that each of us has his or her own unique signature.

Over the years I became a professional astrologer, giving personal readings as well teaching classes and writing a monthly column for my website and local newspapers. But astrology alone wasn't enough to provide an intimate connection to the Divine. So even though I had found a valuable tool, my quest for spiritual connection was not complete. I realized that the missing piece was a way to relate directly, something that could be provided by meditating. After trying different types of techniques and finding each one insufficient,

I was given a copy of *The Autobiography of a Yogi*, by Paramahansa Yogananda.

Yogananda was an enlightened being, the first Hindu yogi to come to the United States from India with the sole purpose of teaching Westerners about Eastern thought. Some of those ideas lead the seeker directly to the enlightened state. Reading the book was a revelation, and I felt as if I was transported into an expanded state of consciousness. Yogananda died in 1952. He was in incredibly prolific writer, leaving behind books, commentaries on scripture, and weekly lessons for each student/seeker. By studying much of this material, I was able to find my place in the universe. Even today, some forty years after connecting with this great being, I find his words inspiring and uplifting—a wonderful way to regain my perspective about life and what really matters. It is my honor and privilege to bring you some of his ideas and concepts in this book.

Introduction

The world, existing in God's suggestion of a relativity of time and space, is merely a condensed thought of God. The wonder I behold is that everything in this universe God has created out of nothing but His own dream, His own ideations. Man's difficulty is that this dream is imposed upon him, like a cosmic hypnosis. When he supinely surrenders his own will to delusive somnolence, he has little or no control over the dream happenings.

—Paramahansa Yogananda

What is a mystic? A mystic is someone who believes in existence beyond human comprehension; someone who values inner spiritual experience rather than relying on external authorities or scripture. A mystic is someone who has the drive and courage to look both within and outside himself or herself in order to discover the true nature of life. But it's not an easy or quick path.

Some people have a deep yearning to transcend the mundane reality of daily routines and long-range professional goals. They seek a deeper understanding of how the universe works. They have an unyielding drive to know why we are here. They want to discover who they are in the grand scheme of the universe. These are some of the prerequisites to becoming a mystic. This book is an attempt to provide the modern mystic, the contemporary spiritual seeker, a way of perceiving and relating to life in a way that will enhance and expand his or her consciousness. It describes ways of integrating individual awareness within the historical time frame in which we live.

Consciousness development is perhaps the ultimate purpose and prime reason that life exists. It is something that has fascinated me since adolescence. This book discusses different techniques that help us develop our consciousness. Commitment to that process is one quality that defines the mystic. The process takes us beyond the limitations of the rational mind. It takes us outside the boundaries of the physical plane. The mystic's goal is complete identification with Divine Spirit. It is the desire to have access to limitless information, wisdom, and healing power. Ultimately, the mystic can perceive life as a never-ending, always unfolding creative force in a reality in which everything is interconnected.

Mysticism is a path that views life from a transcendent perspective. It accepts and acknowledges experiences, even if they don't seem logical. Emotions are examples of human experience that are universal yet illogical. We all know what it feels like to love, to fear, or to be angry. To analyze why those feelings are present can limit our experience of them. Mysticism allows for the liberating loss of boundaries that separate self (a person, a temporary individuated soul) from Self (Spirit, the Divine, eternal). In *Earthy Mysticism* William McNamara states:

> The mystic is not a special kind of person; every person is a special kind of mystic. The mystic is one who consciously and thoroughly immerses himself in the mystery of life and enjoys communion with ultimate Being. Everyone is partially immersed in the mystery, and to some small degree, enjoys communion with ultimate Being. ... Little by little, quite imperceptibly, the Spirit of God seeps in and takes possession of the mystic. The same Holy Spirit that christened Jesus in one way christens the mystic in another.

Some people have inherent talents that provide a relatively easy journey to consciousness development. Their mystical orientation is obvious. All they have to do is tune in to a rich, intuitive awareness

Introduction

of the world around them. For the majority of people, however, the path is neither easy nor obvious.

Most mystics—or those who strive for mystical attunement—share a sense of spiritual alienation, a discontent with the accepted metaphysical and philosophical beliefs of their time. To avoid dogma and live in truth, they are willing to endure tremendous deprivation and suffering in order to come face to face with the Divine. The mystical path can be joyful and enlightening, but it is rarely risk-free. In the traditions of many indigenous cultures, the shaman is a mystic. He or she may be required to face and overcome fearsome enemies. Some of these are terrifying demons who may or may not be external to the shaman. Like the shaman, we have to confront our fears, to overcome feelings of emotional suffering and spiritual alienation in order to gain access to knowledge of how the universe truly works. The rewards of this pursuit are wondrous. We can tap into the limitless light, joy, and creativity that are the essence of life itself. With this understanding we can serve as teachers, healers, and prophets. We can move beyond the physical and mental limits that restrict others. Yet this is a path that requires patience, perseverance, and commitment. Christian mystics of the Middle Ages wrote about the pain of the temptation to leave the mystical path and pursue sensual pleasure and material security. They revealed their terror in confronting the devil and his minions. Today, we might frame this as their having to deal with their own internal conflicts, blind spots, and neuroses. But regardless of whether the obstacles on the path are external or internal, personal or universal, this path can be painful. It also can be dangerous. It is not unusual for a young, aspiring shaman to die or get lost and never be seen again as he pursues his goal of spiritual connection. There are many, however, who successfully walked this path, overcoming the demons and temptations and acquiring the mystical goal of God consciousness. Who are some of our forebears who had the commitment and ability to overcome the obstacles? Who are some of the more well-known mystics throughout history?

The prophets of the Old Testament were mystics. So were Jesus and Mohammed. So are all the yogis and living Buddhas who seek to quiet the mind of all thought in order to experience a transcendent state of awareness. They have experienced direct, firsthand knowledge of the Divine through personal contact with Oneness. Mystics such as these focus their attention away from physical reality and identification with ego-driven desires. They also are able to realize that intellectualizing about God is futile, because it takes them farther away from Source. The path of the mystic relies on intuition and creativity in order to perceive Spirit and to share it with others. Transcendence from self-awareness to Self-Awareness can take place only by quieting the mind. There is a saying, "If you've been there, you know." The same could be said about mystical experience.

Around the time of Jesus there was a group of mystics called the Gnostics. The term Gnostic comes from the Greek word *gnosis*, which means knowledge. The Gnostics integrated beliefs from Asia, Babylonia, Egypt, Greece, and Syria (all of which practiced paganism at that time). Through this integration, the Gnostics came to believe that the ultimate Creator lives beyond the physical plane, but that each person carries within him a spark of that Creator. The big bang theory to which contemporary physicists and cosmologists ascribe is not all that different from the primary Gnostic concept. By becoming aware of our own divine spark, we can be consciously connected to God. As mystics, the Gnostics believed that they could connect directly with the Divine and needed no intervening religion or clergy to facilitate that process.

To the mystic, the important thing is to be at one with the Divine, not to discuss or define it. The focus and result of the subjective experience of the seeker is to experience the transcendent state of consciousness in peace and with the fulfillment that accompanies that state. With that transcendence we can feel in a visceral, intimate way the divine qualities of being. These qualities are the birthright of every human being. Among them are the states of love, joy, peace, bliss, light, wisdom, transformation, transcendence, intuition, and harmony. By tapping into one or more of those states, our mundane lives are transformed. As mystics, our satisfactions in life come from expanding and deepening our connection to those states. The need for external stimulation and material-plane fulfillment becomes less of a priority than the drive for immersion in and communion with Divine Oneness.

Mysticism has never captured the imagination of the public. Although there have been mystics throughout history and in all cultures, the demands on the time, energy, and resources of the seeker are too much or simply uninteresting to most people. Nevertheless, it has been an acceptable and understandable path within many cultures for most of human history. That acceptance declined in popularity after the Copernican revolution of the sixteenth century. Copernicus was a brilliant philosopher, astronomer, and mathematician who intellectually surmised and boldly stated that the sun was the center of the solar system, not the earth. Hence, the sun was the real source of creation, not humanity. Prior to Copernicus's breakthrough realization, it was taken on faith that the earth was the center of the solar system. Humanity, as the most complex life form on the planet, was seen as central to the entire scheme of creation. Gradually, his ideas were accepted, and science was born, but the shock to the human psyche—and our place in the universal scheme of things—continues to have consequences, even into modern times. For example, we are no longer to assume that anything other than quantifiable facts is true. The Copernican revolution prioritized rationality over intuition and the intellect over the mystical. Henceforth, if something couldn't be quantified and logically proven to exist or be true, it wasn't. The good news about the Copernican revolution was that it opened the door to industrial and technological innovations that have radically altered the human experience. Unfortunately, with the earth no longer at the center of the solar system, it ceased to be revered or seen as central to our human experience. Aspects of life that derived their power and prominence from their connection to the earth, the intuitive, the emotional, and the feminine principal, in general, were all assigned second-class status. Any information derived from one's own inner knowing was demeaned and denounced. The mystical path was no longer seen as a valid way of perceiving and defining reality. Science has provided us with tremendous benefits, but the logic of the scientific revolution has also led to alienation from our intimate, mystical connection with the earth and the universe.

It is my belief that the intention of Original Source is that all individual beings experience life in the spirit of joy and bliss. If this is true, there must be laws that can be perceived, understood, and worked with beyond the physical plane so that a seeker can achieve that goal. There must be an order that underlies life. I believe that we can achieve the qualities of joy and bliss by becoming aware of the universal laws, truths, and principles of life and by aligning our values, choices, and behaviors to coincide with those truths. Laws are defined as binding rules. Who created these laws, and who enforces them? Why should we discover and follow them? What are these universal principles? How do we know they exist? Why should we strive to work with them? What happens if we don't? How can they help us to know who we are in the context of the universe?

We can discover answers to these questions by developing our consciousness. This can be done by paying attention to our daily experiences, by following the teachings of enlightened masters, and by utilizing the techniques described in this book. As we contemplate and internalize these principles, we can enhance our freedom and happiness. The purpose of this book is to provide insight into what those laws are and how we can live in accordance with them. By following and living in truth, in a willing and open-hearted way, we discover the ultimate meaning and purpose of life. Our energy flows with the intention of Spirit.

Spiritual masters teach that in the beginning was the One, the Source of Being from which everything was created. The One was not created, and it will not perish. It is the essence of life that exists beyond all material phenomena. The One has always been in perfect harmony with itself, yet it can assume any form or expression of energy. We have learned from telescopes that points of light can suddenly appear in deep space. Most of them will exist only for miniscule fragments of time. Scientists believe that one of those points continued to exist and exploded in the big bang. This event, occurring billions of years ago, began life as we know it. All the elements, minerals, chemical combinations, and limitless forms that we perceive are emanations from that same point of light. It's as if that single point suddenly became an endless series of points, every one of them containing the qualities of its origin. One theory maintains that there is a similar spark that happens when a sperm cell connects with an egg. As it does, it attracts a discarnate soul and a new life is formed. Everything that exists today in the physical universe contains particles, molecules, and atoms that were generated at the time of the big bang. Within this endless series are forms, colors, and sounds that can inspire profound awe in the eye and ear of the beholder. I am reminded of the photographs from the Hubble telescope that showed pictures of star clusters, black holes, emerging solar systems, and dying stars. Amidst this profusion of manifestation, everything contains the seed of its source. At their core, all things contain the same germ. Everything is the center of the universe.

These universal laws function in all areas of life and on all levels of consciousness. For the sake of clarity and understanding in this book, I will define them separately, but they operate simultaneously.

This book uses the philosophical concept of universal law to describe states of consciousness and ways of accessing them. My challenge is to use words and logical concepts as vehicles to help the reader transcend logical and linear awareness. Some of these ideas are philosophical, metaphysical theories that I accept as true, such as karma and reincarnation. These concepts are defined in "The Law of Karma" (chapter 10) and "The Law of Eternal Life" (chapter 8), respectively. The conundrum in using these ideas is that they attempt to explain things intellectually that are more than intellectual. In attempting to do this, I am in the company of the vast majority of scholars, rabbis, priests, and imams who have done and are doing the same thing. Some have been quite successful in this venture. But the obvious problem is that words can create a barrier to experiencing the power of Spirit. It is perhaps impossible to experience the Divine through intellectual understanding, as it doesn't take into account other means of perceiving truth.

The mind and the intellect are useful tools for the mystic, even if by themselves they don't provide the means to connect deeply and immediately with Divine Spirit. I have spent most of my life studying, teaching, and counseling others by using the language of astrology. This is a system that integrates the rational with the intuitive. It is rational because it is based on a complex system that correlates planetary movement with life on earth. It is intuitive because understanding and working with this system requires that we transcend rational thought. Unfortunately, astrology has been marginalized by science, but those of us who maintain a mystical attitude toward life see it as a valuable tool.

Astrology can be a useful tool for the mystic. It is a system that correlates the positions of the planets with human experiences through archetypes of thought, feeling, and action. One of the useful concepts that astrology conveys is that of "synchronicity." This principle simply states that whatever happens at a particular moment shares characteristics with everything else that happens in that moment. It is not the positions of the planets in particular signs that cause something to happen or to create certain traits in a person born at that moment. Simply put, the configuration of planets at the time of a person's birth suggests the nature of that person. If we understand the symbology of the configuration in our lives, we can have a greater understanding of our potential in all areas of life on multiple levels of consciousness. With that knowledge, we can become more self-realized and ultimately expand our consciousness beyond human experience and into connection with the Divine.

The basis of astrology is the twelve signs of the zodiac, each one representing a unique cosmic principle. Astronomically, the signs are derived from designs formed by the fixed stars. Like a cosmic connect-the-dots, human beings have connected these stars to form patterns and images. Each of the signs, with its corresponding patterns and images, illuminates certain potential traits, characteristics, and behaviors unique to that sign.

Astrology connects the micro (you and me) with the macro (everything else). It is a beautiful illustration of the age-old mystical truth: as above, so below. As a conceptual system it helps to delineate the intrinsic order of the universe and how it works, and offers a way of interfacing the individual with the universal. It is a complex system that reflects the laws underlying the nature of life. In this book, the signs of the zodiac are archetypal concepts that contain information about universal laws. I have correlated one of the twelve signs with each universal law. By having a clear understanding of a sign, we can gain greater insight into the nature of the principle that it reflects. The emphasis of signs in our natal chart and the planets that are located in these signs provides us with an opportunity to experience the principles associated with those signs. We find that the astrological archetypes most emphasized in our horoscope correspond to the principles we most need to work with and learn from. Similarly, the lack of planet/sign combinations in our chart suggests laws that are not highly prioritized for us to work with in this lifetime. Knowing which laws are more or less prominent can help us create a strategy for living our lives in a more conscious way. For example, in my horoscope there is an emphasis in the area that seeks answers to the questions: "Why are we here, and what is the meaning of life?" It is an area that taps into the universal laws and mystery of life in order to discover answers to these questions. These laws apply to everybody and everything, but they are not hard-and-fast rules. They could be seen as principles, guidelines, or truths and utilized in different ways, depending on one's metaphysical point of view. My quest to find answers to these questions has ultimately led me to write this book.

Even if you are not familiar with your natal horoscope and have no interest in astrology, the universal laws or principles are at play throughout your life. Of course, there are other systems besides astrology that provide ways of perceiving the underlying order of the universe. By understanding and working with any of them, we can feel more connected to and less alienated from or overwhelmed by life. For example, from the scientific perspective, the periodic table of the elements is a template that provides information about the physical properties of all known substances. Yet it also can connect us to life in a mystical way, once we realize that those qualities exist for those substances anywhere in the universe. From that table we not only understand the inherent qualities of each mineral and gas but also how they combine or interact with other minerals or gasses and, ultimately, how all these substances emanate from the same source and are all intimately interconnected—a truly mystical realization.

Another such system that describes universal laws in terms of the physical plane is sacred geometry. This system describes the symmetries and proportions that are the basis of geometric forms. These patterns exist in molecular formations of minerals as well as musical harmonies, proportions of the human body, and the regulation of the movement of celestial bodies. Sacred geometry is the blueprint of creation. It describes the self-organizing process of nature and the inherent order that pervades the universe. It is a system that interfaces laws of the physical plane with that of the Spiritual Essence behind it. Sacred geometry is based on pure mathematical principles, as are art forms such as mandalas of both Eastern and Western cultures, Islamic mosaics, and various architectural designs from around the world. It also remains connected to nature and the earth through its correspondences to the forms and patterns manifested here.

In lieu of a mystical connection—a transcendent way of perceiving and relating to life—humanity has developed a tendency to become attached to things. Possessions, identities, experiences, or relationships have become primarily what we value and through which we seek meaning. However, attachments can be devices that limit us and that block us from seeing other, more expansive possibilities for fulfillment. Each of the signs of the zodiac and the principle that it represents has its own attachments. Being aware of the potential pitfalls of these attachments can allow us to become more aware of the positive potentials of each zodiacal archetype.

As a professional astrologer for over thirty-five years, I have seen how astrology provides a vehicle for mystical awareness. So although this is not an astrology book per se, I include astrological parallels in each chapter with the universal laws, or principles, because I think the system provides a useful, accurate, and practical framework for understanding and working with archetypes.

Just as you needn't be an astrologer to read this book, so also you needn't feel restricted to read the chapters sequentially. You may have a personal need to know more about your connection to the physical plane ("The Law of Survival," chapter 2), or you might be curious about social behaviors ("The Law of Harmony," chapter 7) or need a clearer understanding of family dynamics ("The Law of the Eternal Present," chapter 4). Or maybe you'll be interested in the laws that embody the more prominent signs in your birth chart or those of friends and family. Feel free to skip around and read the book in whatever order the chapters call to you. This is a good way of tuning in to your intuition. And because all the laws are continuously in play and completely interactive with each other, there is no real "order" or logical sequence of one law leading to another. The chapters and their enumeration of fundamental universal truths are ordered by their association with the signs of the zodiac as a useful framework, not in order of their significance. The order of significance is a personal matter. Thus, chapter 1 explores creation through its association with the first sign of the zodiac, Aries, and chapter 12 examines transcendence through its association with the twelfth sign, Pisces.

Each chapter begins with a definition and discussion of the main characteristics of the principle. Each of the universal laws operates within a framework. In order to successfully take advantage of any law, that framework must be understood and integrated. I offer guidance and examples of how to approach this. Then I define and discuss the astrological sign that embodies and reflects qualities of the law. Each chapter also has a section called "Flowing with This Law." This offers suggestions about various spiritual practices as well as practical activities that you can employ in order to work effectively with that law. Another section, "Not Flowing with This Law" (or "resisting this law"), defines some of the attachments and traps inherent in each principle. This will also suggest practical ways of either avoiding or changing behaviors that flow counter to the nature of the law. Because all the laws are constantly and interactively in play, some of the ways to accentuate one law may also be a way of accessing others. Similarly, we could misuse more than one law by engaging in certain behaviors. Each chapter also includes a section called "Spiritual Opportunity," which delineates the highest potential for experiencing and expressing the law and helps explain the liberating, empowering potential that each law embodies by connecting it with a specific divine quality. The "Bottom Line" section of each chapter distills the law down to its essence.

I also refer to the "higher" and "lower" octaves of each principle. This refers to levels of consciousness through which we can access the law. The higher octave pertains to its expression in ways that are of benefit to us, especially in terms of transcendent experience, as well as using the principle in ways that are beneficial to others. The lower octave refers to using the law only for personal gain or only in a mundane context. This concept is delineated more completely in "The Law of Love" (chapter 5).

It is my intention to make each of these principles accessible to you by defining them as guideposts and by interspersing illustrative stories, prayers, and affirmations in their delineation. The goal is to make each of them clearer and more understandable, enabling you to move ahead more rapidly on your own path of self-realization. Ultimately, I hope that you can become aware of your Source and start growing on your path to a state of happiness, fulfillment, and love.

This is a good introductory exercise into the mystical state: *Find the space between thought. Have a good feeling.*

Chapter 1: The Law of Creativity

Great indeed is the sublimity of the Creative, to which all beings owe their beginning and which permeates all heaven.

—*I Ching*, Wilhelm translation

Increase and Multiply

I used to live in a pristine part of Northern California on the Klamath River. It was wild and untamed and a perfect place for me to understand more about the nature of life. One of my friends was a person we called a mountain man. When I knew him, Hubert was in his fifties and had long reddish-brown hair and a beard. He alternately made his living by being a fishing guide and by climbing up and down steep mountain slopes, collecting huckleberry brush for the local brush plant. He would routinely pack up to one hundred pounds of brush up those slopes. The plant sold the brush to florists for bouquet filler. As a fisherman, he was without peer. One day after I had been fishing unsuccessfully from the river bank for hours, Hubert came by. He put his pole into the water where mine had been. In about thirty seconds he got a bite. Pulling in the fish, he threw his line out again, twenty feet away from the first cast. Another thirty seconds, another catch. His success in such a short time was a credit to his experience, his knowledge of fishing and of the river. Hubert had essentially lived out of doors most of his life. I assumed that since he was so close to nature that his daily observations of the physical plane would provide insights into the profound truths of life. One day he casually mentioned that everything in life has a purpose. I asked him what was the purpose of mosquitoes. Without hesitation he shot back, "To make more mosquitoes."

I'd asked about mosquitoes arbitrarily. It just popped into my mind. I could have asked what was the purpose of deer, or robins, or even people. The answer would have been the same, and the lasting image would have been more pleasant. But mosquitoes reminded me of my childhood. On summer evenings, when I was put to bed, my father would come into the room with a sprayer containing DDT. He would proceed to spray the entire room, especially the space around my bed, in order to kill all the mosquitoes that were buzzing around, waiting to feast on my blood. This seemed like a good idea at the time, as it did eliminate a potential bump or itch. Years later it was realized that the cure was worse than the problem. In any case, Hubert's words brought consternation. If he was right, mosquitoes have as much right to exist as we do. After all, we both come from the same Source. Yet mosquitoes are loathsome, disease-carrying insects. Isn't the idea to kill them before they make our life miserable? A more delightful take on the image of mosquitoes comes from the Dalai Lama. The Buddhists believe that all life is sacred and that people should strive to protect all forms. As if to validate Hubert's idea, the Dalai Lama has responded to the question of "How do you deal with mosquitoes when you are trying to meditate?" by saying, "We do the best we can." We don't have to allow mosquitoes, or any life form, to hurt us. It is important, however, to realize the common origin of all life. It's also important to realize that what applies to mosquitoes applies to people. If the purpose of mosquitoes is to make more mosquitoes, the purpose of people is to make more people.

In the Old Testament, Jehovah exhorts us to "Go forth and multiply." Assuming that the Bible is, in fact, the word of God, this is more than mere biological imperative. It is the command from the Creator, and we are under that commandment as much as insects. All life forms are connected by their need to create.

The Law of Creativity

The first universal law is creativity. It is the initial and most fundamental of the laws. It's the life-giving spark from which all the other laws emanate. This principle is continually at work. Mosquitoes are being created, humans are being created, solar systems are being created. Recent scientific photos of the outer regions of space have revealed dots or flashes of light. Some appear for milliseconds and then disappear. Some last longer. They suggest that the universe is constantly creating. This is an ongoing, never-ending process that takes place in every aspect of life and most likely on every plane of consciousness. By consciously connecting with the Law of Creativity, we tap into and become a conduit of the vital life force and become a part of the never-ending chain of creation.

Origins of Creation

Our physical universe began at the moment of the big bang. Approximately 13.7 billion years ago, a spark of light exploded in an ultra-hot flash. At that moment, space and time, matter and energy began to exist. All of the physical matter that exists today, anywhere in the universe, was created at that moment. At first, the energy was formless and fluid. As time went by, the nebulous energy began to congeal into gas and dust. Eventually, those elements, too, became denser, forming atoms and molecules. When a gas cloud becomes big enough and is compressed, it collapses under its own gravity and ignites as a star. If the star is big enough, it will attract more dust and gas. This may eventually solidify to form a planet that revolves in the gravitational force field of the star. Some planets form with the proper combination of elements so that they, too, can create significant life forms.

The creation of life on earth began roughly six hundred million years ago when single-cell organisms gave rise to multicellular creatures. What is amazing is that our single-cell ancestors were genetically equipped to generate all the attributes found in more complex organisms, including organs, limbs, and feathers. The process of physical creation is ongoing.

The New Testament describes the beginning of life by stating, "In the beginning was the word, and the word was with God, and the word was God" (John 1:1–3). Thus, in addition to the dust, gasses, and particles, the origin of physical being had another fundamental component: sound. The source of everything is potentially audible. This audible vibration is God, as is the initial spark that gave rise to the big bang

Aboriginal myths from around the world describe the ancient ones who first appeared as being more ethereal than physical. According to many legends, these beings participated in the task of creating everything physical. They also serve as a conduit, connecting the human experience to primal forces. Over time, they actually created everything we perceive in nature: lakes, trees, snakes, turtles, and kangaroos. The Australian Aborigines connect with the ancient ones in what they call "Dreamtime." This is a state of being that enables the Aborigines to experience both the physical environment and transcendent states of consciousness in ways that are harmonious and supportive.

This story has been repeated in many indigenous cultures throughout the world. Human beings have been aware of the process that created life for thousands of years before science confirmed it. In most of the cosmologies, the original beings who made the earth their home began as the physical universe itself: ethereal and amorphous but with limitless potential to generate endless forms. As time went by, and more physical elements and attributes appeared, the beings became more corporeal and physically dense. They came to identify more with their bodies than with their divine potential. Their ability to endlessly create was consequently curtailed. This tendency has been inherited through the generations down to us. It has led to the perception of life as duality. Duality conveys the idea that the spiritual plane is "out there," and the physical plane is where *we* are. This leads to the false assumption that we are separate from the Divine and outside of the creative flow. Civilization has evolved in a way that has continued to prioritize the physical and to perceive it as separate from the spiritual.

The truth is that the process of creation is continuous, and we are integral, inseparable parts of that process. It may not appear that way to our perceptive mechanisms, because we have unconsciously programmed ourselves to experience our life as separate, both from each other and ultimately from Source. The One is perceived as "many." This illusion can be strong enough to affirm the assumption that we are outside the creative loop. The more we perceive everything as being separate from everything else, the more disconnected we feel. That perception perpetuates duality. You and me. Us and them. This sets up an opposition of forces and manifestations. From there, it's a short step to mine being better than yours, or ours being better than theirs. Instead of perceiving life as a beautiful, interconnected wholeness, in which every part serves, supports, and reflects every other part, humanity has evolved a fragmented consensus reality. Something is perceived as being more desirable in some way than another part. And of course, if I had that good part I would have to hang on to and defend it. If I didn't have it, I would strive to obtain it. So much for harmony and mutual support. So much for all of the mutually interdependent parts of the One doing their creative dance as parts of the whole.

Creativity is the foundation, origin, and essence of life. In the West, we've been taught that "God created heaven and earth." That's it—a done deal. Some might feel that the best we can do is fit into the construct of that which already is, has been, and always will be. Perhaps one letter of that line was mistranslated; it is the most crucial one and alters the entire concept. The translation could be "God creates heaven and earth." The ongoing manifestation of life suggests that creation is present and continuous. Pollywogs become frogs, oceans become deserts, forests become plains, viruses mutate, and primates became human beings.

What's in a Name?

Consciousness development is the purpose of life. Creativity is the vehicle that enables us to accomplish that goal. Because creativity also implies a Creator, it suggests that there is a Source that generates all that is. The process of the One becoming the unlimited forms of life *is* creativity. It is an expression of that first spark of light that exploded to become all that we experience physically. Depending on cultural context and historical time frame, the One Creator has had many names: God, Jehovah, Allah, Jah, Heavenly Father, the Vital Force, the One, Mother Nature, Love, the Light, the Universe, the Divine, and the Unmoved Mover. Some cultures have referred to this concept as "the Unnameable." The Buddhists refer to this concept of Creator as No Thing, which means that Creator is beyond rational understanding. It is not this or that but is, in fact, everything. It is not male or female but is, in fact, the integration of all that is: universal Oneness.

Regardless of the variety of names, each reflects the same concept and represents an attempt to define that which is ineffable. When we attempt to define this concept in a linear way, we limit it to a mental construct. By doing so, we create two problems. One is the cultural disconnect between people who see these names as actually describing different things. For example, God and Allah are seen as separate, leading to the assertion that "God is on our side" or "my God is better than yours." Attempts to perceive and define something that unifies has lead to a fragmentation among peoples of the world.

The second problem is that the defining or naming of the Source has led to the development of *religions*, as opposed to the awareness of *spirituality*. With religion comes dogma; with dogma comes politics. Dogma has prevented direct, conscious connection to Source, and the politics of religion has created the idea that the deity is simply another politician—someone "out there" who needs to be placated, feared, or followed. The idea that the One is not separate from us—nor we from it—has been lost in translation. This has given tremendous power to those who claim to be intermediaries between God and the people. They can use their knowledge and prestige for personal gain. An example of this comes from ancient Egypt. The priests in that culture were also astrologers. They knew about natural phenomena, such as eclipses. Prior to a new moon solar eclipse, they would announce that the gods required more tribute. If the people did not contribute more to the priestly coffers (in the form of food, livestock, etc.) the priests would block out the sun. At first, the people might have responded with skepticism, but as the moon slowly moved across the face of the sun, and the midday sky grew dark, the people no doubt brought whatever they had to the temple. As the moon completed the eclipse and began moving past the sun, the priests would congratulate the people on their generosity, announcing that the "gods" were satisfied, and all would be well from that point on.

Some people are raised in dogmatic traditions. Their experience of religion or God is limiting and repressive, sometimes to the point of abuse. People from any tradition may tend to avoid spirituality, confusing it with the religion within which they were raised. Their experience of the deity may reflect the negativity with which it was introduced to or forced upon them. Other people simply avoid deviating from the path of their childhood religion. They were taught that spirituality is different from their religion and therefore is either bad or perhaps anti-God. For these reasons I have chosen to refer to the prime deity in this book by neutral names such as Spirit, Source, Oneness, and Transcendent Divine. I want to avoid any negative connotations associated with a name or any associations with any particular organized religion. The reader can then have a clearer understanding of the concepts I am discussing.

What Is the Creative Source?

Regardless of the labels chosen, the question of who or what is the Source of creation remains. Let's answer this question by defining its qualities. Spiritual masters from all cultures and traditions state that it is something that was never created, has always existed, has always flowed through everything, and can never be destroyed. Two attributes that it seems to possess are the intention and ability to create. How can we know more about the nature and purpose of the Divine? We can use our intuition and explore the concept of Creative Source through mystical attunement. We can find validation for this process by analyzing some of the great books of our heritage, written by people of inspired intention and clear vision.

The Bible says, "So God created man in his own image ... male and female he created them" (Genesis 1:27). Does that mean that all people should resemble the familiar, stylized image of Jehovah as an old man with long white hair and beard and flowing robe? In this sense, it seems more likely that we created God in *our* image. Putting Source in a human form has enabled us to feel less alienated and fearful in the face of a physical reality that has been continuously changing and challenging. It has enabled us to avoid dealing with our spiritual potential by defining Spirit in limited, human terms. But I think this biblical passage means that we contain within us the same potential to create—continuously and unabated—that is expressed eternally by the prime Source. In this respect, we are the descendents of those mythic beings who created all the physical attributes of the earth. If the purpose of the Divine is to create, and we were made in the image of that Creator, then we, too, must possess both the intention and ability to create.

One thing that separates humans from other species and connects us even more to Source is that our creative process is not limited to the physical plane. We can generate ideas that enable us to organize ourselves into social groups. We can create technologies that enhance our potential to communicate, to transport, or to make our physical tasks easier. We can generate art that provides a reflection and expression of ourselves, and we can produce situations such as war and peace.

Creation is imminent in all human endeavors. One example is written language. There were four original cultures that independently invented written language. The Sumerian people of Mesopotamia (modern Iraq) created a written form of their language prior to 3000 BC. Other cultures that accomplished this were in Egypt (around 3000 BC), China (1300 BC), and Mexico (600 BC). This is a geographically vast and culturally diverse group, indicating a strong and universal drive to express ourselves through linguistic creativity.

Some people believe that the first creative act we make occurs before physical incarnation itself. It pertains to our birth and our incarnation's choices of time, place, family structure, economic conditions, ethnicity, and gender. I believe there are definite and specific reasons, all conforming to the universal laws, that influence those choices. These circumstantial factors provide the foundation and tools that, in turn, enable us to continue the creative process, once we're actually back in the incarnate state. (The concept and process of reincarnation is explained in chapter 8, "The Law of Eternal Life.") These choices help us create our identity, our reality, and what we want or need to experience during the lifetime. For example, we may have chosen a physical handicap in this incarnation or perhaps a horrible family of origin that left us emotionally and psychologically scarred. These factors were chosen so that we might learn from those experiences, and they were, in turn, based on selections made in previous incarnations and actions taken in those lives. In the best scenario, the lessons learned from these experiences enable us to make different and better choices in the present and future, thus propelling us to be better people who create a more fulfilling life.

If this original act of creation in this lifetime defines the framework of our experience, all ensuing generative manifestations emanate from that first act. But we are also free to make new choices that, in turn, create the ongoing context of our life. It is certainly possible to begin life with a very challenging early life experience, then overcome those obstacles and still create a good and happy life. We don't have to remain in that original pattern and perpetrate the pain. As we create new patterns and behaviors we change the original condition and ultimately will produce a more harmonious life. That's one of the most powerful elements of this law: we are not limited by our past choices. By continuing in our creative process new experiences and realities can and do result.

Astrological Correlation

Each year, the sun passes through twelve constellations, or signs of the zodiac. The sign it enters on the first day of spring is Aries, the astrological sign associated with the Principle of Creativity. Each of the signs partakes of one *mode* (cardinal, fixed, or mutable), which establishes how the sign expresses energy, and one *element* (four fundamental qualities: fire, earth, air, and water). Aries's mode is cardinal, and its element is fire. The cardinal signs are action-oriented. They are comfortable with the trial-and-error process in creating and living their life. Fire is the element of the creative, dynamic drive to express the self in spontaneous, instinctive ways.

The signs also operate through one of the fundamental polarities of life: these are the masculine, or *yang*, and the feminine, or *yin*. Aries, as a fire sign, is yang, meaning that it is outgoing, interactive, and mind-oriented.

Aries represents the instinctive, authentic integration of the mind, creating thoughts and then boldly acting them out. As the first sign of the new season as well as of the zodiac, Aries is considered the sign of new beginnings. Aries is direct, self-affirming, independent, assertive, and sexual. It doesn't hesitate or equivocate. It is straightforward and on point.

Aries tends to look for new projects to initiate or in which to get involved. It has no problem diving into a situation with which it has no previous experience or about which it has little knowledge. It thinks well on its feet and has the courage to act on the fly.

It also can be one-dimensional in its awareness of or involvement in a situation. It can be overly opinionated and impulsive, often having difficulty sticking with a project after the newness and excitement wears off.

Aries represents the vital life force at work. Aries's contribution to the human experience is to get things going. Aries likes trying something new or taking an old pattern in a new direction, based on impulse or instinct. Many of the qualities of the Law of Creativity are similar to the traits associated with Aries.

How to Align with the Creative Principle

Like Aries, the Principle of Creativity is action-oriented. Its fiery nature is reflected in the continuous creation that lies just below the surface of most people's consciousness. We are always creating our own reality. And we always get what we create. Nothing ever happens to us without complicity on our part. It may be active or passive, but we are creating all the same. Similarly, if we don't like the reality we have created, we are free to change it. We can keep creating and changing until we are satisfied with the form and content of the life that we experience daily.

The process of creating who we are is predicated upon the successful integration of the prime trinity of life: soul, mind, and body. The trinity is a primal concept in traditional religions, such as Christianity and Hinduism. In Christianity the trinity is defined as the Father, the Son and the Holy Ghost. The Hindu trinity is Brahma (the Creator), Vishnu (the Preserver), and Shiva (the Destroyer). For our purposes, I define "soul" as that primary aspect of each of us that emerged from the eternal process of cosmic creation. Like our creative source, our soul is eternal. We can become more aware of our soul in many ways, most of which involve tuning in to our inner being. In that process we learn how to recognize our feelings, emotions, and intuition. By becoming more aware of our inner world, these subtle sensitivities shift to the mind and become more conscious as thoughts. As conscious thought, the energy is available to be analyzed by the intellect. Strategy can then be plotted to manifest thought into action. The body is the vehicle that takes action. The body is the dense manifestation of all the feelings, thoughts and actions from the past.

If the journey from emotion to thought to action is conscious, we have completed the circle and are actively, deliberately involved in the creation of our selves and our reality.

For example, we may feel drawn to some form of creative expression, perhaps music. Listening to music might stimulate a whole range of emotions for us. The thought occurs that making music would be enjoyable. No one in the family has ever been a musician. In fact, there might be a family prejudice against it based on moral grounds or class distinction. There is no support, no money for the instrument or for lessons. We might even be berated for having that desire. We could give in to the pressure and pretend that we really don't care or don't want to play music. Or we could be honest with ourselves and realize that to create the reality we want will require a strategy that will effectively overcome the obstacles. So the process and experience of creation is getting from where we are to the point of our holding the instrument in front of the teacher.

Music is an interesting analogy to describe creativity because, as noted, the primal vibration of life is audible. This is the sound *om* or *aum*. We can hear or feel this sound by chanting "Om," or by closing our ears with our fingers and listening to the inner vibration, or by putting our ear to a seashell. Playing or listening to the Australian aboriginal instrument the didgeridoo also creates this vibration of the primal force. The Aborigines take this a step farther. Playing or listening to the didgeridoo (which they call *yidaki*) allows them to access Dreamtime. As mentioned earlier, this concept refers to a sacred dimension where humans are in contact with spirit beings and are thus able to find spiritual and creative inspiration. To the indigenous Australians, it is a place where ancestor spirits as well as archetypal beings live. The beings that can be accessed through Dreamtime are the ones whose consciousness formed the topography, flora, and fauna of the earth, as did Dreamtime itself. It can be accessed in the waking state (with the help of yidaki) as well as in the sleep state. Dreamtime is a mystical state that is accessed in order to find spiritual and creative inspiration and guidance. Dreamtime creates a kind of spiritual loop. Like the Aborigines using the vibration of sound, we can tune in to the Primal Source that reminds us of our birthright as spiritual beings.

Any artistic manifestation will immediately connect us to the creative. Most indigenous peoples integrate art with spirituality. For example, Inuits of the Arctic regions carved faces of important deities into their harpoons in order to enlist powerful forces in their quest for food. There seems to be a consistent thread through human civilization of the arts being a vehicle to connect with Oneness by accessing the creativity that moves through all life. Artists have depicted images of the deity as a way of both invoking its nature and worshiping it. Creating a work of art can be a ritual that connects the artist with the Divine.

Qualities of the Creative Process

Two qualities that factor into the creative process are rate and rhythm. When we understand these aspects and work with them, our creative intentions have a better chance of being manifested.

The Law of Creativity

There is a minister in Los Angeles named Robert Schuller. He has such a large following, and his ministry is so well-endowed, that he was able to take over an old drive-in movie theater and build a church in its place that he calls the Crystal Cathedral. At one time he had a weekly TV show on Sunday mornings. One week, the topic of his sermon was "It's Not the Rhymes, It's the Times." He was encouraging his parishioners not to get discouraged if their prayers were not immediately answered. His idea was that it matters less how we pray (the rhymes) and more when God is ready to answer those prayers (the times). Of course, one problem with this concept is that it assumes that there is a being "out there" who has the power to give us what we want or need in his own time. It conveniently leaves our own creative involvement out of the picture. It also fails to take into consideration that events in life are cyclical. Astrologers refer to the timing of events by noting the cyclical movement of the planets through the signs. When the planets come into certain patterns or alignments, they provide a time frame that is beneficial for a certain activity, a time when our creative power in a certain area will likely be more effective in generating a desirable end. If we attempt something at an inopportune time, we could still be successful through the sheer drive of our creative intention, but the project will be more challenging.

Assuming we have chosen a good time to begin an activity, we also must be patient with the result. Actions on the physical plane take time to transpire, and to be observed. Similarly, if we want to change something that we have created, whether in an earlier incarnation or last week, it takes time. Sometimes we might feel that the time necessary to bring about a change is too long. Other times, it is too fleeting. Part of life's journey is to learn how to be engaged in the creation of ourselves and our reality in ways that allow a comfortable rhythm to develop. People have desires that pertain to both the personal and social parts of their lives. A mundane and personal example of this is my friend Allan. Allan has been trying to quit smoking for years. He is clear about his intention to do this and thus remains undaunted by the fact that he still clings to the habit. At some point, the consistency of his efforts will allow his objective to be realized. The timing of when his goal will meet with success can be based on patterns and cycles of energy: the rhymes and the times. The times when goals can be realized are called windows of opportunity. A consistently and consciously maintained intention, sooner or later, comes to a window of opportunity and that objective is achieved. Even if we have not completed our intended goal while the window is open, it is important that we at least begin the process. If we take advantage of the open window, we will continue to have access to it even after the period is over. Once a window of consciousness or perception opens, it never truly closes. It is a matter of our free will to choose to act or not. We can complete the task in our own time and at our own rhythm. If we fail to acknowledge and work with that opportunity, however, we trick ourselves into thinking that the window never existed, or we simply fail to activate our free will in that direction.

We also can take advantage of this principle by being present in the moment. As Ram Das said, "Be here now." One benefit of such attentiveness is that we can be aware of our feelings and attendant thoughts as they arise, before any words have been spoken or any actions taken. Emotions will often reflect either our past experiences or our present desires. (See chapter 4, "The Law of the Eternal Present," for more information about the emotional life.) Our being aware of our emotional state helps to liberate us from past programming that keeps us in a limited state of being. Because creativity happens both internally and externally, the integration of the two realms enables us to embody the prime trinity: emotions that provide awareness of the need for change, the intellect that creates the methodologies of change, and the body, which is the vehicle through which external change takes place.

Similar to the nature of Aries, present-moment awareness gives us access to spontaneous creativity—the capacity to act on positive impulse. It enables creativity to be expressed—by us and through us—before our judgments or fears provide reasons not to act. Spontaneity helps us tap directly into the creative center of life. We feel full, dynamic, and radiant. It's as if we are super-charged with a force that connects us to something greater than our selves. These feelings give rise to a connection to Oneness, which is a fundamental quality of the mystic.

Courage and Creativity

One of the primary attributes of Aries is courage. Courage is expressed when we step out and do something intriguing but untried. Testing ourselves in new areas accesses the Law of Creativity. This could involve exploring new states of consciousness. It could also manifest behaviorally by overcoming an unhappy childhood to live a happy life. In a very immediate sense, courage enables us to honor who we are and to identify with something greater than ourselves.

One way of demonstrating courage is by taking initiative. Initiative implies the willingness to act independently in getting something started. The first step in doing anything is often the hardest, simply because it is new, just as first gear in a car's transmission is the strongest because it takes a body at rest and begins the task of moving it forward. Sir Isaac Newton was a philosopher who used mathematics as a way of understanding how life works. Among others accomplishments, he deciphered the laws of motion; one of these is the Law of Inertia. It states that an object at rest tends to remain at rest unless acted on by some outside force. By using initiative we become that "outside force." If we are in a static state of being we can change it in whatever way we choose by tuning in to the Principle of Creation.

The courage required to become involved in a brand new experience can feel as daunting as it is exhilarating. Paramahansa Yogananda, a self-realized spiritual master from India said, "Spirituality abhors spinelessness. One should always have the moral courage and backbone to show strength when the occasion calls for it." Courageous creativity can be spontaneous and instinctive in its expression; it is like a lightning bolt. It comes to mind and is acted on right away. No forethought, no deliberation. To be in the moment and to act in a way that expresses our ideas helps us to flow with this law. The immediacy of the experience can enable us to bypass inhibition, restrictive programming, or a severe inner critic. We feel; we act.

Courage requires a certain resourcefulness whereby we rely on ourselves to conceive and execute an action with deliberate intention. Resourcefulness asks that we notice what is motivating us in the process of creating our reality. If our actions aren't in harmony with our intentions, we should stop what we are doing and avoid wasting time and effort, until we realign our actions with our goals. Holding our clear intention, we can then create a strategy designed to facilitate the creative process. In Greek mythology, Prometheus (whose name means "forethought") stole fire (a metaphor for consciousness in this story) from the gods and gave it to humanity. Prior to his action, fire was the exclusive property of the gods. Prometheus's goal was to bring useful tools and skills to humanity through sharing the fire. He was the enlightener. He stood up to the gods and risked retribution. But Prometheus made the mistake of being too resourceful. He relied entirely upon his own skills to accomplish the task. As a result, he was severely punished in different ways. In one, his brother, Epimetheus (meaning "afterthought"), was given the goddess Pandora to marry. It was after this that Pandora opened her box to release disease and suffering on humanity. Afterthought, like hindsight, can be accurate in perceiving the current situation but woefully inadequate in creating a new one. So even though Prometheus had good intentions and did give valuable tools to humanity, he was undermined by his brother and thus, also created severe problems for us. Sometimes we can be successful in what we are trying to create, but unexpected consequences can result.

Excessive or exclusive resourcefulness sets in when we become too single-minded in our intention or too independent in carrying it out. Passion often generates creativity. But we can be overwhelmed with passion and act in such a blinded manner that we actually create resistance to our intentions. If we are committed enough to our objective, however, we might be willing to accept the possibility of punishment or rejection when the drive to express the light of our mind and soul burns so brightly. Prometheus was so inspired by his passion and creativity that his "forethought" became too one-dimensional to be completely successful in realizing his goals. When we act with deliberation and engage assistance from others, we may have a greater chance for success, while minimizing the potential for retribution. The light of our consciousness can bring new awareness for ourselves and others. We are supportive to others expressing their courage and passion, even as we seek their support. By not broadening our intentions in this way, we leave ourselves open for punishment or at least harsh response. For Prometheus, the penalty came in the form of being chained to a rock and having an eagle come daily to eat his liver, which re-grew at night. Prometheus's salvation came from Heracles, who slew the eagle in another courageous act.

Forethought implies consciousness of the future, of the fact that actions have consequences and that tomorrow is created by the choices made today. The Native American Iroquois Confederacy, a union of tribes who lived in the New York area from pre-Columbian times, made decisions based on the concept of the "seventh generation." They were concerned with how people, seven generations from that time, would be affected by the choices made in the present time. Action was taken only if the decision was beneficial to both those living and those to come.

Forethought engages the analytical mind as an ally so that the body can act in a conscious and higher-octave manner. By expressing the intention to do something, we prepare ourselves for action. What do I want to do? Why do I want to do it? How am I acting? Are these actions going to fulfill my desires? Are they expressions of my higher or lower nature? Are those desires a part of me that is only concerned with myself or a part that is connected to all things?

One way to enhance the probability of successfully creating what we want is by working with visualizations and affirmations. When we visualize something we define an intention and focus our mind on its realization. We see in our mind's eye, and sometimes even feel in our body, the completion of our project or goal. Affirmations are mantra-like thoughts or words that provide the confidence that the visualized intention is at hand. For example, if we are sick, we visualize our body as healthy, dynamic, and whole. We picture it in our mind as it was before illness struck. This affirms a state of being. By combining this mental image with an affirmation such as "My body is radiant and in the peak of health," we engage the mind even more as the vehicle of creativity. This is very different from affirming that "I want to get healthy," because the underlying assumption is that you are not. The difference is between wanting a state that isn't there and establishing that what you want already exists.

Spirit and Nature

Mystical tradition teaches that nature is a doorway through which we can access the spiritual. Not only are the physical and the spiritual not separate, but the former actually provides an entrance into the latter. Everything we can know is mirrored in nature. For example, the universal Principle of Creativity can be understood through nature's solar cycle. The sun is the source of physical life in our solar system. Spring represents the vital creative force returning to a hemisphere. As the sun moves north in the Northern Hemisphere, plants grow, and animals give birth to their young. As the sun travels south into the Southern Hemisphere, plants in the Northern Hemisphere die or become dormant, and animals hibernate. This cycle is repeated annually and is reflective of the Law of Eternal Life (chapter 8). The flora and fauna of the area experience new beginnings each spring. The profusion of animals, birds, insects, reptiles, amphibians, trees, flowers, and microbes reminds us that the purpose of life is to create.

One quality uniting all life forms is the drive to procreate. This is also expressed in the sexual drive inherent in the Aries archetype. Every living thing has the inherent ability to be creative, even if only in terms of its ability to reproduce. It must be able to take part in the creative process or its species ceases to exist. Therefore, one expression of the creative force is sex. This is the strongest physical drive that exists, relative to the material plane. A pack of male dogs, starving and thirsty yet remaining outside the house of a female in heat; or a tom cat traveling miles to find a mate—these are examples of the power of the procreative drive. These animals eschew all other forms of satisfaction and security in order to propagate. This is the force that drives insects and birds as well as mammals to fulfill their biological imperative: to make more of who or what they are. In some species, sex is completely dispassionate; insemination followed by spawning of the larva or the laying of the eggs. In some animals, such as scorpions, the female will often destroy and devour her mate upon completion of coitus. In mammals, sex can have multiple functions. The bonobo is a primate that is closest to humans in terms of its DNA. The bonobo uses sex not only for procreation but also as a means of exchange. If a male has a big pile of food, a female is likely to lie down in front of the male, offering him her body. After sex, she will get up, take the pile of food, and walk away. This is actually not unlike certain forms of human sexuality, both primitive and modern. Prostitution, for example, commodifies sex. It's a business arrangement. It has nothing to do with either procreation or emotional involvement. Another similarity between the bonobo and humans is that for both, the sex act can take place literally several times each day with a variety of partners. Unlike the bonobo, however, humans can use sex as a vehicle for the expression of passion and, hopefully, love. It is these last motivating factors that allow an unbridled drive to express itself in one of the most personal and immediate ways available. It mirrors the vibrant dynamism of spring, with its hopefulness and enthusiasm. It is the unrestrained, joyful exploration of a sexual experience that leads to deepening the emotional content of a relationship, increasing its value and investment as a meaningful experience and, ultimately, to creating new life.

Another example of the sexuality inherent in nature as another expression of the Principle of Creativity is the bower bird. In most birds the male attracts his mate by having some physical characteristic that is particularly striking. The bower bird is an exception to that rule. He is often nondescript in his appearance and must resort to doing something other than looking good in order to attract a female. The male bower's strategy is to construct an environment. It is fitting that the dictionary defines a bower as a leafy shelter. The bower bird painstakingly builds a structure that can look like a cave, a hallway, or a tunnel. He also finds colorful objects from his surroundings that he hopes the female will find attractive. These could be bright green leaves or brightly colored berries. If the bird lives near humans, these objects d'art could be pieces of colored plastic or shiny pieces of metal. One thing that is particularly striking about the bird's created environment is that the color scheme is consistent. If he uses berries, they will all be blue, for example. Or if he uses plastic, it would all be green. The female is then attracted to the male bower's nest, and thus, to him. This bird's behavior illustrates how the sexual impulse joins with the creative, and there are many examples of this throughout the natural world. The creative principle is always at work.

Creativity in Action

Another form of physical activity that can enable us to flow more effectively with the creative principle is martial arts. The basis of martial arts is not is not about doing physical harm to others but about aligning our actions with the Divine, such that we act with an awareness of our impact on "other." My friend Daniel, a martial arts instructor with several black belts in karate, insists that his students learn to meditate and do so daily if they are to study with him. This is because martial arts is an active meditative experience, a form of self-discipline and presence that involves doing rather than sitting.

The arts provide another arena through which creativity flows. Painting, drawing, and sculpting are mirrors through which we can see ourselves as the Creator. Writing can also provide access to the Principle of Creativity. When I'm not feeling connected, it's almost impossible to sit down and put anything meaningful on the page. I'm preoccupied by activities that seem more important and require immediate attention: taking out the garbage, sweeping the floor, petting the cat. None of these can wait. But at those times when I'm feeling the pulse of creativity flowing through my mind and body, it's hard to be anywhere other than at my desk, putting down words that seem to flow effortlessly.

The easiest way to find ways to engage in creative pursuits is by being adventurous and bold. Do something new, something outside the realm of habit and routine. Try something that is exciting and that enables us to be true to ourselves. It needn't be something we're already familiar with and know we're "good at," so it might take courage to go out and do it.

Not Aligning with This Law

Resisting any of the laws diminishes the quality of our experience. It could cause us to feel bad about ourselves, as if we have failed in some way. Actually, there is no failure in life, only opportunities to learn and grow. If we understand the lessons of a challenging time or situation, our growth enables a different result in the future. If we don't understand the dynamic of a situation and fail to learn from it, we simply repeat the results until the learning does take place. Once we've gotten the lesson and integrated it into our lives, we can start benefiting from the law by flowing with it, harmoniously and consciously.

As noted previously, Aries is yang. It is outgoing. It is also a fire sign—it thrives on action and new beginnings. If we remain in a comfort zone of habits, clinging to that which we know and avoiding new beginnings, we pass up the benefits of this law. When we prefer stagnation to change, we become limited by yin energy. Perhaps we equate inertia with stability and alteration with risk, but by being timid we can blunt the potential of this law. If we are overly guarded, we allow fear to color our perspective; if we are too prudent, we allow practicality to block creativity.

All action is an expression of creativity, but not all actions are consistently beneficial. For example, if our intention to do something is based solely on self-interest and personal gratification, our choice could benefit ourselves to the detriment of someone else. This is conceit, not creativity. When there is no thought or concern for anyone else, we become blinded by our own light. In the Prometheus tale, the gods were guilty of conceit. They assumed that only they deserved the power of fire: light and creativity. They preferred to hoard their gifts, and thus broke the universal law that creativity is equally available to all. This is an attitude of arrogance. Whether in the mythic realm or the human, we can get so caught up in our momentary interests that our vision of the whole becomes limited.

Limited perspective is often accompanied by opinionated, judgmental words, actions, and a sense of entitlement. We might use a scrap of information to form the basis of our intentions and actions. We could get away with this temporarily, but all of our creative thoughts and acts have consequences. We create a response from the universe with our actions here and now. It may take time for those results to manifest, but sooner or later they will. The focus, then, should be on the bigger picture. How can we create fulfillment in the present as well as a longer-range beneficial reality?

Impetuous activity can also prevent taking advantage of this law. We might get so carried away with the "rush" of courage and creative action that we do something—anything—just for the exhilaration. We affirm the Nike mantra: "Just do it." Here, too, there is little or no thought of results and consequences. Whatever feels good right now is the ultimate goal. An example of this is promiscuity. This is often based merely on the drive for physical release. Our creativity is subverted by impulse or the need for instant gratification, regardless of how destructive those actions may be. Recklessness overwhelms forethought. Sometimes our choices can lead to immediate destructive results.

Even though Aries is the archetype of creative action, Ares was the Greek god of war. Reckless action, especially when taken by a collective body of people, may take years or decades to show their negative costs. For example, a war entered into frivolously or for the mere show of force and power might bring an immediate victory to the attacking army. The long-term cost in terms of resources, goodwill, or the fear of retaliation, however, could prove costly. An individual's ability to alter the course of a political decision may be limited, but it would certainly be an act of courage to try. If we found that our leaders were acting in a self-serving way, we would be acting in tune with the Law of Creativity by opposing them. We would be acting with the clear intention of doing something beneficial for society.

Spiritual Opportunity

The divine quality activated by the Law of Creativity is *light*. This is the light that flows from Divine Source and provides the energy to physically exist, as well as the seed to awaken in cosmic consciousness. In the Old Testament book of Genesis, God manifested light, and thus established the fundamental duality of life: light and darkness. This duality led to the separation of day and night, male and female, etc. Metaphysically, this can also be expressed as the qualities of yin and yang. Yin, the receptive principle, pertains to the physical and represents the feminine. Yang, the active principle, pertains to the light and represents the masculine. The vital life force creative energy is yang. The form that contains that energy and manifests it into the physical is yin. Behind those two complimentary elements is always the One. Thus, integration of the yin and yang aspects of ourselves helps to reawaken the consciousness of our latent divinity and our potential as divine beings.

The Bible instructs us that without light, "the earth was without form." Existence was restricted to "the Spirit of God moving upon the face of the waters." There was no awareness of being, just being itself. This is similar to the Australian Aboriginal concept referred to earlier, that in the beginning of life the "ancient ones" existed ethereally only. It wasn't until they took form that they manifested geographic qualities on the earth as we know it. Out of the darkness came the light; out of the formless came form. We can infer from this that the earth began as an amorphous, gaseous blob. Once light was generated, relativity came to be, and the world and all its creatures came into physical existence.

The light surrounds us at all times. The Gnostics, previously discussed in the introduction, spoke about the light of the *pleroma*. In a manner similar to the ancient ones of Aboriginal Dreamtime, the pleroma was the phenomenon through which divine light could be perceived to exist, even in the material world. They believed that at the time of the fall of Adam and Eve, this light was scattered into divine sparks. As the material plane was forming, the divine sparks chose to identify more with their earth-plane experience than with their spiritual potential. Over time, they forgot their divine heritage. This led to a fundamental relativity, the duality of consciousness (light) and ignorance (darkness). This made the One more difficult to perceive, although it remains present in all. The One can be seen in the light in the eyes of animals as you engage them. It can be noticed reflecting from the leaves of a tree on a bright sunny day. The Gnostics held that the divine sparks have become trapped in matter. This teaching reaffirms that the light of Oneness exists and is alive in all things. It validates the concept that the vital life force has used the Principle of Creativity to both manifest the material plane and to embody itself within the material.

Modern physics has discovered that when matter is investigated and analyzed, it is perceived as waves of light. Physicist/philosopher David Bohm has written: "Matter, as it were, is condensed or frozen light ... all matter is a condensation of light in patterns moving back and forth at average speeds [that] are less than the speed of light. The energy of light and its information-content, form, and structure, is the potential for everything."

In *Republic 29*, Plato describes a cave in which people are chained in such a way that they can only see objects and images reflected as shadows. The radiant light is above and behind them. They not only can't see the light itself, but they don't even know it's there. If they are freed from their bindings and taken into the light, their first reaction is one of pain and irritation. They resist the idea that their previous reality was but a shadow and that now they are in a position to really know what life is. Plato contends that they must change; they must develop a tolerance to the light. Gradually, they do. In the beginning, they can perceive the shadows generated by the light, then reflections of themselves and other objects in water. Then, they can accept the moon, the stars, and the nighttime sky as real. Finally, after going through this process of consciousness shift, they can perceive and accept the light and all that is illuminated by it. So it follows that to take advantage of the truth of creativity, we must first become used to and comfortable in the light. This story is a metaphor for humanity in the journey of consciousness development.

Bringing It Home

Our actions create who we are. Who do you want to be, now and in the future? The choices are limitless and left up to each of us.

The Bhagavad-Gita is the sacred scripture of Hinduism. It counsels that all actions are best executed without attachment to result (see chapter 3, "The Law of Both/And"). By being clear in intention, we predetermine where we are going. Letting go of attachment to the achievement, we become free to focus on Oneness and our connection with it. A mundane example of this is physical exercise. We could be aware of certain factors during the experience: the aches and pains, our desire to lose weight or sculpt our body. We could get discouraged by the amount of time it is taking to reach our goal, the amount of money the health club costs, or the continuous discomfort. We could also engage in exactly the same activities with no attachment at all. We have a clearly defined intention and strive to achieve it through consistent application over time. If we allow the mind to focus on the energy itself, we can feel the juice of life flowing through the body. The point of focus thus becomes the feeling of oneness with our body and with the vital life force that we experience through action.

The most immediate and direct way to access the spiritual light is through meditation. One practice is that of focusing on the "third eye," the point between the eyebrows, until eventually it opens. Parmahansa Yogananda describes the opening of the spiritual eye as "a golden aura surrounding an opal-blue sphere in the center of which is a five pointed star of brilliant white light." Making that connection enables us to tap directly into Creative Source, realizing and manifesting our own personal limitless creative potential. Meditation is a good example of acting with no attachment to results. Most clients and students with whom I've discussed meditation have told me that they stopped meditating because they "weren't doing it right." Most meditation techniques are fairly simple to duplicate, so I was puzzled as to what they were doing "wrong." The answer invariably is that they were unable to achieve the goal of meditation: single-pointed concentration of the mind and the cessation of all thought. My stock reply is always, "Really? And this was after how many decades of meditation?" They smile sheepishly, if not laugh out loud, and respond that they gave it up after a couple of weeks. They were attached to the outcome and overlooked the experience itself. It's as if they enjoyed music to the point that they decided to learn how to play the piano. But they stopped after practicing for a month because they weren't yet able to give a concert.

Most meditation techniques are referred to as a practice. I was always struck by this term and wondered what I was practicing for. The ultimate goal of meditation is experiencing the state of Oneness with the Divine. Until I actually do achieve this, my daily meditation time affords me the opportunity to "practice" being in that state. By being detached from my goal, even as I deliberately work toward achieving it, I can benefit from the insights, inspirations, and peaceful feelings that emerge during my daily practice. Remembering my intention, remaining consistent in creative action, being in the moment, and being detached from immediate gratification is a formula for success.

The same pattern would be true in developing any knowledge (e.g., learning how to build a house or learning quantum physics). By remaining focused on the creativity of learning as well as on the creative action itself, we maintain a conscious connection to Spirit. This relationship provides an inherent and profound sense of fulfillment. Creativity with consciousness is a formula for right action. The light of our actions illuminates who we are as beings separate from all others. The light also unites all separate manifestations with Oneness. If all that exists is a manifestation of divine creation, then all that "is" is the Divine.

The Bottom Line

Spring is my favorite season. In the Northern Hemisphere the beginning of spring also marks the beginning of Aries. As the sign of new beginnings, it signals the time to initiate new projects and behaviors. It provides the confidence to explore new parts of myself. I love the deep sense of well-being that I feel when walking through a meadow of new grass that has just emerged from the ground. The dark, vibrant emerald color brings the feeling of the great cosmic "Yes." All possibilities are opening up, and there is a drive to have new adventures, to experience life through the divine embrace

The Law of Creativity

inherent in nature. Sexual energies are abundant. Being alive and in the "now" feels infinitely comfortable and fulfilling. The universal Principle of Creativity generates life and all of our experiences. This is a force available to us in each present moment at all times. It is Spirit's eternal promise that we are all co-creators of the universe. By using this principle with consciousness, courage, and far-sightedness we actively participate in the creation of life on Earth. By feeling this energy flowing through our body, we affirm our place in the never-ending chain of creation.

The challenge of this law is to blend the courage required to be spontaneous with the groundedness attached by forethought and clarity of intention. This enables us to maintain a pure connection with the universal chain of creation.

Affirmation: "At the core of my being is radiant light."

Just behind the spark of your life is the Flame of Infinity; just behind the glimmer of your thoughts is the Great Light of God; just behind your discriminative reason is the omniscience of Spirit; just behind your love is the all-fulfilling love of God. ... There is nothing to prevent you from feeling that great Power behind your life.

—Paramahansa Yogananda

Chapter 2: The Law of Survival

The supreme goal for the common man as well as for the ruler is survival.

—Lao Tzu, *Tao Te Ching*, Ch. XIII

My family loves cats. The two that we have are very people-friendly and I'm sure would love nothing more than to spend each day cuddling in our laps and purring. Usually, they are friendly to each other as well, spending their days lying together outside in the sun. But in the morning, at feeding time, they revert to more primal behaviors. They hiss and growl at each other, swiping at each other with claws out, and the fur literally flies. When we finally put the food bowl down for them, they quietly eat side by side. The drive to fill the belly is primal.

Survival means the ability to sustain ourselves in the physical world. Maintaining physical existence calls for different strategies to satisfy different needs. The most fundamental need is to eat. To satisfy the need to eat, humans have utilized hunting, gathering, fishing, and agriculture. The food supply is often dependent on what is available in the immediate environment. The most primitive activity in which a life form can engage is looking for food, even as it works to prevent itself from being food. For the youngest members of a mammalian group, the resource of food is the nursing mother. In nomadic groups, the females follow the food supply and the males often follow the females. This is an important point as we try to understand, as modern humans, how best to utilize the universal Law of Survival. By allowing women more authority in determining how humanity survives, we could return to a time-honored, successful formula. The archetypal, traditional female values are protection, physical nourishment, and providing a sense of emotional security. These are all necessities of survival.

Environment is a key to survival. If there is abundant fish or game in a particular place, the people who live there will thrive. The most successful early human communities were those that developed where food was abundant or where there were the fewest predators. The cultures that first developed agriculture were the ones who were fortunate enough to live in environments where the soil was fertile and where the native plants had the highest content of nutrients, as well as the largest seeds that were most conducive for human propagation. These are some of the reasons that people in Mesopotamia, the cradle of Western civilization, thrived and developed one of the first advanced cultures.

Mesopotamia is now called Iraq. Approximately ten thousand years ago it had a temperate climate and abundant water. It was relatively easy for humans to forage for food by gathering native nuts, seeds, and berries, as well as hunting and fishing. The natural-growing flora in that area proved to be easy to find and well suited for cultivation. Grasses, such as wheat and barley, were readily available. Their seeds were large and easy to harvest. Eventually, their seeds were deliberately planted and gradually, agriculture replaced hunting and gathering as the survival method of choice. Planting and irrigating ensured a more stable source of food. This led to greater survival among the newborn, larger populations, and ultimately, the development of art, government, and religion—the foundations of culture.

Survival and the Shaman

The person who has both the ability and responsibility to make personal connection with the spirits of animals as well as with the souls of departed ancestors is the shaman. Either male or female, they are like priests in that they are perceived by members of the tribe as having certain knowledge of things that are beyond the awareness of others. The shaman's knowledge provides another kind of security to the tribe. It reassures them of their connection to the Oneness and the increased probability of survival. Unlike priests, however, the shaman doesn't rely on books or a philosophy in order to make contact. The shaman makes direct, mystical contact with the essence of beings in order to receive special information. This can be useful for healing, for direction to food or water sources, or for spiritual guidance, useful to enable the people to remember and take sustenance from their spiritual roots.

With this type of spiritual guidance, people were able to adapt and survive in harsh environments. The Hopi tribe migrated to the northern Sonora Desert in Arizona and New Mexico thousands of years ago. This was an inhospitable, dry area inhabited by few animals and no other people. But the Hopi perceived it as desirable, the center of their world, a place of salvation. Why would a group choose to live in such a place? One reason is that there were no predators. Another is that since survival was so challenging, it would be seen as undesirable by other, possibly hostile tribes. Thus, the Hopi would be safe. The Hopi lifestyle prioritizes spirituality. Material possessions mean little in comparison to the sense of connection to the Source. Their yearly cycle is based on rituals that honor Great Spirit for all the blessings that are given to them in their quest for survival and peace. These ceremonies enable them to remain close to Spirit and to feel its ever-supportive presence in their lives. Even poisonous snakes are integrated into their spiritual observances, indicating a kinship with and reverence for all forms of life. The Hopi (and hundreds of other indigenous tribes) make significant connection with elements of nature. They relate to animals, birds, and reptiles are as totem animals.

Sustaining the Body

Survival can also mean preservation of the body in the face of a real or perceived threat of attack. We survive by keeping our bodies alive by any means necessary. For some species, this can take the form of individuals fighting each other. The victors gain the right to pass on their genes to another generation.

The most successful forms of animal life have all developed effective, practical tools and skills designed to help them remain alive. Some can run with great speed. Some can climb to great heights, while others burrow. Porcupines and cactus have evolved prickly exteriors. Bees sting. Camels spit. Birds fly. Dogs run in packs. Humans can think strategically and communicate verbally; they developed weapons. Humans also value individuality. A person's size, speed, or the ability to develop certain skills has value in preserving life for both that person and his tribe. Other species, like ants, are more identified as a group and thus oriented to preserving the tribe, even at the expense of the individual.

We honor the creative process by maintaining our physical existence in the face of potential destruction in order to continue the species. One of the Ten Commandments is "Thou shall not kill." The Koran teaches not to take innocent life. But it also speaks of acting in self-defense. In times of war, if our country is being invaded, if our homes and families are being threatened, it is appropriate to do what is necessary to protect ourselves and our loved ones and preserve our means of survival.

Sometimes the drive to survive actually has an unexpected opposite effect and can lead to death for the predator as well as its prey or its host. Viruses demonstrate a fight for survival that can threaten other life forms. If the virus survives, it can kill its host organism, thereby leading to the demise of the virus. As modern medicine discovers potent antibiotics and vaccines to ward off the dangers of microbial invaders, the virus simply mutates into a form resistant to the medicine. For example, malaria is caused by a parasite that enters the human bloodstream when a person is bitten by an anopheles mosquito. Malaria has been around since before we were human. It may even have attacked dinosaurs. In addition to humans, it can attack mice, birds, porcupines, lemurs, monkey, bats, and snakes. Hippocrates documented the distinct stages of the illness. Today, malaria is endemic to 106 nations and threatens half the world population. Because it is so ancient, it has well-developed survival

The Law of Survival

skills. Its ability to adapt and mutate is unparalleled. Whenever we develop a way to fight the parasite, it simply creates a new way to survive within the host human. Ultimately, who will win? The human host with its medicinal allies, or the attacking, mutating microbe?

Every manifestation of life is followed by an expression of the Law of Survival. It may be amusing to me to see my cats go through their daily feeding ritual, but it isn't funny to them. It's similarly not funny to see a human fighting off a virulent virus or bacteria. In both cases, the instinct to survive is the highest priority. Those life forms that demonstrate the ability to continuously and creatively adapt to ever-changing environmental factors and demands are the ones that survive and perpetrate their species.

When seen in macro-perspective, one of the most beautiful aspects of life is the way everything fits together. Is the death of something at the hands of something else happy or sad, good or bad? Or is it merely one form of the life force feeding another? We might have an emotional response to the death of something or someone, but the dance of life continues, regardless. From a spiritual point of view, the virus has as much right to survive as anything else. We may rationalize that somehow humans are more important. Whole philosophies have evolved that grant humans the right to exploit all the earth's resources, including other humans. Due to our intellectual capabilities, we have evolved to the top of the food chain. Humanity has ceased to realize that what enables a life form to survive is the complex diversity of all life forms. The interactive synergy of all species within a specific ecological niche provides the environment within which all can survive. When human beings dominate the earth, ruthlessly and exploitatively, we threaten the biodiversity of this planet and ultimately our own survival. It's as if we have become the invasive microbe threatening the survival of our host, the earth. The concept of our superiority has caused us to become alienated from nature and ultimately unable to use the laws of the universe to maximize our quality of life.

The real question is, if survival is a universal law, doesn't everything have the right to survive? If the answer is yes, then all things need to survive in ways that are in harmony with their environment, so that all life in that environment can similarly survive. If one life form becomes too dominant, it can threaten the existence of the entire ecosystem. How can we access and utilize the Law of Survival in a balanced way that supports human existence, yet does not threaten the extinction of itself or other life forms?

Astrological Correlation

The astrological sign that embodies the Law of Survival is Taurus. In terms of the fundamental trilogy of body, mind, and soul, it represents the integration between soul and body. It is a yin, or receptive sign. It partakes of the earth element, and its image is the earth itself, the living matter upon which we live, and the ultimate source of sustenance and physical survival.

Taurus teaches us how to survive by helping us get in touch with what really matters in life. It values qualities and experiences that focus on physical necessities. It has a bottom-line focus on the necessities that enable us to live a safe, secure lifestyle. The influence of Taurus helps us to get in touch with our inherent tools and talents so that we can rely on what we innately possess in order to function in practical and realistic ways. By being so grounded, Taurus can be autonomous and self-reliant. It is the builder of its own reality and prefers taking whatever time is necessary to create a life that is comfortable and stable. It values its competence and resourcefulness in dealing with life in ways that create a sense of security.

Taurus is a fixed sign. It prefers life to be predicable, routine, safe, and comfortable. It is slow, deliberate, patient, and methodical. In those ways, it reflects the nature of the earth itself—things change on this planet gradually. Taurus enjoys preserving that which it values: a possession, a personal relationship, or a healthy relationship to its environment. It also can be artistic and likes a beautiful environment as well as beautiful objects in it. It will use money as a tool that can help provide the beauty, comfort, and safety that it values.

If Taurus is not in touch with its values and does not look within for the resources that will build a life of quality, its lower-octave traits will manifest. Instead of being patient, it can be stubborn. Instead of being practical, it can be possessive. Instead of being self-reliant, it can be jealous. It can confuse luxuries with necessities and toys with tools. Not being in touch with its inner being, Taurus relies on the outer world and its artifacts to provide a sense of safety and security. In this context, Taurus can see money as an end in itself. The more money, the more security. The more security, the more power. The more power, the more control. This, of course, will minimize real security in the long run. It can undermine harmonious relationships, both to people and the environment. In its power-grabs, it will tend toward being exploitative and ultimately drain the environment of its resources in ways that reflect not being in touch with its own assets.

How to Align with the Preservation Principle

In Genesis 2:15, God puts Adam into the Garden of Eden but commands him to "dress it and keep it." In other words, Adam is the archetypal human being. He exemplifies our task of living in harmony with our environment and working the soil and tending it in order to maximize its productive capabilities. The implication is that if we do our share, Spirit will contribute the means of physical survival and fulfill the promise that the universe will provide our material needs.

The essence of life is energy. Quantum physicists as well as Buddhist philosophers have defined life as continuous flows of individual "packets of energy." You and I are such packets. The most primal manifestation of our energy is our soul. This is the essence of our being. It is our personal connection to Divine Spirit. It represents how we were created and the ways in which we embody divine essence. Matter is created through the manipulation of energy. The nature and development of our soul determines the nature and quality of our body. The body is the temporary residence of the soul. It is the physical form that is the expression of our inner being. The body is the concrete manifestation of the resonance and accomplishment of our being. It illustrates our thoughts, feelings, and actions, both past and present. If we relate to the body in that way, we can find clues about the qualities and experiences that subtly combine to create who we are. The body enables us to manipulate our environment, to survive, and to create new realities, even new consciousness. The first step in utilizing the Principle of Survival consciously is to take stock of our body. Do we feel comfortable in it? Is it healthy and capable of functioning in an autonomous way? If not, realize that the fundamental reason is that we are out of touch with our soul, our inner being. There could be realistic and valid reasons for our physical discomfort and alienation, such as childhood abuse. It could also be something as simple as our body type differing from the media images with which we are continually bombarded. Whatever the causes or reasons, we have the responsibility as well as the potential to discover and overcome them. As we reconnect to our inner being or soul, we also reconnect with Spirit. This, then, enables us to become aware of our ability to affect our bodies, and to find the strength, support, and creativity to change the situation.

Survival and Procreation

The drive to survive is also manifested in the drive to procreate. The drive for species survival can be strong, to a point of self-destructive obsession. We see this throughout the animal kingdom. It can occur as a bull moose fighting a rival for the free access to the cow, or a neighborhood dog traveling to the other side of town, eschewing food, water, and rest in the hope of mating with a female in heat. Eating and procreating are the two strongest human drives. The first helps maintain the body; the second sustains the species. If we don't eat, we can't survive—we certainly don't have the stamina to pursue a sexual partner. If we don't procreate, our lineage—and by extension, even our species itself—won't survive.

Appreciation of the body can also include awareness of its beauty; not media-defined, impossible standards of attractiveness but simply the beauty exuded by our own body as it is. The light shining in our eyes, being physically fit, and paying attention to hygiene can make us more attractive. In addition, we can pay attention to bodily adornment, choosing garments that are attractive and in harmony with our body type, size, and coloring. These are ways to not only make us attractive to others but, even more important, enable us to perceive and feel the beauty in our own physical being.

The human body is innately beautiful. The balance and proportion of the body can bring both visual delight and profound appreciation for all the ways the body can be used and enjoyed. In addition to the obvious needs of physical survival, the body can also carry a deep connection to the Divine. Some ancient pagan cultures had ritual orgies held en masse by the entire tribe. These rites celebrated fertility and coincided with spring, when all aspects of nature were renewed and reborn. In that sense the body acts out the Law of Creativity. The body is valued for its beauty, not because it conforms to some arbitrary standard but because it reflects the beauty of the natural order of life. If for no other reason, the body is beautiful in its ability to sustain physical existence. It is the vehicle that houses us in our journey toward the enlightenment of self-realization.

One of the more pleasurable ways of using our bodies is by tuning in to its sensuality. Notice how touching and being touched in a sensitive, thoughtful way brings a sense of relaxation and satisfaction. A warm hug, a hot cup of tea on a cold morning, or basking in the sun on a clear summer day are all ways of feeling good just being in our body. Adorning the body with garments that are comfortable, like silk or soft cotton, are other ways of honoring the sensuality of our body.

Perhaps the most powerful form of sensual gratification is sexual. This type of stimulation of the body can provide a strong sense of well-being, as well as being a potent connection between two people and a source of renewal within the relationship. Sexual intercourse as a mystical practice can expand our consciousness into a transcendent state. One type of sexual activity is a form of yoga that evolved in India called Tantra. Tantra is part of both the Hindu and Buddhist traditions. It is an ancient teaching that helps us connect to our spiritual nature through sensuality. The word "tan" means to extend, to weave, and to manifest. Tantra uses physical intimacy to create a mystical connection between two lovers that allows each to connect to Divine Spirit. They become god and goddess, Shiva and Shakti, the primary male and female components of life. Through this type of sexual union, partners each are freed from the limitations of their body and can experience the prime Oneness of being by integrating their energy field with their partner's.

Another form of sensual satisfaction is eating. The conscious preparation of food as a healthy, wholesome, nutritious way of sustaining the body is an expression of this principle. If we put effort into the presentation of the food, all the better. One of my sons is a chef. One reason he loves food preparation is that for him, it is an art form that combines all the senses: touch (preparation), sound (the actual cooking), sight (presentation), smell (the food itself), and of course taste. A meal is even more enjoyable if it is designed to ensure our long-term health. The longer we live in a quality lifestyle, the more time we have to experience the universal laws, develop our consciousness, and evolve.

We should remember the importance of mutual survival between humans and the rest of the natural order, and our food choices, then, should take into consideration the needs of the planet. For example, the excessive consumption of red meat is a prime cause of rainforest destruction. Local populations are cutting down their forests in order to graze cattle on that land. Unfortunately, the land is of poor quality and incapable of supporting livestock for more than a year or two. Similarly, land that is of a higher quality and capable of producing grain and other crops that could feed large numbers of people is being wasted to raise and feed cattle, the meat of which will feed far fewer numbers of people. Grain is fed to cattle in disproportion to the amount of meat it yields: twelve pounds of grain are needed to produce one pound of meat. Respect for and appreciation of the body is an important value. How the body—and our earth—is sustained is an equally important question.

Patience

The body grows and changes slowly. To successfully flow with the survival principle, we need to develop patience. Our body did not get the way it is overnight, nor is it going to change immediately.

Being deliberate and patient with physical change does not mean being inert or stagnant. The *I Ching* counsels that it "furthers one to undertake something." This implies that it is important to be active in all areas of life, even while we are waiting to see the results of any kinds of change.

Another benefit of developing patience is that it also enables us to strengthen our willpower. It's been said that everything comes to he who waits. By applying ourselves to realize a certain goal or condition and doing so consistently over time, we eventually achieve the desired end. There is a wonderful story about two frogs trapped in a vat of milk. They kick their legs in a vain attempt to jump out of the vat and save their lives. Soon one of the frogs just gives up. His efforts seem so obviously futile that he simply stops kicking and drowns. The other frog doesn't give up. He applies his will with patience. Eventually, the milk turns to butter, which is solid enough for him to push against and jump out of the vat.

This story applies collectively as well as personally. As this book is being written, humanity is faced with the global warming and the threat of our continued survival as a species. Our collective will needs to be developed and applied to altering this potential. One reason why this problem evolved in the first place was our sense of entitlement as a species. We have gone from people who revered nature and sought to live in harmony with our environment to putting ourselves at the top of the food chain. It's as if we believe that the natural world exists for our consumption or pleasure.

One way we can alter that pattern and return to a more reverent and healthy connection to the world around us is through the arts. The arts can bring us closer to Spirit and to a more secure place in the world because they often reflect nature. Anything that exists in the natural world can be appreciated as Divine Spirit in form. Whether that form is a tree, a flower, a bird, or a human, all forms of life reflect and embody the Divine. Feeling the beauty and order of nature is a way of being connected with Spirit. We realize all the ways that nature nourishes and nurtures us. It then becomes obvious that we have a personal stake in helping to maintain the balance of the natural order and shouldn't take or disturb too much. We can practice "being with the being," employing the word as both a verb and a noun. Our intention must be to connect with Spirit and to do so in an active way, as a manifestation of who we are. We can also use this as a point of attention, even after desirable, healthy changes have been made. Such a state of receptivity helps us become aware of the silent hand of God. We experience firsthand that forces are always at work in the universe to preserve and protect the eternal flow of Oneness.

Survival and the Arts

The visual arts can make a significant contribution to our awareness of the Divine. Images that are realistic renderings with true perspective and color can evoke memories and feelings of times and situations when we felt close to Spirit. Artists' expressions that have no definable forms also can be successful in providing the viewer with a mystical experience.

Dance is another art form that combines beauty with spirituality. Whether we are engaged in moving our bodies to the music, or we are observing the graceful flow of a ballet dancer, we are drawn to a connection to the Divine through the body.

The nineteenth-century poet John Keats wrote: "Beauty is truth and truth is beauty. That's all we know and all we need to know." Music is a sensual art. We can hear it but also feel it in our body. Music helps us to transcend the intellectual, linear mind. It provides an immediate connection to something greater than ourselves through the rhythm and the resonance of sound. A technique that combines both sound and rhythm is mantra. The supreme mantra, the primordial sound of Spirit is Om. This is the fundamental vibration of the universe. It flows through everything, just as the light represented by the Law of Creativity flows through everything. By chanting that sound or other mantras, we infuse our body with spiritual vibrations and facilitate our connection with Source. Chanting *om*, either spontaneously or ceremonially, is a way of bringing oneself into harmony with Oneness.

Qualities of Survival

Taurus is the most self-sufficient and steadfast of the signs. Two Taurean qualities that help us to survive are autonomy and perseverance. Autonomy mean being competent and self-reliant in providing the means to sustain our physical reality. This further implies the importance of being in touch with tools and assets that are inherent parts of who we are. Those resources provide the means to sustain ourselves in a stable, comfortable, enduring way.

The downside of autonomy is that it could lead to feeling so complete within ourselves that we isolate from others, or at least prevent others from providing help or support. Similarly, being too self-reliant could prevent us from seeing others' needs and the ways in which we can help them.

The other quality associated with this law is perseverance. This is the desire to sustain that which already exists and provide a sense of material security. That security, in turn, should be in alignment with our values. What gives our life meaning? Being clear about our priorities and utilizing our inherent resources enables us to create a meaningful life. The quality of perseverance enables us to preserve it.

Perseverance also suggests the importance of not giving up. Once we determine that something is important to have or to maintain, we can use the Principle of Survival in order to ensure its continued presence in our life.

The ability to utilize and integrate these two qualities comes from being centered within ourselves to the point that we continuously weave the strands of autonomy and perseverance. Each quality provides the means to avoid the negative manifestation of the other. As a result, our own needs are met, even as we are there for others in a healthy, appropriate manner.

Survival and Nature

The strongest ecological niches are the ones that are the most diverse. What all indigenous people have in common is the ability to coexist with the natural order and balance of their environment. They created their physical and social reality in concert with nature.

As they lived in support of the natural order, they likewise were sustained. If humans share their ecosystems in sensible ways, they actually support its strength and development. If they attempt to dominate and control their environments, they decrease the diversity and thus weaken that location, threatening its very survival. Consciously or not, indigenous people created a successful strategy of dealing with the potentially overwhelming and terrifying forces of nature. Those forces are also struggling to survive. The successful societies are those that maintain their existence without threatening the existence of other societies or species. They base their survival on a system of fair exchange through which all benefit. They live in accordance with universal law.

Taurus is a sign that defines its value system and then creates a reality that supports and sustains it. In addition to the material plane, we value things that relate to the mental, emotional, and spiritual. Eating, defending, and procreating enable the body to continue its existence, but when a predator pursues, captures, and devours its prey, it benefits on more than just the physical plane. While ingesting the substance of the dead body, it is consuming the life force that was contained in that animal. That energy provides a different kind of sustenance. Some indigenous tribes value the spirit of an animal as much as the meat on its bones. Ingesting the life force of an animal is another way of uniting with the divine force of life. For example, the polar bear is a favorite target of the native hunters of Greenland. Occasionally, hunters have reported that as they pursued and prepared to kill a bear, it turned and stared at the hunter, as if to allowing itself to be killed. The people interpret this as an opportunity for the hunter to acquire special powers from the bear by ingesting its essence as well as its substance. Some hunters kill the bear and accept its power. Others don't, fearing that it requires them to make more of a spiritual commitment to their life than they are prepared to make.

The oldest continuous civilization on earth is that of the Aborigines of Australia. The initial point of arrival for these migrating people was in the inhospitable and unforgiving northern part of the continent, an area now called Arnhem Land, which is a desert area.

For months there is no rain at all, and then, suddenly, rain begins and doesn't end for months. Large parts of the area flood. As in Hopi land, the most dangerous predators in Arnhem Land are poisonous snakes. Although snakes are used as a food source, the people of this area also revere this creature to the point that they consider the rainbow serpent to be the prime deity, the source of all life. Again, there is a sense of oneness: the serpent generated life, including people and all that they need to survive, and in turn, its progeny are used as food to help the humans survive. Thus, the serpent represents a source of both spiritual and physical sustenance.

Survival and Money

The more developed societies use money as the medium of exchange, a tool to maintain physical well-being. It is a strategy that can ensure survival. But like any element of survival, it needs to be used and generated in sustainable ways. For money to function in an equitable way there needs to be a balance of the resources from which products are made, the labor that makes the products, and the creative strategy that plans and generates the finished product. Money functions as a sustainable resource that helps to stabilize an economy when there is a collective agreement about the fair market value of the different elements of productivity. Money—and the economy it represents—becomes less sustainable when it is valued for the power with little regard for the forces and factors that underlie its true worth. As such, a society becomes financially fractured and politically alienated as some groups become significantly subordinated, materially, to other groups. In the long run, this pattern undermines the stability of the entire social and economic order.

Judaism teaches the concept of *tzedakah*, which in English is synonymous with justice. It refers to a state of awareness wherein you share that which you have in abundance with those who have a need for that commodity. To paraphrase Karl Marx, "From each according to their ability, to each according to their need." It could be money, food, clothing, or shelter. It could also be a quality rather than a commodity. If you are feeling happy, share your happiness.

If you have a great sense of humor, tell someone a joke. As you offer that which you have, you share the wealth and at the same time ensure that the flow of energy, from your abundance to another person's need, will circle around. Similarly, if you hoard what you have, you block the flow of energy. Wealth cannot be made available to you if you are unwilling to share. Tzedakah is something that should be practiced consistently and spontaneously, as part of our daily routine. It's more of a lifestyle than a social demand or duty.

My grandfather worked in a factory as a boy. The factory made silk handkerchiefs, which were very popular during the early years of the twentieth century. He was very astute and after a few years, he realized that there was one step in the manufacturing process that was costing his employers too much money. He borrowed some money and at the age of eighteen, opened up his own factory. All his workers did was put a hem on the handkerchiefs. This saved a great deal of time and money for the other factories, and his idea was a success. Then the Depression hit, and silk handkerchiefs became an unaffordable luxury. There were no bundles of unhemmed handkerchiefs arriving at his factory; he was essentially out of business. But this created a dilemma for him. If he closed his factory, his workers would be unemployed, as there were no jobs available. His employees all had families who would suffer if the father or mother were unemployed. So my grandfather kept them all on the payroll for months. He paid them out of his own pocket, and they just sat around all day, every day, with nothing to do. He was willing to put his own family's security in jeopardy just to help those who had less than he had. This went on until one day, he came to work to find his workers on strike for more money. Although he was compassionate, he wasn't a fool, and he used their action as a reason to finally close the factory. My grandfather put tzedakah into practice, even if his workers failed to appreciate his generosity and intention.

Another good example of tzedakah is radio stations that are listener-supported. Several times a year they have pledge drives that are designed for listeners to pledge a certain amount of money. Those funds keep the station alive, paying its bills, until the next pledge drive. Occasionally, a listener will call in with a "matching funds" challenge—the listener offers offer a certain amount of money if the station can raise the same amount from other listeners. The process of matching funds also operates in the relationship between humanity and Source. The universe has an endless supply of whatever it is that we need to help us survive in a stable manner. But it does need us to define what those needs are. If we don't ask, we don't receive. By being realistic about our needs and willing to live within a sustainable context—one that is beneficial to the community as well as to ourselves—our needs will be "matched by funds" from the universe, whatever form those funds may take.

Metaphysically, what is money? It is a means of quantifying a fair exchange of one person's time, effort, and resources for that of another. It is an agreement that everyone is striving for the goal of survival and security. In its most unifying sense, money is a means of improving the material quality of life for everyone.

Not Aligning with This Law

In the *Tao Te Ching*, Lao Tzu states that "the sage avoids excess, extravagance, and arrogance." We block the flow of the Law of Survival if we allow those qualities to pervade our priorities and decisions about how we choose to live. Those tendencies can be generated by the fear that if we aren't proactive enough in meeting our needs, we won't survive. Fear can lead to overcompensation. We lose the clarity that distinguishes necessities from luxuries. We grab as much as we can whenever it becomes available. Eventually, we create the conditions we feared. Being so acquisitive can be an attempt to compensate for internal, spiritual, and emotional needs that are unmet in our lives. We become consumed with greed, indulgence, or attachment. Greed is wanting more than our fair share. It discounts the needs of others and the balance of the natural order. The Law of Survival reminds us that there is enough for everyone, but if we doubt that, we may provide excessively for ourselves at the expense of others. Instead of fulfilling our needs in harmony with the universe, we do so in a way that creates a lack somewhere else. This creates the karmic dilemma of getting what we want now, but sooner or later, we have to replenish that depletion. Greed can manifest both individually and collectively. The greedy individual is one whose primary motivation is to amass possessions, regardless of the cost in terms of the physical resources or the true value of time and work spent by others in their production. In the long run, this creates an imbalance of wealth and endangers the ability of various people and cultures to survive. If we fail to share fairly, by being greedy or seeing money and material possessions as ends in themselves, we weaken the diversity of our economic and social environment. We threaten our survival and perhaps that of our progeny as well.

The same is true on a collective level through the proliferation of multinational corporations. These gigantic businesses are engaged in a multitude of functions in countries all around the world. Their primary goal is to increase profits. If environmental considerations are overlooked, or if the condition of the workers and the quality of their lives is undermined, an imbalance is created. The creators of that situation will, ultimately, in a karmic sense, be required to offset the losses. But all of us suffer due to the disparity. It seems logical that most wars have been fought for one of two reasons: One type of war is initiated by a powerful group or country trying to usurp the resources (minerals, manpower) of a weaker foe. The other type of war is initiated by people who are so impoverished that they feel as if they have nothing more to lose, so they fight against the perceived conqueror. For decades, we in the West were told that the Cold War was about two conflicting political philosophies. That was partly true. The rest of the truth is that those philosophies spawned conflicting economic philosophies. To what degree should those who have share with those who don't? And who gets to make that decision? In more recent times, we have been faced with terrorists from the Middle East. The propaganda this time is that this conflict is about religion or about modernity versus tradition. Again, this only partly explains this phenomenon. The rest of the story is economic. Even if the Islamists themselves think that their cause is for Allah, it is also about economic parity. Suicide bombers voluntarily sacrificed their lives because they have so little so live for in the way of improving their material plane comfort and well-being.

The greed that proliferates and perpetrates the imbalance that leads to these conditions is not necessarily deliberate. It could simply be a lack of understanding of the bigger picture. It could also be the result of such an overwhelming fear of poverty that any means seem justified. In either case, if we work to have more than is fair, we inevitably create lack or scarcity and undermine our own survival.

Attachment and Indulgence

Indulgence implies becoming too focused on material gratification. That drive usually is an unconscious strategy designed to cover up emotional or spiritual doubts, confusions, and fears.

In the 1970s I was living a back-to-the-land lifestyle in Northern California. I was very health conscious and prided myself on eating a primarily raw-foods diet. In the long run, this created severe imbalances in my body, due in part to lack of sufficient protein. This was a metaphor for other elements of my life that were out of balance at that time. When I left the land and moved to a more urban environment, I was soon caught up in the culinary temptations of town. Due to the protein deficiency, my body craved sugar as a way of providing quick energy. I was trying to reestablish a healthier diet in general, but in the meantime I became obsessed with doughnuts. I would deliberately alter my errands so that I could stop at as many doughnut shops as possible. Of course, this indulgence was totally out of keeping with the desire for a healthy diet. I allowed myself to continue this indulgence until one day, when eating the first of two jelly doughnuts I had just bought, I got sick to my stomach. A greater, more inclusive balance, including values and lifestyle, had returned, and my indulgence in doughnuts was over.

One reason that my doughnut indulgence seemed desirable was the sense of instant gratification that they provided. I was unwilling to do the work necessary to assess the problem and change the habit and values that supported it, so I persisted in the pattern. One of the challenges of modernity is to look beyond whatever is providing immediate satisfaction or pleasure to perceive values and patterns that will persist. And that will provide a greater payoff in the future, both for us and for others.

Attachment is another strategy that externalizes our internal emotional and spiritual hungers. Feeling insecure, off-center, or unable to create internal, enduring meaning in our life, we become too attached to material possessions or even to our own body. When the object of our attachment breaks, becomes lost, or leaves, we experience pain and unhappiness. The more we feel or express a desire for something, whether an object, a relationship, or a job, the more it remains just that: something we don't have. Sometimes, attachment can lead to dependency. We think that the only way we can feel good is by eating a certain food, or by gazing upon a certain mountain, or by having a certain possession or person close to us at all times. Qualities and experiences that are more mystical and transcendent get overlooked. In that process, we forget that even though everything that exists is Spirit in concrete structure, attachment makes us focused on the forms and forgetful of their Creator. However enjoyable those forms may be, none of them is as radiant, as inspiring, or as fulfilling as direct connection with their Source.

All material existence, be it a human life or an object, is temporary. If we become too possessive of our bodies, of material objects, or even of who we are, those attachments limit us. We overlook the importance of the Law of Impermanence (chapter 11), and the result can lead to alienation and dissatisfaction. All the laws are working simultaneously. Living a centered and conscious life requires each of the laws to function fully and effectively. If we try to make who are and what we have too stable, or if we have so little connection to anything solid that we exist only in the continuous flow of change, we do ourselves a disservice. We must look within and seek the frustration that causes one extreme to manifest to the exclusion of the other; then we can we discover the eternal elements of salvation and fulfillment. One of the prime teachings of Buddha is that the nature of life is suffering, and the suffering is, in turn, based on attachment. To strive for detachment from the material plane helps to alleviate suffering and leads to the peaceful state.

Even being self-sufficient has its potential drawbacks. Feeling the need to always be in control of your life could imply lack of connection to the Source of all providence. We need to be able to take care of ourselves, to take advantage of desirable opportunities available to us, and to be at the forefront of advocating for our best interests and well-being. And a healthy bond with Spirit reminds us that there are always allies to help achieve our goals, be they material or spiritual. All wealth comes from and is an expression of Spirit.

Spiritual Opportunity

The physical plane is the densest manifestation of Spirit. Seeing all physical manifestations as expressions of divine creation enables us to be aware of Spirit's omnipresence. Relating to the material, corporeal world as part of that divine expression enables us to identify with and feel closer to Spirit.

The spiritual quality associated with this law is *peace*. We can access peace when we put our house in order. According to Paramahansa Yogananda, peace is the most easily accessible connection to Source. In this sense, the house implies our body and what it needs to function and survive, as well as anything that enables us to create a healthy, stable relationship to the world. This is a three-step process. Step one involves clarifying our values. What are the most important and meaningful qualities and experiences in life? Are these present in our life already, or have we created a strategy that is helping us to get closer to realizing them? If our value system is sustainable—that is, not taking more than our fair share—we will feel as if our life is in tune with Oneness, and we will experience a deep sense of peace.

The second step involves getting in touch with our inner being. What feels good? What feels right? By acting in accordance with what gives us a good feeling, we create peace in our lives. If we feel unsettled about something, that part of our life needs creative attention.

The third step involves patience and perseverance. Survival can be tedious. Whether we are doing it consciously, in a spiritually focused way, or just showing up on the job every day, boredom can set in. To overcome the monotony of daily routine requires the discipline and diligence to remain mindful of the big picture. Why am I doing this? What is the immediate payoff, and what are the long-term goals? One way to develop those qualities is by developing willpower. Our strengthened will ensures that we will be able to meet our material responsibilities. It also increases the probability that our clearly defined values will become embodied by who we are and amplified by how we live. Working at this is a process and as such, it requires patience. Remaining clear about our values and pursuing meaningful things as best we can will bring peace. The process is as important as the achievement.

The serenity experienced through a task well done leads to the realization of our own competence, our own ability to preserve our existence in a self-reliant way. By extension, this also strengthens our relationship to Source.

Patience is also a prime requirement in the process of developing higher states of mystical awareness. Christian mystics refer to "practicing the presence." By showing up every day in a clear and conscious way, it becomes easier to feel that we are in the company of the One. Another term they use as a synonym for Spirit is Providence—that which creates life and provides the means to sustain it. Becoming clear about values and working to put them in place allows us to surrender to Providence. Trust in Spirit to provide. If we are doing our part, our efforts will be responded to in kind.

Peace of mind leads to stillness of movement. When we are in nature, we can afford to be more observant. We become aware of life on a grand scale, noticing and feeling the seasonal cycles and their effects. We can become aware of more subtle occurrences, like the interplay of birds on air currents, the behavioral dynamic among animals in a herd, and even the symbiotic relationship between parasites and their hosts. Those observations show us the immediacy and oneness of life. Everything is part of everything else. What might seem predatory actually are interdependent forms of mutual support. Within these realizations are peacefulness and security.

When we are in a peaceful state, we can be guided by the "inner mentor" rather than by habit, external authority, childhood programming, or logical analysis. We will be more likely to do the right thing. For example, how we earn and share our wealth can bring a profound sense of well-being. The word "charity" comes from the Latin word *caritas*, which means love. To share our wealth, therefore, is an act of expressing love. In the modern Western world this usually takes the form of making a financial contribution to a worthy cause.

Gratitude

Gratitude is another way of using the Principle of Survival as a means of enhancing our spiritual growth. Gratitude is a way of being aware of all the blessings and bounty that we have, in all areas of life, on all levels of consciousness. Instead of lamenting how little we have in one area of life, we should strive to allow ourselves to feel overjoyed about those areas where the energy and fulfillment flow abundantly. Part of the process of developing self-awareness involves being realistic about what we have and what we don't have. Being able to survive means having awareness of and access to resources. How we allocate them is a matter of free will. Resources are like tools: we can use some to compensate for lacking others. We develop our resources like we invest and save money. We create our reality so that the riches we have in one account can always be transferred into another account that is in need.

According to the Law of Creativity, the purpose of life is to create. The Law of Survival provides the means to remain and function effectively in the body in order to have a physical awareness of the Creator. The earth plane is very dense. Things move slowly. This gives us ample time to be aware of our options and to make choices that will serve us well. Everything on and pertaining to the earth is impermanent. Nothing lasts forever, and everything is in constant movement. Being aware of and grateful for our material plane gifts and comforts—indeed, even working to maintain them—is but a step on the road back to the light.

It's been suggested that God created the material plane and gave its inhabitants free will in order to give them the framework, means, and opportunity to conscientiously and deliberately turn their attention and intention back to Oneness. This is why the Law of Survival is so fundamental.

From a spiritual perspective, we can understand that everything that exists in material form has the same point of origin. If we assume that the big bang did, in fact, initiate the universe as we know it, then everything that we perceive as being in a form was originally an expression of that energetic explosion. Relating to our bodies as condensed light and as ancient as the universe itself enables us to realize the spiritual nature of our bodies and, ultimately, who we are as beings.

The Bottom Line

The drive to survive is universal. Everything that walks, flies, swims, or slithers has an innate impulse to maintain its physical vehicle. The question we must ask ourselves is how to do this in a spiritual context.

The sixteenth-century Italian poet Ludovico Ariosto wrote "Man proposes; God disposes." The concept of free will can be a hotly contested topic. Some people believe that there is no such thing, that we are destined to do certain things and have certain experiences, and there is nothing one can do to alter that. Others believe that people have the freedom to do what they choose, given their personal limitations and within the confines of the commonly accepted mores or laws of their culture. Beyond that debate is Divine Will. One of the more compelling qualities of astrology is that it is a system for understanding cycles of life experience. Understanding these macro cycles enables us to live our lives in accordance with the big picture, which is an expression of Divine Will. Thus, the most practical, realistic option of activating our own personal will is to align it with that of the Divine. This is a receptive action and is a significant part of developing a mystical awareness. By putting ourselves in the service of the Divine, by acting in accordance with its nature, we help to maintain the balance of life on the material plane and in the process strengthen our access to and usage of the universal Principle of Survival.

Similarly, working within the context of Divine Will helps to strengthen our own individual will. The debate about whether or not we have free will can be concluded with the agreement that we all have the freedom to align with the Divine—or not. Choosing to do so enables us to be open to the gifts and bounty that surround us, that fill our bodies, that *are* our bodies. We realize that taking care of ourselves and helping those closest to us can create an environment that is beneficial to all. We realize that we are using our gifts to create a life that is in harmony with the rest of the universe. Life provides the sustenance for our physical existence, and we help to support others in maintaining theirs. The perfect win/win scenario.

Along the way, we are free to enjoy the physical world and all that it can give us—but see it as the tool that it is. It is impermanent, not something to which we should connect forever. It provides the physical vehicle that enables more permanent and significant growth to take place. My friend Betty Bethards enjoyed referring to the body as our "earth suit," a great metaphor that helps us remember that the body is something we put on, then take off. We can enjoy, protect, and care for our earth suit without seeing it as who we are, or as the point of the whole earth/plane experience. Ultimately, it is merely a vehicle to help us become more self-aware, to evolve, and to align with the Divine.

Affirmation: "I am living comfortably and gratefully in the temporary house of my body, preserving and protecting the Divine light presence on earth."

The Lord is my Shepherd, I shall not want …

—Psalm 23

Chapter 3: The Law of Both/And

Distractions, such as self-pity, despondency, cowardice and irresolution, can be removed by the practice of concentration upon the single truth of God.

—Aphorisms of Patanjali,

Diversity within Unity

My friend Nancy goes to India periodically to visit her guru. He is a silent yogi who teaches by the written word and meditation. When asked one time about the true nature of life, he held up his first and second fingers and shook his head from side to side, expressing no. Then he pulled down the second finger, leaving only the forefinger pointing upward and nodded his head up and down, as if to say yes. Thus, he told his students that there is no two, no duality in life. There is only Oneness.

From early childhood most of us perceive life as multiplicity, and we overlook the unity. Ultimately, this is an illusion. The truth is that the seemingly endless manifestation of phenomena is really Oneness in many forms. This is the basis of the universal Law of Both/And.

As noted in chapter 2, duality is a necessary part of the material plane. The Bible even mentions it almost as a commandment from God. A benefit of duality is that it provides the perspective from which things can be perceived relative to each other. Without relativity, you and I wouldn't exist. We couldn't mark our progress and growth or even define our values, priorities, and goals. We wouldn't know that we have a body. Species, both human and nonhuman, couldn't physically survive if they didn't know when to plant and when to harvest or when to migrate north or south. The categories of dualistic separation seem endless. There are distinctions of rich and poor, young and old, traditional and avant-garde, pragmatic and artistic. Of which categories are you a member? All of these divisions are relevant to help us identify who we are. They enable us to see the choices available for determining who we want to be and for creating the life we want for ourselves.

Divisions of reality also reveal the diversity of life. They help us to awaken to the Law of Creativity by displaying the endless forms that Spirit manifests. These expressions mirror the varieties of creative options available to each of us. The stream of manifestation provides a richness and complexity to life that can be beautiful, amazing, comforting, and inspiring. The varieties of experiences and perceptions provide an unlimited menu of ideas that we can share with each other as we learn more about who we are and can be.

As children, it seemed obvious and natural to us that things are separate from each other. We noticed the differences between ourselves and our parents, between our mother and father, and between our family and the family of our friends. It seemed like a normal part of growing up to learn to distinguish what is from what is not, where we felt safe and where we didn't. Survival requires that we perceive life as a duality. However, when everything is seen as relative to something else, it leads to the obvious assumption that duality is what life is. Identifying with the duality prevents identification with Oneness, and there is also something confusing about diversity. We can feel overwhelmed by the multiplicity of choices and alienated from the endless series of distinctions and phenomena. Focusing on diversity can obscure the perception of Oneness, and, in effect, the Creator.

Good Enough or Not?

Separation from the Creator leads to alienation. Anxiety develops when we perceive ourselves as separate from everything and everybody else. There is "you," and then everybody and everything that is "not you." Relationships, events, experiences, and other people are judged when compared to something else. You are more or less intelligent, attractive, talented, or wealthy than someone else. You are taller or shorter. Part of a desirable group or an outsider. There is no acceptance of things coexisting and each being okay as they are. First comes the awareness of the differences, then the tendency to choose sides. Sometimes the choices are obvious. It is better to be prosperous than poor, better to be healthy than ill. But being poor doesn't make one bad. Being ill doesn't make one wrong. It's one thing to strive for a better quality of life, another to feel lost or not-as-good-as if we are unsatisfied with our current condition.

In spite of how many ways and times we tell ourselves that we are better than so-and-so because of this or that, there always will be times when we come up short, seeing ourselves as not-as-good-as. The perspective of not being good enough restricts our access to the Law of Creativity because it leads us to believe that either we aren't capable or we don't deserve it. Maybe we don't even know the principle is possible for us to access. If we see ourselves as better than other people, we may limit our potential behind a veneer of entitlement. Perceiving ourselves as being on either end of the spectrum of good or bad prevents our establishing ourselves in Divine Oneness.

It also limits our access to the Law of Survival. Perceiving life only as duality causes us to wonder why some people's circumstances are more comfortable or desirable than our own. It appears as if God is blessing others but not us. This assumption is similar to the doctrine of predestination that arose during the Protestant Reformation. Predestination is an aspect of Calvinism that rationalizes that the well-being of certain people is due to their being "chosen" by God. This may be due to their race, health, wealth, wisdom, or some other identifiably desirable quality. To the Calvinists, the chosen enjoy assured entry into heaven. The rest of us need to work harder, produce more, and enjoy life a lot less in the hope of gaining the recognition and acceptance of God. Otherwise, we are doomed to hell or at least to our current state of misery. Calvinist doctrine goes hand in hand with the repression of the unique, the creative, the interesting. Everything is subordinated to the need to please an external authority figure, be it the high priest, the dictator, the father, or God himself—to become "as good as they who are already chosen." The strictness of this belief system limits any form of individual expression, from political to artistic to sexual to emotional, as it would jeopardize the individual's and his family's chances of being "saved."

As we work on the process of centering ourselves in this Principle of Both/And , we integrate dissimilar aspects of who we are into the wholeness of who we are becoming. In so doing, we realize that beyond the diversity of our various parts, we are one being. We can see the connectedness between ourselves and everything else, that nothing is separate from anything else. There may be shades of this or that, but eventually everything folds back into Oneness. The apparent dualistic differences are actually different phases and aspects of the same thing. Everything is both/and.

In a transcendent state of mystical attunement, we can become aware of the connection between all life forms. We perceive the vital life force—the cosmic energy—permeating and activating all phenomena and all action. Everything is connected to everything else through that energy. The only reality is the vibration that is everything, even as it takes on temporary forms and functions, shadows and shades. In the Oneness, we perceive life as it is, and we are free to direct the creative power inherent in life in whatever manner we choose.

Evolution of Consciousness

The state of evolution of the human race is reflected in the consciousness of individuals. In turn, human consciousness is reflected in a culture's perception of life as Oneness. Ironically, some of the so-called "primitive" cultures maintain an awareness of life as Oneness, while most modern cultures do not. In areas as geographically diverse as North America and Africa, for example, the prime deity was— and still is—known as the sky god, an image of unification. Four thousand years ago the matrilineal Mesopotamian civilizations worshipped the great goddess, an image implying a common universal source. One of the names assigned to the great goddess was Sophia, also known as the goddess of wisdom. The goddess-oriented cultures of Mesopotamia were interrupted by invading hordes from the north who brought with them a more pantheistic and patriarchal cosmology. The goddess archetype also appears in the Celtic culture, where she was called Sheela-na-gigs. Here again, the goddess was disempowered when first the Romans and later the Christians conquered Celtic lands and culture. In both the Mesopotamian and Celtic cultures, the great goddess was fragmented into several goddesses, each one presiding over a different facet of life. With that split began the movement from total connection to Oneness to a separation through the fragmentation of duality. The goddesses were ascribed counterparts in the form of male gods. This pattern became more refined and expanded by other pagan cultures, from the Sumerian to the Egyptian, until eventually the Greeks developed the concept of twelve Olympian gods and goddesses. Those archetypes form the basis of both astrology and the twelve principles defined in this book. Greek culture formed the basis of Western civilization and thought. The distinction between the various gods and goddesses in any pagan culture mirrors the fragmentation of Oneness.

The Greeks focused on "bringing order out of the chaos" by emphasizing rational, analytical thinking and demeaning the feeling and intuitive aspects of consciousness. Ironically, Greek philosophy stipulated that it was the goddess Sophia who was the creative power that emerged out of the original chaos. The great philosopher/mathematician Pythagoras coined the term "philosophy," which means lover of Sophia. The feminine archetype and influence were present in the early Greek culture in a primal role. But ultimately, she became only a part of the whole. Not only did the duality become emphasized, but one side of it became more acceptable and valuable than the other. From the Greek point of view the Olympian pantheon arose from the overthrow of Uranus, the sky god, an image also projected by the indigenous people of Kenya and Zimbabwe. To the Africans, the sky god represents unity and stability. It is possible that the prehistoric Greeks embraced the same idea, but as time went by it changed and came to be an archetype of restriction and control, reflecting two ways of seeing the same concept. Unlike the Africans, the Greeks portrayed Uranus as being domineering. He tried to restrict his offspring, the Olympians, from fully embodying their power and potential, thereby preventing them from utilizing the Principle of Creativity. This led to the overthrow of Uranus by Zeus and the other Olympians (Uranus's own progeny). This dispersion reflected the perceptions of reality of the Greek people, as well our own, to this day. We perceive and prioritize the many and overlook the One.

In contemporary astrology the planet Uranus symbolizes change. Uranian energy brings inspiration. If one is open to the awakening of consciousness, the inspiration can lead to innovative, experimental change and ultimately personal liberation. But Uranus's momentum for change also can create restlessness and frustration, leading to endless changes born of reaction, boredom, or frustration. Uranian energy can feel cold, relating in a detached, aloof manner that brings a "better than" or "above it all" demeanor. This view of Uranus contrasts with that held by the Chagan people of Kenya, who believe that the sky god is inclusive and inspires the perception of and connection to the big picture. And then we have the Greeks, who saw Uranus as divisive. He was removed from the human experience in both awareness and concern. His focus was on domination and control. We see, then, how Uranus can be reflective, either of the overriding both/and Oneness that flows through and brings all life together, or of the fragmentation into different attitudes and behaviors that keep us limited in a dualistic reality.

Another significant cosmological shift in the evolution of consciousness came from the Hebrews, who embraced the concept of one God. Prior to that, the early Hebrews believed in a dualistic deity in which Sophia was the source of creation, and Jehovah was her consort and assistant. This later evolved into Jehovah's being the dominant force as well as primal cause. Eventually, Jehovah was questioned by some, as was Uranus before him, as being too removed from human experience and too vengeful to do people much good.

The early Christians returned to the early Hebraic dualistic view but later added a new concept. Perhaps wanting to make the prime deity more accessible or more caring, or perhaps as a form of propaganda in which they appealed to the people who maintained allegiance to the great goddess, they conceived of a fundamental duality in which Jesus represented the Divine masculine and Sophia represented the Divine feminine. At a much later time, the feminine principle was renamed Mary. This primal duality eventually became a trinity that the Christian Church called Father, Son, and Holy Spirit. This can also be defined as Divine Spirit, humanity, and the energy that connects us, which has been defined as Christ consciousness. In our time this concept is redefined as mind, body, and soul. Each of us is responsible for maintaining our own integration of these three levels of being. The self was integrated in that way embodies and mirrors Oneness.

Male and Female

The Bhagavad-Gita also discusses the need for personal integration. In verse 1 there is a discussion of the proper motivations and behaviors of people. It is noted that all people, regardless of gender, have both masculine and feminine qualities. The masculine qualities are reason and intellect, self-control, discrimination, and judgment. The feminine are tenderness, love, sympathy, kindness, and mercy. However, no one is either all male or all female. Biologically, we now know that everyone has both male sex hormones (testosterone) and female hormones (estrogen), each in a way that manifests uniquely, both behaviorally and biologically. The challenge and the opportunity is to maintain our male/female balance in a healthy way. There is a vast spectrum of gender expression based on genetic makeup alone. At one extreme of the biological spectrum are the XXX males. They can have so much testosterone that they seem to be driven to superhuman feats of strength but can also be prone to rage and violence. Although there is no comparable genetic YYY signature for women, there is Turner syndrome. Occurring in one out of 2,500 births, it affects genetic females by causing a short stature and underdeveloped ovaries. In the middle of the spectrum are so called "intersex" people, who defy the standard categories of male or female. For example, Klinefelter syndrome describes a genetic male whose chromosome makeup leads to low testosterone, decreased libido, infertility, and female hair distribution. This occurs in one out of five hundred to a thousand births. For most people the combination of male and female characteristics is neither genetic nor extreme. They exist in terms of behavioral choices. These people feel comfortable manifesting traits that society might define as masculine and reserved for men, or feminine and reserved for women, regardless of whether they are male or female. In some cases, sexual orientation (heterosexuality, homosexuality, or bisexuality) may be established prior to birth. Gender identity (perceiving the self as male or female, regardless of biological sex, such as exists in trans-sexuality) may also be genetically determined. In either case, it is a mark of modernity that diversity is becoming more acceptable, and that we aren't trying to force ourselves to conform to culturally defined and accepted behaviors based on obvious genitalia. By extension, it becomes easier for each of us to express our own unique gender identity/duality in an integrated, balanced way. That balance represents and reflects our potential to be at one with unity by working with the Principle of Both/And.

Astrological Correlation

The Principle of Both/And is an expression of the sign Gemini. Gemini is oriented toward mental social activity. It experiences life in a spontaneous way and focuses on the phenomena of its immediate environment. Gemini is the sign of communication and prioritizes sharing information with others as both giver and receiver. It can enjoy conversation, writing, or expressing itself with its hands through craftsmanship or other forms of manual dexterity. The totem for Gemini is the twins, which suggests that Gemini has the capability to relate to a number of different ideas by sharing with a variety of people. Gemini is the ultimate multitasker. Its strength is its ability to relate to anyone at any time about anything. It is the consummate networker. At best, it is clever, quick-witted, intellectual, and inspired. At worst, it can feel overwhelmed by too much information and confused about the significance of any of it. Similarly, its diversity of social contacts can lead to superficiality and lack of deeper interaction.

The image of the twins can be misinterpreted as implying that someone with Gemini energy in the horoscope is two-faced and duplicitous. A more accurate interpretation is that twins signify Gemini's ability to perceive life from many perspectives and to then share the information gleaned from them.

The twins can also imply duality. If we get stuck seeing ourselves and others as separate, without simultaneously being aware of our similarities, we are stuck in duality. This can lead to communicating in a "right" or "wrong" mode, rather than as an open-minded networker. This needlessly limits our ability to learn and continuously expand our mind. We can get stuck in a "better than/less than" judgmental pattern in our relationships with others, which limits the nature of our social experience.

The contribution that Gemini makes to the human experience is mental agility. Its higher octave is to tap into the universal mind, to be able to perceive and understand anything at any time from any point of view and to communicate it intelligently to anyone.

How to Align with This Law

The Principle of Creativity allows access to the vital life force in its most authentic sense. We are free to use that energy at any time. The Principle of Survival enables us to provide the means to maintain that which we have initially created on the material plane. The purest way to integrate the creative force within the body is through sound, a vibration that is both audible and sensual. As mentioned in chapter 2, the *om* sound is the most primal vibration. The first two principles, creativity and survival, put emphasis on the body and on feelings; the Principle of Both/And amplifies the mind. The primal experience of sound as a sensate experience in the first two laws becomes more complex when applied to the mind. It is utilized as a vehicle to communicate ideas and concepts. Language is an extension of the mind and an expression of what's in it. So, with the Principle of Both/And, language develops as a fundamental tool that allows a society and a culture to evolve. We can share our perceptions and feelings as we become more individuated and yet more integrated into our social order. Thoughts are forms of energy. They arise through an integration of present feelings and perceptions with past experiences.

The mind is oriented to gathering and sharing data. It is that part of us that perceives, thinks, and understands information and files it in the appropriate place. The mind uses data to invent, calculate, strategize, and create empirical definitions of reality. It recognizes the difference between our inner world and the world that exists outside us. It is also the part of us that can note the similarities between inside and outside, and the fact that one mirrors the other.

The mind also is capable of perceiving data or phenomena that may appear to be dissimilar, perhaps even in opposition to each other in some way. Things in seeming opposition to each other can help to expand our awareness. Noting the contrast between things can lead to clarity about each one. Becoming aware of their similarities and integrating their differences enables us to perceive them as a complementary unit. By observing how the two parts of any complementary pair differs from each other, we can become more aware of how all seeming differences combine to create the unity of life. This is another example of the uses of the Principle of Both/And.

Perception and Mental Discipline

In order to utilize the Law of Both/And properly, we must be able to perceive the unity that connects all opposites. It is important to keep two things in mind when striving to do this: First, what appears to be in opposition to something else is an illusion. Any one thing is a fragment of a much larger thing. There are a limitless number of reference points that separate different perspectives. So instead of allowing ourselves to be limited by either this or that, we should try to see how many points of view we can become aware of that pertain to the subject at hand.

The second task to keep in mind is the overview perspective. The Christians of the fifth century defined God's presence on earth as being perceivable through "divine sparks." The Jewish Hassids of the eighteenth century had the same idea. Contemporary quantum physics has arrived at a similar conclusion. The challenge in this is to achieve awareness of the source of the sparks and strive to perceive the many perspectives as manifestations of the same unity. Through this integration we can create continuity in our life and an awareness of the flow of energy within us, through us, and around us.

Perception is determined by our state of mind. One way that we can exercise free will is by choosing the quality of our thoughts and the contents of our minds. Our state of mind is our primary reference point, the condition through which we perceive and distribute information. It is the only "place" in which we are always present. Is that state joyful or fretful? Optimistic or worried? Accepting or judgmental? Curious or dogmatic? One of the basic tenets of Buddhism is the concept of mindfulness, which instructs, above all, to pay attention. Be mentally present. This requires discipline and the ability to maintain concentration. Mental discipline is a fundamental requirement of being able to embrace all seeming opposites.

One way to become aware of the state of mind is by learning how to control the mind. One useful technique for doing so is controlling the breath. As we slow down our breath, we slow down our mind. We can actually notice what's going on in there. Breath control is one aspect of the yogic technique of pranayama. Pranayama is an ancient teaching of unknown origin. Prana is the creative vibration or energy that activates and sustains life in the body. Pranayama is the conscious control of prana. It involves much more than just controlling the air passing in and out of our lungs. As pranayama techniques are practiced consistently, they help increase our health and vitality as well as help discipline and control the mind.

Many years ago I was at the Langley Porter Institute, which is the mental health branch of the University of California, San Francisco. Some researchers there had been conducting experiments in which they monitored the brain waves of meditators. The subjects were all masters of their particular technique. The study involved attaching electrodes to the brains of people who were meditating. The electrodes were connected to an electroencephalograph (EEG), a machine that detects patterns of brain waves. The study showed that any technique of meditation changed the brain waves from what they were prior to and subsequent to meditation. Furthermore, different techniques produced different graphs. What was even more interesting was the fact that they found particular energy waves, previously recorded but never in the context of a human brain, that appeared during meditation. Most fascinating was the discovery of new waves, never known or recorded before, showing up in the brain patterns of meditating masters. Here was scientific proof that the brain itself is altered through mental discipline.

In addition to pranayama, there can be different points of attention on which our mind can focus during meditation. We can concentrate on a sound, or mantra, which is repeated continuously throughout the session. Or we can visualize an object or form, such as a flame, a cross, or a star, in order to quiet and control the mind. No technique is better than any other. The study proved that when practiced with consistency, each worked to produce an alteration of the mind. The point is that mental discipline serves the process of consciousness development.

Other forms of controlling the mind are not so esoteric. For example, another type of meditation is walking meditation. While walking, we pay attention to what is around us, what we may be feeling, our breathing, being hot or cold. No judgment. Walking meditation allows us the freedom to go where we choose and, while there, to simply be. We perceive the animated life of a tree, the radiant glow of a fern, the continuously expressive sound emanating from the flowing water in a creek.

One of the best places to experience a walking meditation is in a quiet, pastoral environment. Being in nature is the simplest, most immediate way to transcend duality and feel at one with life. Children, in particular, respond to nature. The best way to teach children about God or any concept of a transcendent Divine Being is by allowing them to experience nature in a personal and immediate way. As adults, we experience nature in a conscious way; we can also express our gratitude for all the blessings of our life. The expression can be silent or verbal. Remember, language is one way to access the Principle of Both/And. We can communicate appreciation for a specific blessing or simply for the beauty surrounding us at that moment.

Over time, mental discipline leads to the attentiveness that awakens the observer to the underlying unity of all phenomena, the perception of Oneness. It is most beneficial to practice either a sitting or walking meditation in a ritual manner. We can, however, also develop mental discipline by simply being attentive in the moment while we are walking around and living our lives. Some people focus on a mantra while engaged in daily routine and mundane activities. My client Gary practices another type of walking meditation. A devotee of the Taoist spiritual path, he has committed the *Tao Te Ching* to memory. While walking, he recites its passages. He uses this as a technique to still his mind. He eliminates random, intrusive, or negative thought and replaces them with inspirational messages. We can do something similar by memorizing poems or prose passages that we find particularly uplifting and significant to us.

Writing is another method that can serve to slow down and focus the mind. Creative writing of prose or poetry accesses the Principle of Creativity as well as helping develop our concentration. Keeping a journal can also help attentiveness. One useful example of this is a "feelings" journal. Rather than focusing on the events of our life, we can take time to note our emotional responses to the events of life. Getting in touch with how we feel, at which times, in which relationships, and under which circumstances can help in the process of consciously creating ourselves and our life. It can also be a vehicle for mental discipline.

Writing down our dreams each morning (see chapter 12) can be another aid to mental focus. In addition, it can help access the Law of Transcendence. Dreams are reflections of our soul. They provide insight into parts of our psyche that are otherwise unknown to us, parts that are usually blocked by the ego. A dream journal can aid us in developing more consciousness about who we are and what resides in the recesses of the mind. It can offer yet another way to develop mental focus.

Educational kinesiology offers a series of physical and mental exercises that can produce mental focus. These are highly effective techniques when used with children in classroom situations. The exercises are designed to promote integration between the left and right brain. This is another way to incorporate opposites in order to create a unity. With these exercises, unity is created within the mind, which then enables us to go about our lives in a centered and more attentive way.

The keys to maximizing the beneficial potential of any of these tools are clarity of intention and consistency of application. It doesn't matter which "technique" of tuning in we choose, as long as we remain aware of the goal. If we seek to perceive life as unity and choose to live by the Principle of Both/And, any tools that help to slow down the thought process and control the mind are useful to that end. It's important, though, to choose at least one such tool each day in order to make significant and consistent progress. If the goal is fuzzy or our application of techniques is sloppy or inconsistent, we may not notice enough progress to keep us motivated.

The Polarity of This Principle

The polarity of the Law of Both/And is talking and silence. Talking is an opportunity to share information with others. It provides a means of letting others learn more about who we are by letting them know our interests, opinions, and points of view. They don't have to agree with us. A stimulating debate between people who have different perspectives can help both sides have a more well-rounded understanding of the topic. Through sharing, both parties can partake of the Principle of Both/And, by realizing that Oneness incorporates all possible perspectives. It benefits the development of our consciousness if we communicate in ways that are inclusive and respectful of other people's points of view. Prior to speaking, we should strive to make sure that we are clear about the topic and that our ideas are lucid in our own minds.

Silence implies the absence of sound, especially speech. Silence involves emptying the mind of thought. This is harder than it seems. Slowing down the mind through pranayama and other forms of mental discipline is a good way to work toward the empty mind. The Buddhists call it "finding the space between thought." By stilling the mind from its normal thought patterns and perspectives, we open it up to new insights, realizations, and intuitive clarity. An open mind also can expand consciousness into the limitlessness of Divine Spirit.

One way to experience silence is by undertaking a word fast. We could choose to do this for a few hours or a few days. We might notice that in the beginning of the self-imposed silence, ideas come to consciousness, and we feel that they just have to be communicated. We could write them down or simply allow them to subside. As time goes by, those thoughts will recede completely and a greater sense of calmness will pervade the mind. That state is conducive to triggering a mystical connection to Spirit.

As more information is taken in, through conversation with others as well as through silent contemplation, it's easier to realize the inherent interconnection among all things, a fundamental part of accessing and living in the state of both/and.

Life Is a Hologram

It's been suggested that life is a hologram, in which everything is an aspect and a reflection of everything else. Rather than judging something based on what it is or isn't in relationship to something else, our challenge is to see how everything complements and reflects everything else. Several years ago my mother was in the intensive care unit of a hospital following open-heart surgery. She lived several hundred miles away from me, and I was flying to see her weekly. I wanted to offer her supportive company in the hope that it would affect a rapid healing. I am an only child, and my mother was a widow, so after a few months of wandering the corridors of the hospital or sitting by her bed for many, many hours a day, I was feeling isolated and alienated. My only conversations were with nurses and doctors about her condition. My mother was unable to speak, so there were many hours of silence. Most of my time was spent listening to my own thoughts.

I value the diversity of humanity and think of myself as open-minded to all cultures and ethnic groups. So it was somewhat shocking to hear little judgments creep into my mind, based on observations of patients, staff, and other patients' visitors. I noticed that I was comparing myself to everybody and finding something in everyone that was not as good as something in me. Was this a way to feel less alone? It was actually making me more lonely. Maybe it was a way of covering up my feelings of inadequacy in taking care of my mother. Or perhaps this was an unconscious attempt to compensate for my insecurities. In reality, it was probably all of the above. But it didn't make me feel good about myself. I vowed to alter my perceptions and quiet the judgmental mind. I assumed it would take days, even weeks, of hospital hall-walking to rectify this tendency. It actually took a few minutes. Instead of looking at people as not good enough in whatever way, I noticed how we were similar. In that process I saw the light that shined in the eyes of each and how everyone manifested a unique, radiant quality. The more I looked, the more I recognized that residing in and emanating from everyone is the face of God, the radiance of the Divine. Everyone included me, and this realization helped to dispel feelings of loneliness and fear. I felt more connected and less insecure.

Not Aligning with This Law

The lower octave of this experience occurs by twisting this law into "either/or." This is the embodiment of the duality. In duality we perceive self, other, and the act of perception as being three separate entities. This type of perception and thinking causes us to remain in a disjointed state of mind, confused by the multiplicity of life. The mind remains restless and attuned to a superficial understanding of information. Ideas seem fragmented, and we are left feeling agitated, worried, and overwhelmed. The inattentive, undisciplined mind drifts within polar oppositions. Impatience becomes the action of choice. Tuning our minds solely to the drift of a conversation or to the random flow of ideas restricts us to our immediate mental environment. In this condition we perceive who we are and what we are looking at as two different things. We never bridge the gap between "me" and "not me" by attaining the mystical, transcendent state of consciousness. We become judgmental. We continually walk down the corridors of our lives, making judgments about everything and everybody in a vain attempt to feel better about ourselves and to bring order out of the chaos of our minds. Being judgmental causes attachment to duality and limits consciousness. When attached to duality, we perceive everything and everybody, including ourselves, as being at one pole or the other. Either I am this, or I am that. Either you are this, or you are that. If you are this, and I am that, we are different. You are either with me or against me. This can cause us to feel excluded. After all, if we judge everyone else and find their flaws and faults, we create creating an arbitrary barrier between ourselves and them. We are different, on the outside. Alienated. To overcome the habitual perception of an attachment to duality requires a clear focus on the present.

Without that focus, we easily become involved in too many interests or relationships. We trade off depth for breadth. But instead of experiencing the breadth in a centered way, we flit from topic to topic, person to person, and conversation to conversation. If we are centered, we can pull together the seemingly random situations to see them all as interconnected parts of Oneness. Each point may be fine and interesting in and of itself, but there is no central reference point that enables us to pull it together and recognize the central theme.

We also block the flow of this law when we dial in to one point of view and assume that it is (and consequently we are) "right." Once we stipulate something is more or less desirable, it's as if we are compelled to defend that position, locking ourselves into one perspective. All the other "sparks" of possible truth are discounted. This is a dangerous tendency that also can develop within media and political circles. It involves narrow, doctrinaire thinking. Progressive-minded people are criticized and demeaned for taking into consideration the values and perspectives of other people and other groups. This type of thinking not only limits debate and the possibility of making decisions or policy based on consensus, but it also creates the fear that if we speak our minds, expressing our ideas and points of view, we may get hammered by someone who disagrees with us. So we all go off into our respective corners, protecting ourselves and hiding our information. We are penalized by having less information and a narrower perspective than we would if discussion were encouraged in the public sector. It also enables those who have greater access to the media and more power over the media to have dominion in shaping public opinion. Instead of both/and, we are left with divide and conquer.

Similarly, if we become identified with our ideas, we can be attached to the information. That attachment can cause us to seek validation from others for "correctness" of our ideas and support for who we are. We confuse what we know with who we are. We could assume that someone who disagreed with us doesn't like us. Love me, love my ideas. This form of emotional attachment could cause us to limit or to stop sharing our points of view.

Another potential problem in accessing this law is how we arrive at our conclusions. We may be single-focused in mind and dedicated to understanding whatever topic interests us, but if we don't share what we know, and we aren't open to others' points of view, we are limited in our knowledge to our own experiences. We could be so convinced of what we know that we don't listen to anyone else. The *I Ching* says, "There is something ponderous about the self-taught person." We could be so heavy-handed in the communication of our ideas that we pontificate and give a monologue, rather than discuss and have a dialogue. We could be so dogmatic that our style turns off the listener, and shared learning stops. It blocks the flow of the Law of Both/And.

Spiritual Opportunity

Spiritual wisdom advises one to be in the world but not of it. We should strive to function effectively in the material world without identifying or becoming attached to it. Similar advice can be given to governing our state of mind. We should use the information at our disposal to positive end, share it with others, and not be limited by its scope. The key is to be alert to the immediate flow of information, while simultaneously being aware of the divine mind. We remain centered in the mystical state of transcendent awareness, while at the same time being aware of the mundane thoughts, conversations, and experiences that circulate within ourselves and between ourselves and others. This is the mental equivalent to rubbing your stomach and patting your head simultaneously. Or chewing gum while whistling. Keeping the mind focused simultaneously on both the transcendent and the mundane can, however, be done. It is a form of mental discipline combined with consciousness development. Learning how to concentrate and to direct our thoughts is the crucial element in this undertaking.

Each of the universal laws can be accessed through a divine quality. These are forms of being or behaving that connect us to Oneness. Everyone has the right to employ them as a means of connecting to Spirit. The more we connect or identify with each divine quality, the more we employ each as continuous reminders of who we are, and the more we exist in the consciousness of Spirit. As we exist and function in that context, we are more aware of our potential for creative expression and personal fulfillment. For example, the Law of Survival is associated with the divine quality of peace. If we focus our mind on peace, even as we are interacting with others and going about our daily routine, we function in the realm of Oneness. We function in the world and act appropriately, but we are also aware of the unity flowing through and connecting all things.

If we choose to ground our minds in the divine quality of the Law of Creativity, which is light, we feel a sense of courage that enables us to experience life as a self-generating adventure. Light can also help us remain clear about the intentions underlying our actions. The more consistently we affirm and employ the divine qualities of being, the more we actually become peace or light or whatever qualities we need to experience ourselves as being more centered in a more exalted state.

Proper use of the universal Law of Both/And manifests the divine quality of inclusion. This state enables us to perceive everyone and everything as a part of Oneness. We learned from the Law of Survival that our bodies are condensed molecules of light. Everything that exists in physical form has its origin in the beginning of life itself. The same is true for the mind. Whatever we perceive is an expression of Oneness.

The Buddhists teach that we should strive for the spacious mind, one that is capable of embracing all thought and all phenomena simultaneously. In that state, we embrace our inherent Buddha nature and relate to life as an interconnected whole. We can relate to others with acceptance, rather than judgment, and realize that our desires, goals, fears, and drives are reflections of everyone else's. Instead of judging others as a way of feeling better about ourselves, we can learn from them. We are each other's teachers.

The spacious mind also enables us to be mentally adaptable. Our minds can flow to an interesting or stimulating point of attention. This can prevent mistakes from recurring, as well as allowing us to adapt to the unexpected contingencies of life. Humanity's ability to change in the face of environmental shifts and challenges is one of the reasons our species has survived.

Yin and Yang

Taoist philosophy is based on the concept of yin and yang. These are the fundamental constructs of the dualistic world—the receptive and the active. To the Taoists, all existence partakes of both qualities in different proportions. Everything is in a state of flux, moving from one to the other. What is receptive now will be active later, and vice versa. This is the Tao, the way of all life. To remain attached to only one or the other, to identify with one to the exclusion of the other, is to work against the nature of reality. To embrace both, to be at one with the Tao, means being aware of the continual interaction between those forces within and noticing how they are affecting and being affected by energy around us.

The Bhagavad-Gita is to the Hindu what the Bible is to the Jew or Christian and what the Koran is to the Muslim. It is a scriptural reference about the Divine. It is a story in poetic form about the nature of life and how to function on the earth plane in order to experience transcendent consciousness. It discusses the basic nature of life and the journey we undertake by being here. The Bhadavad-Gita states that every being is an essential soul, neither male nor female but having qualities of both. The masculine tendencies are the powers of self-control, reason, and logic. The feminine are the qualities of sympathy, kindness, and mercy. The former express overt strength; the latter, inherent tenderness. There is no judgment that one state of being is preferable to the other or more dominant than the other. There is no mention of the weaknesses or limits either. They both represent fundamental qualities of being. Through behaviors defined by these qualities, people reflect the nature of the Divine.

When we integrate the masculine and feminine parts of ourselves, we are practicing the Law of Both/And. Whether we are in a male or female body in our current incarnation is significant. It is not arbitrary; it is part of our karma and our evolutionary process. In any culture there are strictures that are specific to each gender. Some of this is useful and valid. Division of labor is useful for survival. Men and women each have strengths that are unique to their gender and that are important for the continuation of the physical existence of the people. On an individual basis, however, we should each strive to be who we are and to manifest our responsibilities in a balanced way that expresses the Law of Both/And. A man, then, even when handling the responsibilities of hunting, defending, and achieving can do so with sensitivity and understanding of others. A woman can, even while performing her tasks of family nurturing, can do so with strength and intellect. Ultimately, this helps produce a society that values individual freedom. Metaphysically, we are not limited by gender in our choices.

My client Gretchen is a practitioner of Tibetan Buddhism. She once attended a retreat at which two young monks were imparting important teachings. During the question-and-answer period, a female student asked why the lamas and rinpoches, the upper echelon of the lineage, were almost always male. At first the monks didn't even understand the question. When they finally got it, they roared with laughter. They responded by saying that they incarnated as males because at this point in time, men were perceived as being more authoritative than women, and the important thing was for the greatest number of people to be open to their message. But if that were not the case, they could just as easily have taken on female bodies. To these beings, the choice of male or female is based on their determination to best to serve humanity.

The quality of inclusion allows unification of the apparent dualities. We can see ourselves as reflections of each other and all humanity as a reflection of the Divine Source. Inclusion will enable us to perceive everybody and everything as being part of the same Oneness that we are. It also will enable us to realize that everyone is included. As we relate to and embody the divine quality of inclusion, we feel a personal connection to Oneness, to the all and everything. Similarly, we can perceive all parts of ourselves in more accepting ways. We don't have to like everybody, every experience, or even every part of ourselves. By starting from a point of inclusion, however, we create a framework within which to work on improving that condition, relationship, or trait.

The divine quality of inclusion, therefore, enables, stimulates, and promotes the realization of the oneness of humanity. When the world community separates people by race or nationality in the realm of international relations, it is working against this law. This is also true in any society that makes distinctions based on caste or clan, ethnicity, or gender orientation in such a way as to deprive certain groups of the advantages and freedoms of other groups.

The Law of Both/And functions within as well as beyond the material plane. We all have the potential to perceive the physical and the metaphysical, the incarnate and the discarnate as parts of the same unity. The African writer Malidoma Somé tells us that in his tribal tradition, it is both accepted and expected that one can perceive and communicate with beings "on the other side." To his people, this is not a big deal; it is part of the natural order of things. By allowing that to be part of life, there is an infinite amount of information that can be gained, information that is beneficial to the tribe both in terms of physical survival and spiritual sustenance.

In order to be successful in any endeavor, it is necessary to have a confluence of thoughts, words, and deeds. By cultivating our state of mind, we take care of the mental part. By being in a peaceful state of mind, connected to the Tao and grounded in Oneness, we are more creative in choosing words that accurately express our thoughts. We will then be effective in letting others know our points of view and more successful in imparting useful information to others.

The Bottom Line

Columbus called the native people of the New World "Indians" but not because he mistakenly assumed that he actually had sailed to India. The word "Indian" is actually a corruption of the Spanish term *en Dios*—in God. He perceived correctly that these people lived in harmony with their environment. They placed a higher priority on the interactive connection among all beings than on the singularity of this or that.

The more we are centered in the awareness of ourselves as separate and different from everything else, whether better than or not as good as, the more we tend to experience life as an overwhelming, confusing, chaotic mess. As we develop the ability to be present in the moment, residing in spiritual Oneness, and to include all parts of ourselves in our experience, we cease to perceive life as fragmented.

We realize that life is a beautiful, harmonious, flowing, supportively interactive unity. Living in Oneness, we perceive all phenomena from that state. However real it may appear, duality is an illusion. The only truth is the One. We are all the same in that we share a common life force, were generated from a common source, and have the same fundamental needs and desires.

Part of being mindful is being grateful. It is helpful to remember that the blessings in our lives are our own good karma matched by the boundless potential of Spirit. Part of being conscious is to remember to express gratitude for these blessings. It's been said that what we praise is what we become. By praising Spirit for the splendor and variety of creation, as well as for the unity of creation, we eventually perceive that we are both an inherent and interconnected part of that creation and the Creator.

Affirmation: "I am included in the flow of divine creation. Everything around me reflects the light of my own divinity."

There is one body and one spirit ...

—Ephesians 4:3

Chapter 4: The Law of the Eternal Present

The way to peace and fulfillment in union with God, the divine Beloved, is a daring dive into the "eternal now."

—Meher Baba

The Mother Is the Source

Many years ago when my son was small, he gave me an impatiens plant. It was healthy and pretty, but I liked it most because it reminded me of our connection and love for each other. Impatiens are somewhat delicate plants, but I took good care of that one. Time went by, and eventually my son grew up and left home. Shortly thereafter, the impatiens started to die. Having a sentimental attachment to the plant, I wanted it to remain alive and a part of my life. I took a cutting from a remaining healthy branch and rooted it in water. When roots were sufficiently developed, I planted the cutting in a pot. I took as much care with this plant as I had with the original, but eventually that one, too, started to die. So I took another cutting and repeated the process over again. This process has since been repeated many times over the years. The plant that I nurture today is not the same one my son handed me years ago; its roots, branches, leaves, and flowers are physically different. Yet while the plant today is several generations removed from the original, it contains the same genetic and vibrational material of its progenitor.

The Law of the Eternal Present

This plant is special to me because it is a living symbol of my connection to my son in the here and now. It reflects the continuous growth that he has experienced throughout his life. It connects me to the past and inspires me to welcome the future.

The plant is also a metaphor for my own life. Alive in the here and now, it embodies the physical presence of its ancestor. As such, it represents my connection to my family's history. My family is the foundation of my life; it is my root. The emotions generated within me, though my relationship to my family connect me to my core. This is a common human experience: the link between the family bond and the feelings generated by that bond is the basis of the universal Law of the Eternal Present.

My source in this life is my family. The source of all families is the Source of life itself. By honoring my ancestors, I honor who they were as well as where they came from. Ultimately, this leads back to Divine Spirit. Just as the impatiens plant lives on in the form of the multigenerational cuttings, so too does our ancestral line live on in the people that we are. The universal Principle of Survival tells us that the purpose of any life form is to "go forth and multiply." In doing so, we generate progeny. By having children, our forefathers and mothers enabled their lineage to continue. We honor them by also choosing to procreate. In the process, we continue the survival of our family. The emotional support we received is passed on to our children. Relating to our children in present time connects us to both the past and the future. By being present in the now, we honor the undying past and ultimately help to maintain the continuity of life.

By being present to the moment, we are able to feel the fullness of our being and through that fullness access a connection to Source—the origin of all that is, was, or will be. Source is the basis of all families and tribes. It is also where each of us comes from prior to birth and where we shall return upon dying. The mother is the agent of Source, as it is through her that we all come into this world. The ancient cultures and indigenous people that exist today revere the mother for this reason. In the Navajo culture, land is passed on through women. To the Australian Aborigines, the female is the gender of life. The basis of the Aboriginal culture in the northern territory of Arnhem Land is *yothu-yindi*, which translates from the Gumatj language to "mother and child." All relationships stem from and are based on that fundamental union. The most sacred relationship is that between the Creator and the offspring. Our mother is our immediate connection to the Creator. By honoring our mother, we honor all women; by honoring all women, we honor the Source of life. By honoring the Source, we connect to and ultimately identify with Oneness. Identifying with Oneness we immerse ourselves in divine love.

Astrological Correlation

The Principle of the Eternal Present is represented by the zodiac sign Cancer. Cancer signifies the experience of pure, immediate, subjectively experienced feelings. These enable us to be emotionally self-aware and sensitive to the needs and feelings of others. Emotional awareness helps us develop empathy for others and to relate to them in warm, caring, nurturing ways. In Western cultures, feelings tend to be undervalued and under-expressed. It seems it's more acceptable to interact with others in cold, uncaring ways or at least in ways that allow logical understanding and communication to trump feelings and sensitivity. Human abuses and brutality are typically reported by news agencies as "business as usual," with no counterbalancing collective emotional response of outrage.

Cancer is the sign of the family, especially the mother. The earliest Western cultures perceived and defined the prime deity as female. She was the great goddess, or Divine Mother. She is the female aspect of creation. Paramahansa Yogananda says that due to our physical and emotional bond with her, we are closer to our mother than our father. The relationship to the father develops later. Yogananda suggested making a conscious effort to connect to the mother each night while falling asleep. Affirming the female aspect of Spirit makes it easier to have an immediate emotional tie to Source-as-mother and to feel nurtured and at peace.

Cancer is also the sign of the parent/child relationship. Regardless of our situation, we all have the *potential* to relate to others in a warm, supportive, nurturing way. We also all have the need to feel protected and cared for. This potential is harder or easier to manifest and fulfill, depending on the placement of Cancer's affiliated planet, the moon, in our astrological chart.

When we are off-center, these qualities of nurturing and protection can manifest in our being overly controlling or demanding in our parental role. We also could be hypersensitive, moody, or excessively self-protective in our childlike nature. Centering in this universal principle requires learning to recognize our emotional state and responding to it gently and effectively.

Cancer also prioritizes its connection to the home as a place of security and family. Family implies both one's immediate family and family of origin. As such, Cancer can be sentimental and enjoys researching and learning about its genealogy. Off-center, this can lead to being overly possessive of both physical and emotional reminders of one's past.

The relationship to the childhood family can, in turn, suggest a connection to one's past as a being. I am not just the partner to my spouse, the parent of my children, or the child of my parents. I am a singular and unique being who has been formed by the many personal experiences I've had since the origin of my life as a being, an eternal soul.

Origins, Childhood, and Past Lives

Our lives as souls began prior to our birth in this lifetime. Our core being was generated by Divine Spirit. In this life, the core self is reflected in the relationship to our family during childhood. Our membership in our family honors the accomplishments of those who preceded us and who created the vibrational matrix that attracted our soul as a haven for growth and development. Similarly, our spontaneous emotions can mirror our core self in the present. Having no emotional self-awareness limits access to our core. Limiting access to our core limits access to our roots and family. Collectively, a rootless society is a throwaway society, one in which human life and its fundamental experiences are not valued. Conversely, remaining connected to our roots ultimately connects us to our common origin. Union with Source bonds us with the rest of the human family. When people start perceiving reality from that perspective, the resulting change of consciousness will affect everything, from primary relationships, to international relations, to systems of economic distribution.

Our past in this life, reflected by our family of origin, can mirror our past lives. How our family related to us as children suggests how we related to ourselves and others in past incarnations, as well as the way we are likely to relate emotionally to ourselves and others in this life. The legacy that determines the quality of our future experiences is a by-product of childhood programming and present-time experience. It's as if the details of our past free-will choices are etched on our soul, programming our hard drive. Those engravings create a vibrational resonance that is reflected in the conditions and circumstances into which we were born. How we respond to that environment will either maintain or alter the initial soul harmonic, which is the essence of who we are. If we experienced a warm welcoming in this life, the nurturing we received will be easy to continue to manifest in our behavior toward others. The body is the parents' gift to the child. Being happy in the moment is our gift to our parents. Our well-being is an expression of gratitude for their time, care, and love in a supportive, encouraging environment. At minimum, it expresses our thankfulness to our caregivers for providing us with a body and a chance to be on this plane of consciousness, growing and working through our karma.

But there may well have been nurturing patterns that didn't feel comfortable to us as children. The family may have been significantly dysfunctional. There may have been little warmth or feelings of well-being and security in our experience with the family of origin. We could choose to continue to manifest the self-serving, abusive, or hostile patterns that we learned from our parents, or to not continue. These are free-will choices that we make daily. Our parents' behavior was only reflecting parts of our fundamental essence back to us. Our free-will choices prior to this lifetime could suggest a lack of self-worth or difficulty responding to nurturing, as programmed from past-life experience. Or we might have formerly been a perpetrator of child abuse or other forms of power misuse. Maybe we never developed the sense of empowerment, deservedness, or self-love that enabled us to say, "Stop! No more." Whatever the past-life programming that led to the experience of a painful childhood and a difficult relationship with parents and family of origin, we can consciously reject those patterns. If we choose not to repeat them, we change our karma accordingly. It's also important to realize that abusive parents probably started out their lives as abused children. They didn't break the pattern, but we can. By consciously breaking away from negative patterns, we not only liberate ourselves but also create new karmic habits, even as we demonstrate to our family a different way to be.

Our parents are our first teachers. They create an environment that provides the opportunity to learn some primal lessons in this lifetime. That we chose these people can be hard to accept if the parents were abusive, neglectful, or unavailable. It doesn't mean that we aren't deserving of love and attention. It also doesn't necessarily follow that we were so horrible in a past life that karmically, we are being punished by having to withstand our parents' abuse or dysfunction. It could simply signify a lack of self-love or a sense that somehow we don't deserve to be loved, cared for, and nurtured. For example, I did a past-life regression session with a client I will call Bernice. She was born to a teenage mother, a single parent who gave the child to her parents to raise. The grandparents were old. They had raised their children and resented this child's invasive presence in their life. They related to her in a cold, indifferent manner. As an adult, Bernice had not been able to create a healthy, fulfilling relationship and blamed her upbringing for this. During the regression she discovered that she had lived in Europe during the bubonic plague. She was married and had a daughter. Her husband and daughter both contracted and died from the disease, despite her efforts to save them. She survived. She went to live in the city where she continued to care for the ill. Again, she survived. Although she displayed unswerving dedication to the ill, she was left with terrible feelings of self-recrimination. She blamed herself for her family's death. She considered herself a bad wife and mother, undeserving of being loved or cared about. The family with whom she incarnated in this lifetime and the relationship she had with them was based on what she assumed she deserved. Her family of origin provided the setting that allowed her to live out her expectations. With consciousness, however, she saw that her assumptions about herself were wrong to begin with. She had done all she could as a loving, devoted wife and mother. She had simply been fortunate enough to escape the disease. Learning to value herself in this lifetime requires her to overcome her family circumstances. The off-center patterns she grew up with reflect her previous life experiences but don't need to limit her in her current life.

Our childhood experiences connect us with people whose vibrational frequency is similar to our own. It is not our parents' fault that we grew up as we did; it's ours. If we blame our family for an unhappy childhood, we perpetuate our own misery. We are stuck in the past and unable to access the Law of the Eternal Present. There is no blame; there are only lessons. By uncovering the reasons why we chose our childhood experience, we can let go of the past and move along on the path of new growth in this lifetime.

Our childhood reflects our past lives, which in turn provide our foundation in this life. Our new life allows us to make new choices and decisions about who and how to be. Some of these patterns may be hard to change, because our childhood imprinting creates some of the deepest grooves in our psyche. When other parts of our life fade, it will be our early life experiences that remain to remind us of the most basic part of who we are. An example of how enduring childhood programming and experiences can be is seen through my friends Joe and Lee, who are taking care of Joe's aged mother. His mother suffers from Alzheimer's disease. She is in her early nineties, but all memory of her adult life has been erased by the illness. The only thing she does remember is being a young girl. Sometimes in the middle of the night, she calls out for her mother and expresses the needs and fears of a three- or four-year-old child. These are the oldest and deepest parts of herself. They are the only ones left that she can access. Even though they are inappropriate to express as an elderly woman, they nonetheless are accurate expressions of her core experiences in this lifetime.

The most direct way of relating to ourselves is by accessing feelings. Our emotional state is the most reliable way to determine who we are. It is also an excellent way of sharing our core self with others. If you and I to go a movie together, read the same book, or view a sunset, we can discuss the meaning or impact of the experience. We can have a certain understanding of how we each experienced the activity. The emotions that got stimulated within each of us, however, are not as easy to convey. If we try, something gets lost in the translation from the emotional to the verbal. Even if we do not, being in conscious awareness and expressing this awareness are two entirely different things.

Overcoming a Difficult Childhood

One way to break some of our dysfunctional programming from our parents is by tuning in and developing a relationship to Divine Mother. In his autobiographical book, *Of Water and Spirit*, Malidoma Somé details his initiation rites of passage in Burkina Faso, West Africa. The first rite involves sitting in the hot African sun, staring at a tree, with no food, water, or sleep. He is told to remain there "until something happens" but isn't told what to expect. Days go by, and he just sees the tree as a tree. It's not particularly remarkable in any way. His muscles ache, his throat is parched, his stomach is growling. Suddenly, he notices the tree begin to turn green. The whole tree—trunk, branches, and leaves—radiates a deep, soothing green. It begins to move in slow, graceful patterns. Suddenly, it becomes a beautiful woman who gently caresses the sore, sensitive body and soul of the young Malidoma. Her warmth and love heal his pain, and he knows that his consciousness has been altered in an important and fundamental way. He was visited by Divine Mother. By being in the moment and concentrating on what was directly in front of him, he transcended his mind and body. He became more inwardly focused, tuning into an emotional flow. This is one way to feel a connection to Source.

Anyone can experience the mother firsthand in the waking state and in present time. One way to do this is by observing or creating rituals that honor her in nature. For example, the moon is responsible for tidal flow. As the moon moves through its monthly cycle, the tides rise and fall accordingly. In astrology the moon pertains to emotion. It can indicate how we respond to the immediate flow of life experience and how we deal with and express our emotions. Our emotions are like our personal tides that flow with the cycle of the moon. If we observe simple monthly moon rituals around the new or full moon, they can help us to track our own emotional cycle. These are the times each month when our feelings are more heightened, and we can be more aware of what is going on inside.

The sun represents the source of creativity in our solar system. As with the moon, periodic observances of the annual sun cycle also provide opportunities to track our personal life experience, as expressed outwardly. The solstices and equinoxes mark the beginnings of each of the four seasons. Those seasons also reflect the life cycle of an organism—it is young (spring), comes to adulthood (summer), goes through middle age (autumn), and finally, elderhood (winter). By celebrating the changes of season, we celebrate the cycles of our own life experience.

The ancient Greeks introduced the concept of *logos*, or logic. Logos is a quality that is uniquely human and that can help us understand ourselves and create our own reality. The logical mind can comprehend everything from how to plant crops to the underlying order of the universe. With such understanding comes the ability to control our lives to create a reality that is safer and more secure and that conforms to more of our needs. Without logic, we are left with unpredictability. Without logic, the universe would seem chaotic and could treat us as it chooses. We would have no awareness, no perspective, and no choices. It is much the same with individual human experience.

How to Align with This Law

Tuning in to Our Emotions

Emotions are not so easily controlled, yet the first response we have to an experience is emotional. Before the logical mind chimes in with its ideas, judgments, or strategies, we have a feeling about what confronts us. To act from that emotional perspective may be the most real thing we can do, as it is an expression of our true, immediate, subjective experience. However, it won't necessarily help us respond effectively, safely, and appropriately with the immediate reality. That is something that can be best done by accessing the linear, analytical intellect. The Principle of Both/And would suggest integrating the two ways of dealing with the situation—logically and emotionally—in order to manifest the best response. Western culture is out of step with the universal principles, and it has created an imbalanced reality as a result. We have been taught to primarily value the analytical process and to overlook, even repress, our feelings. The poet William Wordsworth referred to the "meddling intellect" as a deterrent to being in touch with emotions. The ultimate result of locking up our sensitivities in the chamber of the logical mind is that we tend to dismiss our feelings and emotional needs.

For some people, consciously accessing inner sensitivities requires reprogramming the psyche and the behavioral patterns learned in childhood. Some children are raised in an environment in which expression of feelings or emotional needs was dangerous. The parents may have felt overwhelmed by their responsibilities, had personal problems, or were simply unaware of their own internal experience. For whatever reason, the child learned at an early age that to be vulnerable lead to being hurt. Children learn from experience. Hiding feelings from others leads to masking them, even from the self. This pattern needs to be broken. Working with a therapist or practicing meditation exercises can help break the cycle of emotional self-abandonment and enable us to be continuously present within our emotional awareness.

We can also break this chain of detachment and alienation by striving to tune in to our immediate experiences and situations. This can, in turn, help us get in touch with how we feel about others and to make wise choices about the people to whom we open ourselves.

Being aware of our spontaneous response to the flow of our life enables us to be present at all times. When we notice that feelings of negativity, depression, or fear are manifesting, we can take steps to change our state. Something as simple as smiling can alter our emotional condition. Sometimes we might have to get up and leave a situation. Other times, choosing to do something that we know we enjoy will shift the energy. We need to learn what is sustaining and what is draining. Spending as much time as we can pursuing the former and limiting the latter are ways of taking care of ourselves. We can become more adept at becoming emotionally self-nurturing and capable of giving ourselves an "emotional feel good." Aligning with the Principle of the Eternal Present allows us to be self-aware to the point that we recognize our inner state and can decide whether to maintain it or change it.

Emotional Self-Care

As we become aware of our feelings, we notice when the state of our inner being is unpleasant. This is a time to use techniques of "psychic first aid." These won't necessarily resolve the problem that is causing the unpleasantness, but they can make us feel better in the present, enabling us to be more effective in recognizing what the big picture is and planning useful strategies to resolve the situation.

Techniques of psychic first aid are very simple and easy to access. They are best when tailored to who we are and when pertinent to the situation at hand. One person could feel better calling a friend for a short chat. Someone else might prefer to read a chapter in a good book or a story in a magazine. For another, a cup of hot tea in front of a fireplace could help shift his or her emotional state. These measures rarely take longer than ten or fifteen minutes, but they can completely change the way we feel and how we experience and create our day.

Another way to become more emotionally self-aware is to keep a journal that focuses on emotional experiences. This is especially useful if we tend to be linear and more oriented toward ideas than emotions. The content of this "feelings journal" is not external events or interactive experiences with other people; the point is to note our immediate internal state or mood and express that through the written word. This enables us to develop a strength to compensate for a weakness. We could use the first page or two to write down words that describe emotions we can't identify. We can turn to that page and scan the words to locate the one or ones that seem to fit our state. Then we can write about it. With practice, we will be able to recognize emotional states more spontaneously and accurately and won't need the linear reference.

Qualities Connected with This Law

Two important qualities connected to the Principle of the Eternal Present are receptivity and self-protection. When accessing both of these qualities, we are aware of other people's feelings as well as our own. To be receptive means to be open to the energy of the moment, including that of others. Does the energy surrounding us feel safe, comfortable, and supportive? If so, we can express our feelings openly, allowing ourselves to be more transparent. Similarly, when we feel protected, we can be more open and receptive to those people. We cocreate with them a social environment that is caring, warm, and enjoyable.

Being overly receptive can cause loss of identity and lead to being completely caught up in the emotional mood of the environment. This can leave us open to being drained.

We might also tune in to the energy of our immediate social environment; we might feel that others are being too emotionally demanding or draining or are too cold and unavailable to respond to us in a caring way. In such situations it is appropriate to resist internalizing their emotions or revealing our own and to adopt self-protection as the appropriate mode of response. Being emotionally self-protective enables us to remain emotionally self-aware and self-nurturing without being hurt or taken advantage of by others. Taking care of ourselves doesn't mean being cold or indifferent to others. We can remain attentive to them and interact with them in realistic ways without putting ourselves in emotional jeopardy. However, at the extreme, we should also avoid being overly self-protective, as that can excessively limit emotional involvement. We could become so resistant to emotional interaction that our relationships remain superficial. We might be the most sensitive person in our social circle, but unless we let others in on that reality, we shut off from emotional support and connection to others.

Not Aligning with This Law

There is an inherent paradox in the Law of the Eternal Present. That is, even though we strive to keep our consciousness in the here and now as a means to a mystical communion with Divine Spirit, this law also helps maintain our connection to our familial past. If that connection remains the priority, we are not so present. If all we do is remain present, we could overlook the valuable support we receive from our ancestors. One resolution to this dilemma comes from an essay by Argentinean writer Jorge Luis Borges. In his essay "A New Refutation of Time," Borges discusses vertical time and horizontal time. Vertical time is chronological time—yesterday, today, and tomorrow. This enables us to remain in continuous contact with our family and our past, even as we plan and prepare for the future. As Borges says, "I never pass the Recoleta Cemetery without remembering that my father, my grandfather, and my great-grandfather are buried there, as I shall be."

In horizontal time every instant is autonomous. Everything that is happening in that moment is connected to everything else existing in that moment—but that's all. To Borges, nothing preceded that moment; nothing will follow. He says, "Time is the substance of which I am made. Time is a river that sweeps me along; I am the river."

This is similar to a quote by German philosopher Arthur Schopenhauer, who said, "No man has ever lived the past, and none will live in the future; the present alone is the form of all life." We can tap into vertical time to learn, to remember, and to honor those who preceded us. Ultimately, however, we align these two concepts so that they function like cross-hairs, a cross, or a plus sign. By remaining at the center of the cross, we integrate the eternal present with the awareness of where we come from and where we are going. Without that alignment, we could either remain attached to the past and our memories, or live for a future that has not arrived and maybe never will. Or we could just live moment to moment and be oblivious of how we got here and where we could go from this point.

The key to integrating these two perspectives of perception is tuning in to our inner self and the emotions that flow there. Not being in touch with our immediate feelings can prevent us from flowing with the Law of the Eternal Present. Our emotions provide clarity about our experience in the now. This clarity, in turn, helps us to connect to our core self. If we negate or overlook our feelings, we become disconnected from our core. Denial of feelings can take us right out of the awareness of the moment and our experience in present time. Emotional alienation can block connection to our past, in terms of both family and Spirit. It can also cause us to remain stuck in the past; in the emotional, psychological, and behavioral programming of our childhood, for example. As such, we continue to identify with who we were, how others related to us, or with past experiences. We seem to live our lives by looking in a rearview mirror. This doesn't help us see where we are going, nor does it provide a clear, accurate perspective of where we are. In so doing, we allow our past to define and limit our future. In neither case are we present in the now.

Emotional self-awareness, therefore, is our most immediate access to Spirit. When we overlook how we feel, we disconnect from our origin as a soul. If we identify with our past to the point that our emotional attachments to our history define who we are in present time, we deny ourselves access to present time awareness. We continually project those experiences into the situation at hand. Rather than "being here now," we merely re-experience our past in the present. We could also perceive people in the present time as those from the past and unconsciously re-create past relationships. These tendencies limit our identity and growth and prevent us from being anyone other than who we were.

Our childhood relationship to our parents and the programming from them that we internalized could have left us feeling undeserving, fearful of rejection, or fearful of being prideful. Being prideful refers to putting awareness of self in a higher priority than awareness of God. One of the liberating lessons of the universal principles is that everyone and everything is a divine manifestation. As we learned from the Principle of Creativity and the Principle of Survival, everything about us, from our being to our body, partakes of the essence of the Divine. To enjoy that reality is part of our birthright. Exalting in being who we are—maximizing our abilities and sharing ourselves with others in joyfulness and love—enables us to flow with those first two laws. It also helps us to establish a base from which to experience the eternal present.

It is possible, however, for us to be so caught up in ourselves that we are unaware of everything that surrounds us, human or otherwise. This degree of egocentrism suggests insensitivity to others and a high probability of not being in tune with our inner self. The obverse would be people who are also self-absorbed but who are continually feeling so overwhelmed by their own emotional responses to external stimuli that they are unable to openly express their feelings in appropriate ways. Thus, even though they might be aware of their emotions, in effect, they become prisoners of them. This can lead to emotionally dependent relationships in which the individual needs others to provide him or her with a sense of emotional well-being, because left on their own, they feel insecure and out of control.

Even if we are in touch with our feelings, we can also undermine the Principle of the Eternal Present by failing to integrate these feelings into our life in a good way. For example, we might act in a way that is based on emotion but without real understanding of where the feelings are coming from or what they reveal to us about who we are. Thus our actions fail to produce a sense of emotional well-being, let alone a mystical connection to the Divine.

If we are sensitive to others but still out of touch with our inner self, it could be that we are the source of emotional support for others and tend to be the "emotional carriers" of the relationship.

Taking responsibility for others at the expense of our own needs is a good definition of codependency. We put others' needs so far ahead of our own that our time for personal fulfillment never arrives. We take responsibility for other people's emotional well-being to the exclusion of our own.

Similarly, if we seek out others to emotionally care for us, allowing us to feel safe and secure while avoiding our own emotional self-awareness and self-nurturing, we again create codependent relationships.

We also might avoid being present to our own experience by being reactive to others. In reaction mode, we focus solely on the external and in the process, limit and repress our internal process. We attempt to protect ourselves by putting attention onto someone or something outside ourselves. This can also lead to codependent behavior. Our sense of well-being becomes predicated on meeting someone else's needs or making her happy, perhaps at the expense of our own needs. Obviously, the desirable state is mutual fulfillment; a relationship in which both parties relate in thoughtful, considerate, cooperative ways with each other. In order to cocreate such a situation, we must first be in touch with how we feel and what we need. We also must be clear in communicating that information to others.

Being Responsive

One way of creating a healthier emotional environment for ourselves is by changing reactive behavior into responsive behavior. In reaction mode, the only point of focus is "other." Others' needs and how they want us to behave in order to feel good about themselves are our only point of attention. In response mode, there are two points of focus. The first point is ourselves. For example, we might become aware of someone else's needs or expectations in a situation through verbal exchange or by intuition. Or we know what someone needs based on past experience with that person. Then we have to determine how much time, energy, drive, interest, or motivation we have to meet those needs. The second point is informing the other person, either through words or actions, how many of his or her needs we will choose to react to (or are capable of reacting to). In this way we are true to ourselves, affirming our emotional reality in this present situation and establishing healthy emotional limits and boundaries between ourselves and the other person. We are not being insensitive; we are simply being honest.

Being in touch with our emotions and expressing them clearly and consciously can also help us to be better parents. When we share our feelings with our children, we encourage and support them to share their sensitivities with us. This mirrors the sacred relationship every human being shares with Divine Mother. It creates a bond of nurturing and love that is the foundation for a child's growth. Experiencing our children becoming independent from us is a mixed blessing. It can liberate our time, energy, and resources, but it also can create a longing, a tendency to cling to that special relationship that we shared with them when they were younger. We remember all the cute ways that they were, things that they said, and ways that we helped them when they were confused or in trouble. These are precious memories, but attachment to them also draws us into the past. If we identify too much with the past, our growth in the present is limited. The challenge is to build on our past success, even as we pay attention to opportunities and challenges that present themselves to us now. This growth will aid in our relationship with our children. As we continue to develop, we give them the message that life is about advancing to new levels of awareness and experience. This offers them the support to continue that pattern in their own lives. As we grow, we also create emotional space within the family for them to develop. We don't continue to relate to them as young children when they are adolescents, for instance. Our parenting skills and patterns shift as their maturation requires. This promotes a healthy family dynamic.

A person's birth is an event that has always seemed like a mystical experience to me. It is clearly a moment when we have the opportunity to feel connected with Source. The development of Western civilization has diminished the awareness of that connection by putting such heavy emphasis on logic and the development of the intellect that mystical experiences are either no longer noticed or are undervalued. For example, consider how modern hospital births are so oriented toward technology and man-made drugs that the mother is either overwhelmed by the experience or is completely unconscious during the birth itself. Although the intention is to provide a safe environment for both mother and child, the resulting experience often comes at the expense of the spiritual experience of birthing. This is an example of how the imbalance between the intellect and the emotions affects most of us. On a collective level, if we maintain that imbalance, we perpetuate an alienated society. We are left in the limbo of a left brain/right brain duality with no sense of a transcendent Oneness and no connection to our shared origin. This pattern fosters the separation between the genders. Men are supported as being dominant, and women are limited to being subservient second-class citizens. The denigration of women undermines the sanctity of the mother, the human vehicle that brought us here to work for ultimate liberation. Nurturing, caring, and human warmth remain second to the masculine qualities of achievement, control, and emotional abandonment. The concept and experience of family—our own and ultimately the human family—remains fractured and fragmented.

Throughout human history the primary vehicle of survival and evolution has been the extended family. If a mother died in childbirth, there were always grandmothers, aunts, or older sisters who would contribute to raising the child. If the father died while hunting or in battle, there were always grandfathers, uncles, or older brothers who would supply the growing child with food and instruction. These relatives also assisted in child-rearing, even if the parents were present. They could offer emotional support, spiritual growth, or survival instruction beyond the ability of the parents themselves. This also worked in the reverse direction, so that no elder was ever left bereft of sustenance as his or her productive years declined. No one was left without support. Over the past couple of centuries, the growth of "progress" through the industrialization of the world has led to the decline or demise of the extended family. With the rise of the factory, beginning in the late eighteenth century, people began leaving the land. Whole family groups spent their lives in service to the production of machines and material goods.

Their health suffered, their family lives declined, and the support they had disappeared. Today, people have become isolated in their nuclear families. Families have become alienated from each other. The unified support of the past doesn't exist. If adults in their prime become ill or incapacitated or die, the surviving family members may be at great risk. Our cities are littered with senior citizens living on the street. Children are growing up with no place to call home. The physically and mentally ill suffer broken lives, living from handout to handout or from bottle to bottle. The world seems to have successfully put the Greek ideal of *logos* into reality. We have brought the order of the intellect out of the chaos of emotion. But there has been a great price: the disconnection to our inner self. We have become materially prosperous, even as we have lost our soul, our core being that knows how we are connected to the world emotionally, spiritually and in a familial sense.

A further challenge in aligning with the Principle of the Eternal Present is the potential conflict with the Principle of Creativity. In creativity, emotion experienced as instinct is the basis of action, as it provides the impetus to initiate action. The Principle of the Eternal Present, on the other hand, uses emotion as a vehicle to deepen self-awareness. Whether or not that awareness impels us to action is immaterial. Those emotions connect us in deep appreciation of our family or our spiritual origins. They stimulate us to be supportive of others, recognizing that we are all part of the one human family, and they help us to be more aware of the potential available in each moment. The eternal present is more about *being* than *doing*. Getting too caught up in the doing can limit our access to this law, just as too much being can limit our access to the Law of Creativity.

Spiritual Opportunity

When we work with the universal principles we sustain ourselves and simultaneously help to create an environment that supports the survival of others. Like many other immigrant families, mine has stories of extreme acts of single-pointed selflessness (not to mention determination and strength of will) that enabled us to survive and thrive in the United States. One such story is about my maternal great-grandfather, Barnett Bornstein. He emigrated from Poland in the late nineteenth century with no money and speaking no English. He immediately realized that to survive, let alone advance, he had to learn English. There were no English classes available and no Polish-English dictionaries. There were, however, Polish-German dictionaries and German-English dictionaries. So over the course of two years, he taught himself German in order to learn English. During that time he worked as a manual laborer to survive, sleeping in doorways and saving whatever money he could. His goal during this time, and the reason he came to America in the first place, was to send for his wife and then start a family. With amazing grit and determination and an unbending willpower, he succeeded in achieving his goal. The result was the growth of his family and ultimately, me.

In traditional cultures, having children meant that the tribe would continue to survive. Children were also a form of social security. They would provide the care and nurturing of the elders. In effect, this system of family heritage is a positive feedback loop that reflects life: we are born and cared for, and we in turn give to those who have cared for us. This cycle mirrors our relationship to Spirit: we are created by Spirit, and as we care for other manifestations of the Divine, we are provided with means of survival by still other expressions of the Creator.

The continuity of family is represented by the generations present on earth at any given time. Our families are present in the here and now as a result of that continuity. The achievements of my great-grandfather are carried forth by the way I live my life, by what I accomplish, and by the way in which I parent my children. This pattern is a reflection of the divine presence in life. Jesus maintained that the universal consciousness present in him is the consciousness of the eternal now. In Spirit there is no past or future, only the everlasting present.

Astrologers look at the motion of the planets to determine cycles of time, within which different energies are in play in our lives. Understanding these planetary cycles can be useful for personal growth, planning strategies, and defining ways to achieve goals. This is beneficial in maximizing our potential in the linear dimension; it also limits us to a realm in which space and time are prime coordinates of reality. It perpetuates the illusion of duality. It is possible that as human consciousness develops, we will perceive reality in a way that is more sophisticated. A different state of the collective consciousness could function in a way that enables us to tap into total consciousness by living in the eternal present. We can realize that we *are* forever, not that we were or will be.

When living in the awareness of the present moment, we could be more identified with Divine Spirit. We could experience our bodies as incorporating the entire physical universe. Our minds could function in the state of universal awareness at all times. We would be able to reconnect with the original purpose of our creation: to be conscious manifestations of the limitless Source of love and light.

The great astrologer Dane Rudhyar pointed out that if there was a cord stemming from the base of everyone's spine and passing down into the center of the earth, all the cords would unite at that center point. He used this as an illustration of how we are connected at the core of life. Being here now enables us to remember that interconnectedness and use it as a point of reference when relating to others or making decisions that impact our lives.

Compassion

Accessing the eternal present helps us to awaken emotionally. We tune into our most immediate and personal experience and become aware of both our own and others' feelings. In actualizing this principle, we create a state of emotional well-being from which point we can provide emotional support to others. But there is another form of tuning in to others' needs that transcends family and friends.

The divine quality associated with this law is *compassion*. Compassion means sympathy and caring for another person or any number of beings. We get in touch with their pain and suffering and respond with love. In Tibetan Buddhism, Avalokiteshvara, the

Buddha of Compassion, is often depicted as having a thousand eyes that see all the pain in the universe and a thousand arms that reach out to extend his help. In its truest sense, compassion requires action—a clearly defined, sustained, and practical determination to do whatever we can to alleviate suffering. If we perceive life from the point of Oneness, it becomes obvious that we are all striving for the same things. To act in accordance with the principle of compassion leads to happiness for others, satisfaction for ourselves, and the development of positive karma. With compassion, we feel the afflictions and joys of all beings in a personal way. In trying to decrease others' suffering and increase their joy, we increase our own happiness.

Our soul patterns manifest as behavioral habits. In Buddhist thought as well as certain Sufi groups, these are called *samsaras*. The mirror through which we can perceive our fundamental soul vibration is our immediate emotional responses to life. By developing our consciousness so that we are continually aware of our feelings, we become connected with our core self. We understand that the condition and quality of our situation is an expression of our karma. By working through that karma we are free to be in touch with our core self and, ultimately, Self, the eternal Oneness. To be continually in touch with something that is ever-flowing and changing we must be here now, creating our lives in the eternal present.

Being in the moment offers access to a limitless array of emotional experiences. Some are honest interpretations of our experience in the here and now; some are free to be chosen—feelings like love, joy, and bliss. These are part of our birthright and are available to us all at all times, if we choose to access them. Being in the moment enables us to perceive and experience the continuous miracle of life that surrounds us at all times—a pregnant woman, a nursing baby, light reflecting off the ocean or off a thousand leaves on a giant oak tree, the silence of the falling snow and the pristine landscape left when it stops. The Principle of Creativity teaches that life creates itself anew, minute by minute. The Principle of the Eternal Present teaches that we can experience and participate in that creation.

Present-Moment Being

Being emotionally aware and self-nurturing, we can generate a sense of belonging, peace, and well-being. Behaviors that create misery and suffering are those that take us farther away from our connection to Spirit. This is part of the plan. Even though we were given a unique set of tendencies, characteristics, and desires when we were first formed from Spirit, the journey of our soul can either lead us back to Source or farther away. If we notice that we perpetuate a pattern that alienates us from others, or that certain words or actions generate hostility between ourselves and others, we can choose to change or stop that pattern, sometimes by removing ourselves from a certain environment. When we generate loving feelings, compassionate thoughts, and harmonious actions, we affirm our divinity.

As we get in the habit of being in the emotional moment, we realize that there is an energy that connects us to that moment and to everything and everybody else with which we are involved in that moment—some call this intuition. Intuition is the power of knowing something immediately without reasoning. Intuition provides access to our conscience and inner wisdom. It enables us to draw spontaneously upon inner knowing as a guide to right thought and action in the here and now. It helps us to remain simultaneously in contact with ourselves and to access Higher Self and the emanation of information flowing from Spirit.

The Bhagavad-Gita defines intuition as communion with the infinite. It is a voice from Higher Being that produces all prophecy. The Bhagavad-Gita discusses five forms of intuition. The first is the awareness we all have of being present in the body on the physical plane. The other four are varying ways of being aware of higher vibrations that emanate through the body. In these states we can hear subtle sounds, see subtle lights, feel subtle sensations, smell subtle fragrances, and taste subtle flavors. These are not physical sensations but part of the process of transcending the body and becoming aware of our connection to and our ultimate presence in the Divine. Seeking to become aware of these experiences, we must shift our sense of identity from body to soul, and from soul to Spirit.

The Koran, the sacred scripture of Islam, means "the recitation." The prophet Mohammed recited the words of the Koran as he heard them when he was in divine communion with the archangel Gabriel. Mohammed was illiterate. A humble, modest man, he didn't think himself capable of proclaiming anything of value to anyone else. But Spirit had other plans for him. At first, Mohammed resisted the concepts and words that were flowing through him. When he finally surrendered, he found the words flowed effortlessly, and through them an entire society became galvanized by a new understanding of the nature of life. Ultimately, such a spiritual union leads to ecstasy. The Koran 4:103 says, "When your prayers are ended, remember God while standing, sitting, and lying down." Being attentive to the Law of the Eternal Present allows us to be aware of the presence of the Holy Spirit, our connection to Oneness, at all times.

Genesis 2:7 says, "And the Lord God formed man of the dust of the ground, and breathed into his nostrils the breath of life; and man became a living soul." At the beginning of a soul's journey, the soul contains all the clarity, purity, and potential of the Creator. Each soul is also given certain qualities that render it unique. We each have a specific set of tools to work with and desires to satisfy. We also have the freedom to choose the desires we fulfill and the way in which we fulfill them. How we exercise that freedom determines the nature and quality of our life and, ultimately, our very being.

The Christians speak of being "reborn." This refers to the life process of overcoming the desires and karmic samsaras of our soul and reclaiming our birthright as a divine being through feeling the connection to Source. On the physical plane, we honor Source through remembering and honoring our ancestors. They represent the nurturing and care that are always available to us from Spirit. The choices are ours. By honoring our ancestors and caring for our elders, we recognize a path from past to present. By keeping our point of attention in the moment, we honor our feelings. By tuning into feelings, we can access intuition. With intuition, we connect us to Spirit.

The Law of the Eternal Present helps us to remain focused on Oneness, the source of our beginning, and the end of all our striving. Mastering this principle enables us to see beyond the transitory attachments and temporary sensations of the material plane to a reality that is both nurturing and eternal.

The Bottom Line

I have seen several interesting television commercials in which a person's face morphs into another face, which in turn morphs into another, and so on. Each person is of a different race, gender, and age than the one previous. The array of changing humanity revealed is fascinating; it illustrates some of the similarities that unite us all. It also brings to mind the connection between my ancestors and myself. It would be intriguing if the computer could take the images of the previous ten generations of my family and morph them, one into the other, until it stopped with me. Visually, it wouldn't be as diverse or as extreme as the TV commercials, but it would be much more personally meaningful to me. If this family movie were extensive enough to show not just the faces but also some of the life experience of these people, it would lend perspective to my own life. These people are the background, the foundation, of who I am. Who they were, what they did, and how they did it presages my own life experience. I could use that realization to become attached to them, suffer their pain, and celebrate their joy. Or I could celebrate their lives by taking as much advantage as I can of the gift of life they provided me. A good way to do that is to be here now—to be so focused on who I am, what I am doing, and the nature and quality of my interaction with other people that I am perpetually living in the fullness of the moment. Within that context I have access to both my own personal qualities and the traits handed down to me through the generations. Going back even beyond that would unite me with the divine origin of all life and matter on this planet.

To be truly present, to direct all my faculties and awareness to the situation at hand allows me access to the limitless creative potential that lies inherently within all people and situations. That focus also frees me from attachment to the sentiments of the past or future, whether those concerns generate exciting anticipation or fear, doubt, and worry. This type of concentration enables me to experience the fullness of the moment, to be aware of all the gifts and potentials that this moment provides. And it enables me to perceive and relate to others with compassion, nurturing, and intuitive understanding.

Affirmation: "In this moment I am connected to Source and all the limitless possibilities contained in the eternal flow of life."

> *Pure Divine Love is no meek priest*
> *Or tight banker.*
> *It will smash all your windows*
> *And only then throw in the holy gifts.*
>
> *It will allow you to befriend*
> *Life and light and sanity*
>
> *And not even mind waking*
> *To another day.*
>
> *It reveals the excitement of the Present*
> *And the beauty of Precision.*
> *If confers vitality and a sublime clarity*
>
> —Hafiz

Chapter 5: The Law of Love

Stop the words now
Open the window in the center of your chest,
And let Spirit move in and out

—Rumi

Love Incarnate

My son was born in a cabin I built on a gold-mining claim on the Klamath River in Northern California. It was a simple one-room structure, created from boards I had found and reused. It was ten feet wide, twenty feet long, with two lofts at either end of the room. It was isolated from any neighbors, and we rarely had company. On the day of his birth, six of my male friends separately and spontaneously came by to visit. Since it was a month prior to the anticipated due date, I was enjoying a rare opportunity to socialize when suddenly labor began. During the delivery, several of us were up in one of the lofts, helping the expectant mother. The social pleasantries had given way to the controlled chaos of men heating up water, calling the midwife, tearing sheets into rags, or winding a pocket watch to ensure accuracy in recording the time of the child's birth. All these men were doing the work usually reserved for women—ironic. We were all excited and in a frenzy, making sure all went well. The climax was, of course, the emergence of the head, followed by the first cry, the first breath, and the cutting of the cord. I was a father! It was the most awesome, amazing, magical, wondrous, spiritual-peak experience I had ever had or could ever imagine. The most incredible part of the whole experience was the feeling in my heart. It opened to the extent that I thought it would burst from my chest. My son had been born in body, and love had been born in my heart. Feelings of devotion to this child were awakened in me that rendered me committed to his well-being beyond anything else. Everything else in my life shrank in importance beside caring for and raising my son. Nothing before or since has ever so grabbed me and altered my thinking, feeling, and indeed, the very course of my life as this experience in the cabin on that chilly, late-April evening.

As a student I had extensively read poets, philosophers, and metaphysicians on the nature and feeling of love. But until I had felt it in my own heart, its power and limitless ability to create had remained mere wordy thought-forms of the mind. Through this birth experience I finally encountered, experientially, the principle that motivated, manifested, and maintained all the others. Although all the universal laws and principles are always in play, and none is more prominent than any other, the Principle of Love is the foundation. The principle that motivates all the others, the source from which everything else emanates, the father/mother of reality in all its expressions, formed and formless, is the universal Law of Love.

As the days and weeks passed, and the love energy didn't subside, it became obvious that this love was a quality of life that seemed to be flowing continuously throughout all experience and phenomena. In my newly altered state, it was something I could perceive and feel at all times. I recognized this quality as a gift, something issuing from the core of the universe itself, a freebie that comes from being part of Oneness. It seems likely that the quality of love that I felt upon my son's birth is the same quality of love that Spirit experiences upon the creation of each soul.

When our children are conceived in love and born in love, they are actual manifestations of the principle. Yet each of our children has unique qualities. We love each one in a slightly different way and relate to them in ways that reflect their uniqueness. The relationship we have with our children mirrors the myriad possibilities of relationship we share with our Creator. For example, Divine Spirit loves us unconditionally, and we have the option of tuning in to that love and feeling safe, protected, and provided for. Similarly, Spirit provides us with the necessary means of physical survival. Sources of food, clothing, shelter, and medicine exist abundantly in the world. We, in turn, can share that love with our children and provide them with the knowledge and tools of physical survival and emotional well-being. But there are also differences in the two relationships. In human relations, it can be challenging to be unconditionally loving and supportive of a child who acts out or treats us with disdain and disrespect. It can be difficult to pass along our knowledge of life to a child who may have vastly different tools and needs than we do. When we parent our children, we, as adults, are the ones who define the nature and quality of the interaction. If we don't like how our children are behaving or developing, we should look to ourselves for the reasons. Young children reflect the patterns of their parents in the time-honored "monkey see, monkey do" mode. They relate to themselves and to others as they are related to. They act in ways that coincide with the tendencies they observe in their parents. The things we dislike about our children tend to parallel qualities we don't like in ourselves. If we want our children to change who and how they are, we need to work on changing ourselves first. It may take a while for them to catch on, but sooner or later they'll notice the change and begin to emulate the new patterns. Basically, the more love we feel for ourselves, the more love we have to share with them. And the more they will love themselves as a result.

Types of Love

We can characterize love as existing in four primary forms. The first and most primal is the love we feel for our family—parents and siblings. The *I Ching* states that the family is the foundation of society. The loyalty, security, and shared common experiences of family combine to create a safe and loving home. These are the same qualities we strive to create as a strong, viable culture. The sense of security we feel in our family emanates from everyone's knowing who they are within that context. Some families and cultures are firm in the delineation of the roles of the father, the mother, and each of the children, from eldest to youngest. Other families prioritize individuation over roles. Each member of the family is encouraged and supported to be who they are, not just who they are supposed to be within the family structure. As long as each individual acts in a polite and accepting manner with everybody else, the individual is accepted. This is also reflected in some cultures at large, in that people relate to each other in an accepting manner, assuming that they act in accordance with the laws of the land. This form of love is beneficial beyond its familial template as a mini-society, for it also provides the structure that promotes material and emotional security. The children feel the supportive strength of stable and loving parents. They learn early lessons in socialization by interacting with brothers, sisters, and cousins. Eventually, the children provide the emotional, physical, and sometimes financial support to their aging parents. We might call this the familial loop of love.

The second type of love is the love shared between friends. These are people with whom we share common interests, values, and goals. One quality that exists in friendship is acceptance. We don't usually have expectations about what our friends are supposed to do, how they should act, or what they should look like. As long as they share with us in supportive and enjoyable ways, that's enough to feel accepted and offer the same. The freedom to allow our friends to be who they are gives us the same freedom. We can be ourselves openly with others, as they are equally open with us. The limitation of this type of relationship is the depth and emotional bonding that we offer and share.

Sometimes the open, accepting friendship evolves into a union in which emotional sharing becomes a point of focus. It can't be forced; it either develops within both people over time, or it doesn't. If it does, the third type of love develops—romantic love. Sometimes one person feels the emotional connection while the other one doesn't. This is an unrequited love that leads to pain and heartbreak. Even when shared, romantic love can prove difficult for several possible reasons. One reason is the idealized expectations that one or both parties have with regard to romance. Gone is the mutual acceptance developed during the friendship stage. Once it becomes obvious that the ideals have not manifested, the romance is over—and so is the loving friendship.

When two people feel that their friendship is deepening, they usually feel motivated to be on their best behavior when relating to their beloved. They are attentive and thoughtful to their partner and express affection to each other in warm and spontaneous ways. Often, after a period of time, one or both people stop being so conscientious and don't work as hard to maintain their expression of love. At that point the relationship begins a slow decline in meaning and fulfillment. Unless both people wake up to their negligence and begin to be more present, the relationship will eventually die.

Another potential difficulty in romantic relationship occurs if it is based on erotic stimulation. This isn't necessarily a problem, assuming both people are aware that sex is the primary point of attraction and purpose of the relationship. The interaction is limited and probably not very emotionally interactive, but at least the partners are aware of the reality and satisfied by it. This type of relationship is really more about fun and playfulness than it is about a heart connection. Too often, the individuals involved are coming from a point of self-interest: how does this person satisfy my needs?

Unconditional Love

The fourth type of love—and by far the rarest but most important and impactful—is unconditional love. This is what sustains life itself and what is available to us continually from Divine Spirit. The Creator loves us unconditionally at all times. Our relationship to Source is the connection to our common, universal parent. The basis of that relationship is sustenance and support. These are qualities we can also enlist in the parenting of our children, as the guidance and understanding needed are always available to us from the Creator. If we overlook or are unaware of the qualities of this principle, we may be unaware of the acceptance from our Creator and fail to tune in to its ever-present love. When we don't relate to ourselves with acceptance and love, we abandon our connection to Source. Likewise, if we relate to our children without offering acceptance and support, they grow up without unconditional love, and it becomes difficult for them to establish a positive, loving relationship to themselves or to the Creator. It's very hard to connect in an open way to Divine Spirit if we never felt that positive connection on the ego level as children. Noticing our children growing up without self-love could, in turn, lead to more self-loathing as we note our lack or inadequacies as parents. Instead of seeing what we don't like about ourselves when dealing with our children, we could choose to see what we do like about ourselves by noticing how our behavior and attitudes emulate those inherent in the Divine. We can do this not simply when dealing with our children but at all times and in all situations. In the Bhagavad-Gita, Krishna says, "Again listen to My supreme word, the most secret of all. Because thou art dearly loved by Me, I will relate what is beneficial to thee." It is our job to behave in ways that reflect that love.

Early Christians created a ceremonial celebration that was a feast of charity. We might think of it as a love feast because it provided an opportunity to make charitable contributions to the poor. It was called *agape*, and it evolved to mean the unconditional love that Spirit has for all its creations.

Unconditional love gives all and requires nothing. Beyond the ephemeral material plane exists the love that the Creator has for all aspects and manifestations of creation. The universe loves us completely and unconditionally. Why feel less about ourselves than Spirit feels for us? It all starts with the relationship to ourselves. If there are aspects of ourselves with which we are uncomfortable but aren't willing to change, we accept a self that is less than complete. This type of relationship to ourselves does not reflect the love that Spirit has for us, and it makes it difficult for to us to respond to that love in kind.

Similarly, if we live our lives totally on an ego-based perspective, seeing self as the primary reality of life, we are probably unaware of Spirit altogether. Even if we like ourselves and assume that we are a good person, we could still be ignorant of the love available to us. By developing a transcendent, spiritual, mystical perspective, we realize that the transitory self is merely an actor with a small part on a very large stage. The stage manager is Divine Spirit. As we develop an awareness of the cosmic play in which we are involved, we begin to realize that at all times we are connected to Spirit. We are, in fact, an extension of Spirit, a reflection of Spirit. From that point of view, we can feel and appreciate the power and comfort of the universal Principle of Love.

Western culture has evolved such that the concept of self-love has gotten confused. Consciously feeling good about oneself and demonstrating that state has become equated with conceit and narcissism, and this may be the case for some people. They are motivated only by self-interest. They feel good about themselves based on the amount of compliments and recognition they receive from others or the dominion and control they can exercise over others. But to assume that it is somehow wrong to feel good about ourselves based on our accomplishments, or by how we affect others, or the feedback we receive from others is to misunderstand the nature of love. My client Amy played volleyball in high school, an interesting choice as she is quite small. Prior to the beginning of an important game, she overheard an opponent say that their team should "watch out for the little one. She's the best player on that team." She was surprised but happy to hear that. At home that evening, she conveyed that statement to her sister. Their mother overheard the conversation and made Amy quit the team because she felt Amy was getting too self-important. In the mother's belief system, the only entity who deserves praise is God. Apparently, he is—or is perceived as being—above us and separate from us, and it is he alone who deserves to be complimented and revered. The irony of that assumption is that it minimizes the nature of love as well as Divine Spirit's fundamental intention. We are not separate from Divine Source. Life is Oneness. Nothing is truly separate from anything else. The greatest desire of the source and creator of life is that we feel self-love and feel good about who we are. In that way, we embody the truth of life and reflect back to Spirit the energy that it is sending to us.

Astrological Correlation

The sign associated with the universal Principle of Love is Leo. Each of the twelve signs of the zodiac is ruled by one planet or coruled by two planets. The energy represented by a planet coincides with the qualities of the sign it rules. The sole planet ruling Leo is the sun. The sun is the center of life in our solar system. Without its light and energy, there is no solar system. Leo and its characteristics are as central to life, as is the sun.

Although the planet Venus does not rule Leo, it too is associated with love. Because Venus also pertains to relationship, Venusian love can be primarily experienced in a romantic context. But it can suggest *what* we love as much as *whom*. Because Venus also involves beauty, it can signify our love of an object, such as a work of art or piece of jewelry. Venus is obviously not as primal or powerful as the sun, but it expands our ability to give and receive love when we fully understand the nature of love and the many ways we can experience and express it, including the influence of Venus.

Leo partakes of the element fire. As such, it is outgoing, dynamic, radiant, and expressive. Leo is also spontaneous and creative. Its primary point of orientation is love: feeling, giving, and receiving love. As stated above, love has many levels and connotations. We can love romantically. We can love our children. We can love our pets and our hobbies. Love can motivate us to be heroic or chivalrous. We can love ourselves as well as others. We can love what we do and how we do it. But most importantly, love is a quality that connects us directly to Divine Source. Love can provide the motivation and means to be of service to others.

Many years ago I knew a woman who was a gifted mystic. Zoe grew up in pre-revolutionary Russia and lived with her family in a small, crowded apartment. Another family also lived in the apartment, but they never left a certain corner of the living room. One day she asked her mother why these people always stayed in that one place. Her mother became extremely angry and told the little girl to never mention anything like that again. She said that if the authorities knew that she could "see things that weren't there," they would lock her up.

As the years past, my friend Zoe developed her psychic talent and was able to heal people whenever she was asked. She eventually immigrated to the United States and married a man who worked as a logger. Her husband was seemingly not as gifted. In fact, he was completely skeptical of her abilities to the point of being derisive. Because of his work, they lived in logging camps in a remote area in the Pacific Northwest in which there were no doctors for hundreds of miles. When someone in the camp, a logger or a family member, became ill, they would ask Zoe to heal them. Sometimes the patient's condition was too dire for her to help, and then they would call on her husband. Although he claimed no mystical or healing power and, in fact, was skeptical, he would take his Bible and sit by the person's bed. He would stay there all night long, perhaps even well into the next day, if necessary. Almost invariably, the patient got well. No one knew how this happened, and it was never talked about. But Zoe noticed. She also knew that her husband's sun sign was Leo.

Leo is the sign of the emerging individual—one who separates from others in the demonstration of uniqueness. What Leo contributes to the human experience is the realization that we are individuals who are capable of creating the kind of person that we choose to be. In this respect, the Leo energy reflects the power and potential of Spirit itself. Tuning in to love, we *are* the Source of life and the substance of Oneness. As such, we realize that love exists to be utilized by whoever wants it. There is a limitless, inexhaustible supply; thus, it is impossible to drain the universe of this quality. As freely as it is given, it can also be received. Zoe's husband may have been unaware of any transcendent reality, but he cared deeply for his friends and their families, and the quality of his love took on divine proportions. Ultimately, love was the healing agent, and he was merely the one who delivered that energy.

When people with planets in the sign Leo are centered, they will feel love flowing through themselves and outward to others with supportive generosity. They will give love abundantly and freely, the same way they will experience it coming toward them. But if they are off-center, they will not feel the love present within them at all. They could assume, therefore, that love must be external to them, and they experience a primal drive to acquire it as much and as often as possible. This could lead to their being dramatic in order to get attention, the assumption being that the attention will be in the form of love. Or they could be very demanding of recognition for a quality they have or something they have done. Again, the assumption is that recognition from others will feel like love and fill the gaping hole they feel within themselves. As we will see, the only way that hole can truly be filled is by working to become and remain centered.

How to Align with This Law

When we are truly centered, we are the center of the universe. There is no separation between ourselves and everything else, and we exist in the realm of Oneness. When we incarnate, we may appear to lose this inherent bond and have to work to get it back. With incarnation we develop an ego, which gives us a sense of ourselves as being separate and different from everything else. We become aware of self, usually at the cost of our spiritual awareness as Self. Eastern philosophies have stressed the importance of transcending the ego. In this context, the ego is defined as the temporary self. To perceive life merely from the point of our own needs, feelings, desires, and goals limits our connection with the Divine. Anything that affirms the ego-self as the center or point of life is an illusion, with shades of narcissism and a limitation to consciousness development. Narcissism occurs when self-love becomes exclusive, and we forget to include others in the scope of our love and care. We are narcissistic when we are so self-absorbed that the only thing that matters is getting what we want. Sometimes pride is confused with narcissism, because it can indicate an overly inflated opinion of oneself. But pride can also represent a dignity, the intention to conduct oneself with integrity and relate to others in honorable ways. If we assume pride is merely a synonym for narcissism, it could lead to extreme forms of self-denial and the unnecessary limiting of our sense of personal satisfaction, happiness, and fulfillment. This is not what the doctrine of ego loss really means. In the mystical sense, ego loss means that getting one's desires met is not the prime point of life. We differentiate between needs (those activities or possessions that enable us to function in a grounded, effective way on the earth plane) and wants (activities or things that provide only a sense of personal gratification). Ego loss means to value our connection to Divine Spirit above our need for personal satisfaction.

Another way to define the ego is as our state of I-consciousness. It reflects how we define, understand, and relate to who we are. Without an ego, we would essentially cease to exist on this plane of being. Human beings function on three levels of experience: the physical, the mental, and the emotional. For the ego to be healthy and to be a positive influence, we must integrate all three levels in a balanced, harmonious way. Too much emphasis on sensual gratification, too much focus on logic and analysis, or too much yielding to feelings leaves us out of balance. This puts us off-center. To get centered again, we need to be self-loving. The process of centering is the path that generates a healthy ego, one that enables us to take full advantage of all our inherent tools, talents, and resources without assuming that life is all about us. The more consistently we are centered, the more easily we can feel the ever-present love that is Spirit's gift to creation.

Centering

The process of getting centered involves integrating body, mind, and soul. On the physical plane, we must be grounded. Grounding involves being aware of our material responsibilities to both ourselves and others. When we are grounded, we also define, establish, and enforce healthy, appropriate limits and boundaries in relationship to people and to tasks. Becoming aware of and discharging our obligations on the job, with our partner, and in our family is part of grounding.

In relationship to ourselves, grounding involves being aware of our personal physical needs in life and taking responsibility to fulfill those needs. What do we need in terms of financial and material security, health maintenance, affection and sexuality, and our connection to nature? In order to be grounded, we don't necessarily need all these categories fulfilled, but we at least need to be in a process of becoming aware of each and defining and updating those needs as time goes by. These will change over time. The needs of a young adult are not those of a middle-aged person or a senior citizen. As long as we engage in the process of discovering and defining our needs, we are grounded, and all—or at least most—of our needs will be met.

Centering involves integrating the grounded earth plane experience with the mind and the emotions. The emotional work involves becoming aware of our internal drives, responses, and experience, accessing the universal Principle of the Eternal Present. It involves monitoring the psychological process through psychotherapy or hypnotherapy or engaging in self-contemplation and self-analysis on a regular basis. Developing a clear understanding about our motivations and behaviors is important in freeing us from those that are fear-based or that were programmed by our family, schools, or community when we were children. Monitoring our dreams is another method for tuning in to our subtle feelings and intuitive realizations about parts of our lives and the people in them. Emotional health and psychological clarity is a fundamental element of centering.

Spiritual growth and consciousness development are also key ingredients to developing a healthy, centered ego. Meditation, prayer, yoga, Tai Chi, Qigong, or working with visualizations or affirmations are practices that support soul growth and spiritual self-awareness. Aligning with the universal Law of the Eternal Present also can be quite helpful in this process because it helps us to use our immediate subjective experience as a vehicle for tuning in to Oneness.

The mental aspect of the integration process involves refining and utilizing our skills of discrimination. The rational mind is one of the qualities that sets human beings apart from other species on earth. Discrimination is one of the highest forms of rational activity of which the mind is capable at its current stage of evolution. Making subtle distinctions between different options and ranking them in a prioritized order enables us to gain perspective on what we define as meaningful. By then achieving or manifesting what we value, we create a meaningful life.

The universal Principle of Both/And discussed the importance of monitoring our state of mind. Knowing what's going on in our rational mind is an important step in centering it. If we don't like or value our thoughts, why are they there? Replacing those of less meaning or virtue with those of greater value enhances our ability to maintain positive thoughts and to remain focused on them.

When we successfully integrate body, mind, and soul, our ego can function as a catalyst that stimulates the positive interaction between ourselves and the world. In this manner, the healthy ego serves as a bridge that helps keep body, mind, and soul functioning as a unit. This provides the foundation for perceiving life from a unified perspective—hence, from the point of Oneness. Ultimately, the centered ego sees and relates to life as consciousness. Rather than reacting to and identifying with the endless stream of experiences, thoughts, and feelings, the centered ego is free to feel love flowing through everything and to identify with that flow of love. Rather than perceiving and experiencing our lives from the point of self, we do so from the point of Self and are thus connected to Oneness.

Opening the Heart

The purpose of life is to create, and what motivates creation is love. The power of limitless creativity lies within each of us, and we tap into that power by tuning into the limitless love that also lies within. Accessing love can also happen when we do something that we love to do. This could be hobbies, recreational activities, or a form of artistic expression. Being with friends or simply relaxing and engaging in a pleasurable activity can allow us to relax and open our hearts. Or, as suggested earlier, it could involve the ultimate creative act: bringing a child into the world and consciously parenting it—that could be the most immediate and guaranteed way to experience love. That initial opening can inspire us through spiritual devotion to raise our children with the greatest degree of clarity and the most consistent level of love of which we are capable.

For some people, having pets can serve a similar function. The animal relates to the human with absolute trust and loyalty. Those qualities can help to open the heart of the owner, who finds within himself similar qualities to share with the pet. In return, the pet feels the owner's love and responds in kind.

Creative expression also can open the door of our hearts to the ever-present flow of love. We feel this when we sit down to write a poem or recite it; when we choreograph a dance or simply dance; when we paint, sculpt, or sing. Any creative activity immediately tunes us in to the eternal flow of creation. We become a link in the chain of consciousness and feel the mystical connection to Oneness by utilizing our creative talents. We are in sync with the eternal chain of the universal Principle of Creativity.

Love can be expressed and felt in times of joyful celebration. This could be in a formal context, such as noting a rite of passage or milestone such as a birth, a bar mitzvah, a wedding, or a promotion at work. Celebration also can be a vehicle to feel love. It could be in a spiritual ritual that enables the participants to make direct, meaningful, and personal connection to Divine Spirit. Or it can be a spontaneous expression that we manifest because we are centered, know we are alive, and feel overjoyed at the blessing of knowing that we are connected to the One.

Qualities of Love

Two important qualities of this law are humility and self-confidence. The former has more to do with how we feel inwardly, the latter with what we project to the world. When we are centered and feeling the flow of love within, we carry ourselves with a modest dignity, a realistic expression of humility. We know who we are and what our place is in the divine movie. We aren't looking for attention or recognition, but if it comes our way, we respond with graciousness.

Self-confidence defines how we approach other people and external situations when we feel aligned with our own self-love. Equipped with self-confidence, we like ourselves, know what we are doing, and assume that we will both enjoy and be successful in our endeavor. There is no need to prove ourselves to others or for them to validate what we are doing. Through the process of centering, we continually weed and rake our inner garden so that our intentions and methodologies are clear and come from a loving place.

Hobbies or recreational activities have the potential to open our hearts to love and provide opportunities for expressing ourselves with both humility and self-confidence. The only requirement is that we love the activity. A chess player concentrating on his next move; a collector discovering a rare "find," and a hiker coming upon a breathtaking vista can feel the connection to Source through the love they have for their activity. A tennis player acing a serve; a basketball player on a hot shooting streak; a baseball player feeling the bat meet the ball and watching it fly over the fence can all feel the "sweet spot" of love.

Once we have created a centeredness within Self, there are two valuable and realistic ways of tapping into the universal Principle of Love. One is to do something we love to do, which by nature is intended to invite our awareness of love. For example, at times we might feel disconnected from Source, depressed, and alienated. Doing something that is familiar and which has worked in the past to generate love in our lives can help reconnect us. Or we can remember a time or a relationship through which we have felt love. Keeping that memory alive allows us to connect with love in the present. We can remember to be aware of that love energy as it flows and pulsates through our bodies, minds, and souls. Love wants to be discovered and experienced consciously. It is offered freely by Spirit so that it can uplift and fill the receiver who will, in turn, share it with others and reflect it back to the One.

Leo is the sign of illumination. It enjoys bringing things out in the open for others to observe, learn from, and benefit by. As such, the qualities of honesty and integrity are central to the Leonine experience. We don't want to put information out there or act out in ways that are motivated by duplicity or which would be cause for embarrassment. When we are on a centered path, we develop a greater sense of self-love. From this perspective we realize that we can best illuminate and share that love by relating to ourselves and everyone else with truthfulness and sincerity. Keeping things open and honest enables us to embody love. Others see us as reliable and trustworthy; they relate to us accordingly, and this, in turn, provides the sense of security that supports our centering process and our mutually loving and supportive relationships.

Not Aligning with This Law

The universal Principle of Love is misused when we live an uncentered life. If our physical drives and desires are prioritized higher than our spiritual growth, mental clarity, or emotional awareness, we are off-center. For example, we all need to eat to live, but if we live to eat, we are off-center. To focus excessively on eating means we are sublimating certain desires or are in denial about feelings of frustration, confusion, or fear. Rather than face and resolve them, we find immediate gratification in food.

We also minimize this law in our lives if we equate love with romance. Being romantic is fun and enjoyable—while it lasts. But like everything else pertaining to the material plane, it is transitory. One of the challenges committed couples face is what to do when the romance fades. The real question is what creates romantic feelings in the first place?

American culture, which is now being exported to all corners of the world, equates love with romance, and romance with sex. This is prevalent throughout Europe and has even spread to third-world countries such as India. It has reduced sexual gratification to the satisfaction of lust, rather than love. Advertising bombards us with images of young, attractive bodies. It equates sexual appeal with deification, coining such terms as "sex goddess." In the process of selling products, which may or may not be beneficial to the consumer, marketing and advertising interests sell sex. Having the most beautiful body, or being lovers with someone who does, offers the promise of happiness. This is a false promise based on an empty premise. Addictions to sexual or sensual stimulation and gratification in whatever form serve to keep us focused on the body only. The mental, spiritual, and emotional parts of our life are not addressed, and our potential for fulfillment in these areas drops accordingly.

Of course, even beyond Madison Avenue, many people misuse sexual energy. It is a powerful force and can be used to control others through giving it or withholding it. For some, sex is synonymous with intimacy. For them, physical closeness becomes the vehicle through which they share themselves at the deepest, most personal level. True intimacy, however, is realized when people voluntarily reveal sensitive parts of themselves to each other. A client once offered a play on the intimacy as "in-to-me-you-see." Certainly, being lovers with someone in a conscious, giving way is a form of closeness. But real intimacy establishes a bond of emotional trust that can take place only when both partners are willing to take the risk of sharing parts of themselves that they typically do not share with others. Often, we don't share deeply with others due to fear. However that fear might manifest, fear of intimacy is a result of being off-center. If we don't love ourselves, how can we expect anyone else to treat us differently than we treat ourselves? We can only love others to the degree that we love ourselves. The less we love ourselves, the more we attract those who agree with our self-assumptions.

For some people, physically addictive behavior serves to mask emotional discomfort. The addiction is not to the physical experience itself as much as to the experience of emotional exhilaration created by the experience. This is usually followed by an emotional "valley"—a rush of feelings on a roller-coaster ride to nowhere. Sometimes one creates a scenario that demands much emotional drama from other participants. This is a form of control or manipulation that causes intense emotional experience with no sense of connection to anything beyond the drama.

There are those who avoid physical/emotional attachments altogether by limiting themselves to intellectual forms of stimulation. Some people love to read and study. But to focus entirely upon academic achievement, endlessly reading books and taking classes, or simply keeping up with the news of the day creates an unbalanced reality. We must also include physical activity, social contact, emotional self-awareness, and spiritual growth to create the desired goal of centeredness.

When we identify only with the self who is experiencing the immediate phenomena of life, this off-center ego blocks the true experience of love. We create our life as a series of experiences. In other words, we identify with the fragment of reality, and thus overlook the Oneness of reality. We are stuck in a dualistic life in which everything is either this or that. There is me, and then there is everyone else. This also ignores the Principle of Both/And. When we fall into this trap, the ego becomes the limitation of who we are, rather than a vehicle for self-realization. We perceive love as being "out there"; something to be earned or gained. Instead, it should be something that is an inherent quality of life and is open to any and all people who consciously strive to wake up and experience their divine birthright. In order to obtain love, to have what is "out there" be "in here," we do whatever we deem necessary. We might try to become a duplicate of the desirable physique, to become the gourmet cook, or to say or do the right thing in order to attract someone who will tell us that we are loveable. In reality, we are trying to manipulate another to fill the empty, aching hole in our being. Without being centered, however, we have no idea or experience of what love feels like in the first place.

A person might try to compensate for lack of self-love by assuming a sense of entitlement. This is an attitude of thinking "whatever I want should be given to me, simply because I want it." In such a case, wanting and deserving have been confused or assumed to be the same. With a sense of entitlement we might not feel the necessity of doing the inner work required to get centered, feel self-love, and share that love with others. Being centered and loving enables us to be more deserving of whatever we are striving for. Not being centered and loving, we would tend to feel the need for external gratification yet without the necessity of working for it.

We can also limit the flow of love by focusing more on possessions than on Spirit. When we commodify ourselves as some*thing* rather than some*one*, we do the same to love. When centered, we receive love effortlessly and share it openly. When off-center, we love only *if* we are being loved in return in a certain way, by a certain person, at a certain time. This is what is meant by conditional love. We minimize ourselves, even as we reduce love to bartering rather than the divine quality of being.

Similarly, when we are off-center with the Principle of Love, we might relate to our partner with indifference. We might act as if we are unconcerned with what he or she is doing. When the romance fades, so does our commitment to the relationship. If we are centered, we are continuously in touch with love. We feel it flowing endlessly through our heart and out to whomever we choose to share it with. If it is someone with whom we have shared countless experiences, someone in whom we have a major emotional investment, perhaps the person with whom we have had children, our love for that person deepens even as the romance fades. We might also discover that the romance isn't entirely gone. It may show up less frequently but remain just as powerful as ever when it does. Because it's not the point of the relationship anymore, we appreciate the sweetness of the romance even more than we once did. Love can also stimulate creativity within a relationship. We can respond to the changes that take place in a relationship over time by creating new ways to be together. The greater the intimacy, the more exciting the creativity. Only by working to remain centered within ourselves can we stay connected to the source of love within a relationship, feel it flowing in us, and feel genuine love for others.

Another instance of not aligning with this principle comes from being too open. We may tend to give love away so readily that others can easily drain us. They enjoy the benefits of our generosity but fail to return it in kind. Confusing pity with love is another potential problem. Because we feel sorry for someone, we reach out to him or her in a loving embrace. Even though our compassion may be real, our actions indicate that we may be off-center. We may be attached to an expectation that our love (generosity, altruism, etc.) is noticed, appreciated, and can somehow save the other person from pain and suffering. Even if our efforts are genuinely intended to help the other person, attachment to appreciation or response to our efforts could leave us feeling taken advantage of. This is not love flowing effortlessly through us, but our trying to control someone else's life. Love given freely is a spiritual act by a centered person. When love is given with the expectation of recognition it may be well-intended, but is nonetheless a confused act of one who is not centered.

Spiritual Opportunity

Each of the twelve universal principles I discuss in this book has a trait I call its "spiritual quality." It is obvious by now that the trait associated with the universal Law of Love is … love! Love is the most fundamental, motivating, connecting, and powerful force in the universe. As we feel love filling our very being, helping us become who we really are, we understand that it must flow through us and be shared with others. If we become attached to the "amount" of love we have and try to hang on to it, we actually limit its availability to us. For when we share love possessively or conditionally, we needlessly restrict our own ability to receive and experience the fullness of love.

When I attended the University of California in the late 1960s, I used to enjoy walking to campus. Outside the main gate there were tables set up to advertise a cause or an activity. There were also speakers who would stand on their soapbox to espouse their perspective on life. Two such speakers stand out in my mind. One was a middle-aged man called Hubert. He literally would bring a box to stand on and pontificate about Jesus and how we should relate to him. "Holy Hubert," as he was known, was filled with hellfire and brimstone, as if hoping that if he frightened people enough that they would conform to his brand of spirituality.

The other speakers were a couple. They carried a banner on which was written "Karista Is Love." They were hippies in their mid-twenties. Apparently Karista was the name of their group. Their idea was that love is eternal, immutable, and always available to everybody. All we had to do was tune in to feel it. They pretty much ignored Hubert, while he spent days vilifying them for having long hair, not being married, or whatever conventions they flouted that he took as a slight to his message and lifestyle. Their message that God is love failed to penetrate Hubert's dogmatic, black-and-white thinking. The paradoxical image of the conventional holy-roller and the counter-culture eccentrics, both stressing their brand of the truth, was as comical as it was educational. The important points are that they were both espousing a spiritual/mystical lifestyle and that there is more than one way to do so.

When we are centered, we perceive life in a transcendent state. We realize that the ego is a vehicle that serves a twofold purpose. First, it is a bridge that connects body, mind, and soul. It acts as a governor that enables us to keep our being in our body, so that we can physically survive and function effectively while we are here. Second, when centered, the ego enables us to realize that we are not here in isolation, cut off from everything else; that in fact we are part of the limitless flow of life energy, an inextricable part of the whole. The principle that continually reminds us of that connection is love.

Ultimately, being centered enables us to live in a bifurcated state of consciousness. We are aware of our connection to and interaction with material and social activities and take responsibility for our actions therein. Simultaneously, we are also aware of our immediate and eternal connection to Divine Spirit and take responsibility to maintain and strengthen it.

Feeling love enables us to realize the truth of our being; that our individuality is a beloved aspect of Spirit. As such, we become aware of Spirit existing in and flowing through all thought, all feeling, and all phenomena. We realize that life exists as a cosmic play in which all the actors and actresses, props, sets, and stages are reflections of the same life force. The love that we feel so deeply and that is given to us freely is the very nature of life itself, the essence of creation. Our primary goal and desire becomes to share that love endlessly with the Creator. The more we share, the more we receive. The more we receive, the more we have to share. We become liberated from the duality of life, from the illusion of fear, from the pain of alienation. All our thoughts and feelings become centered on Spirit through love. Whatever we are doing on the physical plane, part of our consciousness remains with Spirit. Eventually, we realize that, in fact, there is no separation. The giver and receiver are the same. The actor and the action are one.

In the Bible, Proverbs 10:12 says "love covereth all sins." It doesn't matter how long it takes to discover these truths or what our sins were prior to awakening to them. All that matters is that we do wake up and realize that we are loved more than we have ever dreamed of being loved. All that is asked is that we share the love with the Creator and its creations, rather than remaining ensnared by the material world's gifts, pleasures, and distractions.

The Bottom Line

Being "in love" is not a social experience; it is a state of consciousness. It is a flow of energy inherent within all manifestation. It is the most powerful force in the universe. When we are truly "in love" in the highest, most centered sense, it is impossible to be selfish or self-absorbed. It is impossible to be too open and hence, to share love inappropriately. Since centering is a prime requirement of knowing love, when we love we are able to establish clear and healthy limits and boundaries that prevent our being taken advantage of.

God is love. Whenever we feel love, God is present. Although love generated through a relationship or other external situation can certainly be real, we don't have to base the feeling of love on anything other than the fullness in our heart. We just open up and feel it. When centered, we can understand that love is a continuously flowing energy. All that Spirit asks is that we be open to receiving it, willing to share it, and that we reflect it back to Source.

Affirmation: "In divine love, in the center of life, I radiate and share love with all."

> *We are all parts of God. We leave the comfort of being a part of the Whole when we are ready, and start our journey to become whole enough on our own. We then return to God as a whole, increasing the Love that is God. Our only lesson to be learned is Love. It is surprising how hard it is to learn and how many lives it takes to learn that one lesson.*
>
> —LALAC

Chapter 6: The Law of Service

And it shall come to pass, if ye shall hearken diligently unto my commandments which I command you this day, to love the Lord your God, and to serve him with all your heart and with all your soul.

—Deuteronomy 11:13

Organized and Dutiful

From the early 1960s through the early 1970s, the United States was involved in an undeclared war against Vietnam. Like thousands of Americans, I opposed our involvement with what was essentially a civil war in a distant third-world country. Unlike many of those anti-war patriots, I was of draft age and classified 1-A by my draft board. As such, I was highly desirable to the military and on the verge of being drafted at any time. Determined to avoid that fate, I went to Canada to see about the possibility of becoming an expatriate. Some friends had preceded me and gave me the address of similarly dedicated Americans with whom I could stay. I was warmly welcomed when I arrived but soon discovered that the beliefs, values, and perspectives that they maintained were not that similar to mine. Whereas I was fundamentally opposed to war for any purpose other than self-preservation, they were avowed Communists who, at least theoretically, were committed to the violent overthrow of any government that was not supportive of that philosophy. There were placards posted throughout the house that

The Law of Service

served to continuously remind the "communards" about both their goals and their methodology. For example, one sign read "Political power comes out of the barrel of a gun."

After spending a few weeks with these folks and checking out my own opportunities and possibilities in western Canada, I returned to the United States. I had, in fact, been drafted and decided it was better to come home and fight that fate than to say good-bye to my family and friends.

When I returned to California and the friends with whom I had been living, I was struck by two differences in our living situations. Up north, the people were feisty and argued continuously, but at least their environment was clean. They had sublimated their anger into household chores. Down south, my friends and I got along wonderfully. We were friendly, cheerful, and enjoyed our lives. But the house was a mess. No military organization or attention to neatness and cleanliness. So I decided to borrow a page from my Canadian friends and apply it to my California buddies. I wrote out and posted signs all around the house. But instead of exhorting my friends to armed conflict, I gently goaded them into doing the household chores. For example, my sign in the bathroom read "Political power comes out of a clean toilet." Oddly enough, this tactic worked. Although we may not have been any more politically potent than we had been, we had the cleanest bathroom on the block!

This somewhat convoluted anecdote illustrates to me one important aspect of service—that of duty and daily routine. I doubt whether anyone wakes up in the morning, hops out of bed, and goes immediately and joyfully into the bathroom to clean the toilet—nor is it necessary to do so. But at some time in the course of our weekly activities, paying attention to that kind of detail *is* important. Our immediate environment is a reflection of our state of mind. The external mess mirrors the internal jumble. For most people, household chores are not priority and certainly not fun. But they are done to keep things organized on the domestic front. It can be a drain if only one person takes it upon himself or herself to do this, and it can lead to resentment. If everyone pitches in, the work gets done more quickly and in a less burdensome way. This is the essence of the universal Law of Service.

For Its Own Sake

There's a construction company in Northern California that has a large fleet of trucks and heavy equipment. The slogan written on the side of the vehicles reads "Find a need and fill it." This too expresses the essence of service. To serve, we need to be adaptable to the ever-changing conditions of life. This could be on the home front, in the workplace, or in addressing the needs of the community. The intention behind service is to assist with a condition or undertaking. Repairing something that's broken. Refining a state of affairs so that it operates more efficiently. Creating a system that will produce a more efficient flow in a situation. When such tasks are executed in the spirit of service, they can be done with little or no fanfare. No accolades or recognition are needed. Doing what needs to be done provides its own form of satisfaction. Service offers the opportunity to work behind the scenes and to be more focused on personal gratification than on external reward.

Astrological Correlation

The universal Principle of Service is embodied in the sign Virgo. Virgo combines the qualities of body and mind and partakes of the earth element. One way that Virgo expresses its earthy practicality is through health and healing. It can be very focused on maintaining a vital body and mind and can help others to attain the same state. It also connects with the material plane through a close connection to nature. This could take the form of gardening, hiking, or camping, or it could involve animals. Anything from caring for domestic or barnyard animals to working as a park ranger can provide a way for Virgo to be of service while relating to the instinctual, physical realm of life.

Virgo is also oriented toward analytical thinking and has both the desire and ability to take something apart, see how it works, and put it back together so it functions more efficiently. This could be a

The Law of Service

machine, an idea, or an entire system. This tells us that service is not just a physical act but that it engages the mind as well.

Virgo can be dedicated to a project or an ideal and will devote a great deal of time and effort in service to the activity or concept. It also has the ability to be extremely focused, methodical, and detail-oriented. I have long felt that Virgo is the hardest working sign in the zodiac. If you want something done efficiently and effectively, hire a Virgo.

Virgo is self-contained, relies on no one, is task-oriented and obliging. As an expression of its autonomy, Virgo is often socially shy and modest. It prefers working behind the scenes rather than getting a lot of personal attention and recognition. To the Virgo, being supportive to others or seeing a project through to completion is gratifying enough.

One drawback to being so physically and mentally oriented is that Virgo will often overlook its own inner world, feelings, and emotional needs. This can cause the Virgo to be so overly focused on service to others that it can develop more resentment and frustration than self-satisfaction when helping others. When feeling this way, Virgo can tend to socially or emotionally withdraw from the situation, even as it continues to provide service, or it will become extremely critical of others. Usually, the criticism is reductive; that is, it's designed to hurt or to tear someone down rather than being constructive and helpful. Often, the criticism will take the form of comparing what someone is doing or how he is doing it to an idealized perspective of who that person could be or what he theoretically could do. It is also something Virgo expresses when off-center—in this case, as a result of not doing enough inner work.

Virgo functions best when working in a system of some kind. This can be a system of thinking and understanding, such as an academic field, or it can be a system of service that is part of a job or profession. The system could be a type of daily or weekly routine that enables them to maintain a healthy center within themselves. Systems are helpful to the Virgo because they provide parameters that can limit the devotional service to something functional rather than ideal. Systems also provide Virgo with a framework for learning, something fundamental to the Virgo experience. Without a healthy system, Virgo can get bogged down by expectations of perfection for themselves and others.

One type of system that can be effective for Virgo is a daily routine. There is, however, a potential problem: being overly routinized in thinking and doing is the trap of obsession. This is the excessive side of being detail-oriented. One becomes so aware of doing something specific at a certain time and in a certain way that she fails to take the big picture into consideration. Being overwhelmed with minutiae, all their good intentions and effort lead to frustration when they fail to complete something effectively. Similarly, Virgo can be so focused on work and service that their life gets out of balance—all work and no play.

But when centered, Virgo excels at integration. Mentally, this can take the form of being selective and discriminating so that the best idea or way of doing something is the course taken. Physically, this can manifest as adopting the proper combination of exercise, diet, and rest to ensure a strong and healthy body. And in terms of service, this can take the form of discerning duty from desire. If the Virgo truly wants to be of service, then by all means he or she should have at it. But if they are doing something only out of a sense of duty, and this behavior persists, the sense of satisfaction could be replaced with antagonism and antipathy.

How to Align with This Law

In Greek mythology, Hestia was the goddess of the hearth. Although there were no temples built in her honor as there were for the eleven other original Olympian gods and goddesses, she was revered and respected in every home and temple. Zeus charged her with keeping the flame alive at the hearth in every building in the country. Since the hearth was recognized as the center of each home and temple, when the people gathered to eat there, they would make Hestia an offering of gratitude for her presence. Unlike the other divine Olympians, who were favored by some people yet eschewed by others, everyone appreciated Hestia. What also separated Hestia from her fellow deities was her attitude. The other Olympians expressed needs and desires for attention and worship. They reveled in the grandeur of their temples. But Hestia was humble. Rather than seek the limelight, she was comfortable just being herself. Rather than cultivate a following, she sought to remain self-contained. Her desire was to simply execute her tasks, feeling good about her contribution to each family and the community, while not being limited in any way by needs that she was disinclined to fulfill. Her self-containment enabled Hestia to maintain a more steady flow-of-life experience. She was free to go about her daily chores of keeping the hearth clean and the flame burning. It's easy to overlook how important the hearth flame is, especially as translated into today's modern world. It may seem to simply be "always there." Yet without it, there would be no light, no heat for cooking, and no center around which the family could gather each evening to recount the activities of the day and experience a sense of warmth and renewal.

Humility in Action

Service requires selflessness. To emulate Hestia, we must go about our tasks in a modest yet diligent way. This enables us to be most effective in accomplishing fundamental things without interference. Our payoff comes from feeling good about ourselves because we are doing something useful and necessary. Our focus is on the proficiency and efficiency of our actions, rather than on recognition or approval from others. We are free from the drive for attention and the push/pull of popularity and can focus on what really matters, in a practical sense, with the business at hand. After all, popularity has its ups and downs. Our sense of self can be enhanced or limited by what others think of us and how they perceive and relate to us; we can be deified at one point, only to be vilified later on. We can be coerced to do things we'd otherwise pass on, just for the sake of the worshipful response of others. But the Principle of Service bypasses the popularity seesaw by focusing on work for its own sake.

One way to activate this law and emulate Hestia in contemporary life is by willingly embracing the practical chores of daily life. These are rarely exciting to do and easy to overlook when others do them. Yet when we willingly take on these tasks, our life flows in a smoother way.

Karma Yoga

It is important to consider, while the body is performing all these tasks, where our head is. What is our point of attention? Many service-oriented activities are habitual; that is, they are simple to do and need to be done continuously. Beyond the initial awareness of what needs to be done and figuring out how and when to do it, these tasks don't require much thinking, planning, or strategizing. So we can use the time when we are engaged in these things to focus the mind on more exalted thoughts. While attending to the chores of the day, we can simultaneously access higher states of consciousness. These states can stretch far beyond the tasks at hand and can help us to attain mystical attunement to the Divine. When practiced in a centered, loving way, service is an exalted act. One technique that enables us to be of both material service and expanded awareness is the practice of karma yoga. As defined in chapter 10, *karma* is the law of action, and *yoga* means union. By practicing any form of yoga, we integrate our own sacred, fundamental trinity of soul, mind, and body into the larger Oneness of life. In karma yoga we engage in useful things and practical activity. Our point of attention, however, is not limited to the task at hand but on the intention behind the action. The purpose of Hestia's work was to keep things clean and orderly for the people she served, while ultimately serving the One. Likewise, when we perceive and relate to others as manifestations of Divine Source, then serving them is like serving Source. The daily chores of washing dishes, sweeping the floor, commuting to work, or cleaning out the garage are not particularly glorious or exciting. But if our intention is to provide financial support for our family or a clean, attractive place for them to dwell in, our actions can bring a sense of joy. This concept is similar to the Buddhist aphorism: "Before enlightenment: chop wood, carry water. After enlightenment: chop wood, carry water." What matters more than what we do is the attitude and intention with which we do it. Even the simplest tasks can provide opportunities to connect with Oneness if we perceive the Divine in the dishes, the floor, the car, the road, or anything and everything else that surrounds us and that needs periodic maintenance.

Helping Those in Need

Sometimes service involves paying attention and using common sense. As trite as it may seem, helping an old person who has trouble crossing the street or carrying a package for someone is a simple act of service that requires nothing but care and compassion. Making a commitment to volunteer for any of the numerous causes or agencies that exist to care for our fellow beings, human or otherwise, puts that compassion into serviceful action. Furthermore, our commitment also enables the circle of service to have greater effect.

Service is performed continually in the family. In addition to the usual daily chores, there are needs that occasionally come up in families that should be addressed. We might need to deal with an elderly family member who suffers from a debilitating disease or after an accident. Or perhaps a grandmother suffering from dementia simply needs a smile, a kind word, and a warm meal, or a grandfather healing from a disabling stroke requires service that is performed altruistically by loving family members. Attending dutifully and joyfully to the needs of a disabled partner is an example of exalted service. The indigenous people of the island nation of Fiji place such high honor on service to their elders that they view it as a spiritual act.

We hear a lot these days about the environment. Often the focus is on global warming and sometimes on natural disasters. Valuable ways to offer service in these areas include learning first aid or being a neighborhood organizer to help others in times of earthquake, hurricane, or flood. It's especially gratifying to help those who live closest to us. These days we can be alienated from our neighbors to the point that we don't even know their names. Joining with others in the spirit of community is a wonderful way to break the ice and get to know our neighbors.

In my community, we have a neighborhood park. It was a private property that was donated to the community in the 1950s. This park, which includes sports fields as well as a picnic area and a children's playground, is completely funded and run by the people who use the park; there are no government monies involved. When my children were young, I would be out there with them every week, particularly during baseball and soccer season, when we participated as coach and players. Between seasons we would do field maintenance, which involved everything from mowing the fields to painting the dugouts to picking up garbage. Once a year, there is a fundraiser with a barbecue, pies, drinks, games, and live music. We would always take a turn doing something that would help to bring money into the park. Not only was it enjoyable, but some of the people I met while volunteering there are still my friends.

When I served as a coach of my children's sports teams, I was able to teach the value of teamwork and sportsmanship, traits that would serve these children throughout their lives. Volunteering in this way was very gratifying. What I didn't realize at the time was that some of these young people would grow up to become my friends as well!

Being of service can, of course, involve more than just household or family-oriented tasks. Fields of service work involve everything from the building trades, to the food industry, to sales. In every service field there are things that need to be done in an organized, careful way. There are techniques to learn and skills to refine. Most of these activities require a period of apprenticeship. If we approach our period of apprenticeship with an open mind and willingness to learn, and we study with someone more skilled or advanced in the field than we are, we can eventually become adept ourselves.

Another important aspect of service—and a good way to access this law—is by being observant of others' needs and seeking to satisfy them. When my grandfather kept his factory open at his own expense he was acting on his awareness of the financial needs of his employee's families. When they did not return that service by being aware of his situation, he had to close the factory.

Humble service can be performed quietly and efficiently by doing tasks that need to be done in any situation regardless of how simple they may be.

Healing the Body

Another important area of service is healing. The first point of attention to healing is one's own body. The body is the vehicle that houses the soul. It has been said that our body is God's gift to us, and how we relate to and treat it is our gift to God. Attending to the body properly is similar to a mechanic's taking care of a car. The more intricate the car, the more highly trained its caretaker needs to be. The human body is incredibly complex. Its care requires continuous learning and constant attention. In addition to maintaining a healthy body, we also might have to address health challenges brought on by illness or accident. Aging is another challenge. Even if we remain healthy and accident-free in our early years and in middle age, we all face the inevitable slowing down and gradual loss of mobility, vision, hearing, and sex drive that accompanies growing older. Although we can't stop the aging process, we can certainly retard it by servicing our body regularly through proper exercise, diet, and rest.

The condition of the body can express a person's emotional being just as the physical environment can mirror the state of mind. In order to effectively maintain good health or alter an unhealthy state, it is often necessary to address the inner being by getting in touch with the soul or psyche. For some people, the root cause of their disease is their state of mind or the lack of clarity they have about their emotional or psychological issues. To completely heal requires them to address both the internal causes and external manifestations. An aspect of inner work is developing a connection to our own higher being and through that, a connection to Creative Source. While the intention may be to heal the body, the process can provide an opportunity for mystical attunement.

Events on the earth plane move slowly. Conditions that exist here usually have evolved over a period of time and will require time to be resolved or healed. Similarly, consciousness develops slowly. Putting significant, quality time and energy into learning about body maintenance and health care is an investment in the long-range future of ourselves and our society. Our body's job is to survive. Tuning in to our physical experience is a way of using our body to teach us who we are and what our truth is. Being in service to our body is a way of being in service to Spirit.

Apprenticing one's mind to study the art and science of healing is also a way of being of service to others. It requires the commitment of years of academic learning, as well as the altruism to attend to others who are in pain and suffering from physical or emotional conditions. As a healing practitioner, one can be called upon to deal with the messiness of bodily fluids, to be on call twenty-four hours a day, or to have to tell a patient or family of an unfavorable prognosis. But there are other times when a life can be saved or a condition altered to the point that the patient can go on to live a quality of life that he or she might not have known for years. The extremes of experience known to healers require not only a commitment to the study and the work but also the compassion that calls one to be of service to others. This spirit of generosity can carry the healer through the hard times, when a cure is not found or a patient is lost. This spirit is also a powerful motivating factor impelling us to serve. It can provide a strong foundation from which the healer herself experiences personal growth, as well as a profound connection to the Ultimate Healer.

Healing service can be performed in simple ways. Listening to a friend who is going through a hard time, or sharing what we have in abundance with someone who has very little may seem like small things. But they express the caring and compassion that are essential qualities of service. And, as with professional healing, the benefits we bestow with our generosity can be healing to both ourselves and others.

Healing the Earth

We can seek to be of service to nature and the environment that surrounds us. The two-headed demon of industrialization and human greed has combined to create a tenuous condition in the relationship between human beings and the planet. We are fouling our nest to the point that some scientists fear for the survival of our species. To help remedy this, we can serve humanity and the planet by being more conscientious in our personal use of material resources. We can commit to recycling and a host of other resource-conserving practices. In a broader context, we can also choose a profession involved with environmental preservation or cleanup.

Participating with nature in general is another way to access the Principle of Service. Observing the flora and fauna of our environment helps us to notice, feel, see, and hear the common energy flowing within our body and every other life form. Nature itself is healing. Spending time in a natural environment can prove beneficial to mind and soul as well as body. This could be through something as simple as taking care of pets or houseplants, or growing a vegetable garden. A more committed way of connecting to nature would be through becoming a veterinarian, or working as a professional landscaper or park ranger. If one simply enjoys being outdoors in a park, going backpacking in the wilderness or camping at the beach can connect us to the stream of life force flowing through and within everything. By being conscious of our actions in nature, we can employ the Principle of Service by striving to protect or nurture all the elements of the natural environment. For example, in Oregon there is a law that defines where and how we can have a campfire while camping. Upon breaking camp, we must gather all the coals and ashes of the fire, put them into a receptacle, and pack them out. There can be no evidence of any camping or fire in that environment. The idea is to leave it as clean and cared for as it was on arrival.

Two qualities that are fundamental to this principle, but which can be used either to promote or block its flow, are naiveté and discrimination.

Naiveté

Naiveté is a form of idealism. It can be beneficial in a visionary sense, as it represents the impulse to improve a condition until it achieves a desirable state. This often implies creating a situation in which everybody benefits. For example, the ideals of ending slavery or the oppression of women may have once seemed naive. Yet in time, the value of these ideals was embraced by enough people that these conditions are now commonly considered unacceptable.

Naiveté can also imply purity or an openness to a situation, based on innocence or lack of experience. The positive potential of this is being open-minded about what we are doing at any given time. Without preconceptions or agendas, we are better able to benefit from whatever happens. Often this will mean learning something new or unexpected. As we learn more from a person or a situation, we can then become more effective in our service to or support of it.

The negative potential of naiveté is being unrealistic about something to the point of being overwhelmed or taken advantage of. One way to avoid this outcome is by developing discrimination.

Discrimination is the key to helping minimize the potentials of being drained, disappointed, or trapped by serviceful activities. This quality helps us make subtle distinctions between things, people, or events. It is the antidote to naiveté. Discrimination is one of the most exalted ways of applying the intellect to the process of creating and living our life. It can assist us in becoming aware of what our capacities are, how they can best be utilized, and where they can be most effectively applied.

When we discriminate, we discern the best action to take among several possibilities that might all seem viable. As such, we learn to make subtle distinctions between different points of view, concepts, or definitions of truth. We discern which among all the possibilities is the one that seems right to us. It's like taking a multiple-choice test in which we are asked to pick the "best" of the possible answers. As we scan the options, we might think that more than one of them is correct. Choosing the best requires discrimination of thought. In this sense, the service we are performing is to our own sense of right and wrong. This type of mental acuity can help us overcome any tendencies to become compulsive in our desire to be of service.

One of the problems of service can be a tendency to become a workaholic. We could also become so enamored of the way in which we perform our tasks that we become critical of others who do similar things in different ways. Sometimes we might redo tasks done by someone else because we think we can do them better. Perfectionism is a trap. Under its sway, we become overly analytical and obsessed with details. We fail to see a bigger or more balanced view of a situation.

When we perceive in a discerning way, it becomes obvious that everything is already in a state of perfection. In Tibetan Buddhism, perceiving the totality of life is called the View. Dudjom Rinpoche, one of Tibet's foremost scholars and meditation masters, said, "The View is the comprehension of the naked awareness, within which everything is contained: sensory perception and phenomenal existence, samsara and nirvana. This awareness has two aspects, *emptiness* as the absolute, and *appearances* or *perception* as the relative." In this respect, the full range of perception and experience, phenomena and reality is and always has been perfect, because everything is complete within itself.

Discrimination enables us to remain firm in upholding our ideals without being influenced by what someone else or some ongoing, external condition defines as important to know or to do. We can be selective about what we do and with whom we do it, based on critical analysis.

Not Aligning with This Law

One of the requirements when participating in service is that one act in a selfless manner. There are countless stories of heroes and heroines who have put their safety and well-being in jeopardy in order to assist someone or something. The person who runs into a burning building to rescue a trapped victim is acting out of selfless service. The soldier fighting for the freedom of his people is acting in service to the ideal of freedom.

Service does not always require self-sacrifice. If an employer gives in to his employees' demands, and in doing so puts his own family's welfare in jeopardy, this is where he has to draw the line—as my grandfather did in my earlier example. If he had not, he would have quickly run out of money, and he and his family would have been left with nothing. We can help others, but it is not necessary to harm ourselves in the process.

If we are so selfless that we are willing to adapt to any set of circumstances and do whatever is asked of us, we abandon our sense of identity or our sense of right and wrong. That is not service; it is self-abandonment. Another misuse of this law is being so attached to what we want or need from our service that we are actually serving ourselves, not others. When the Law of Service is used properly, everyone benefits—the server as well as the served. Being self-absorbed or self-denigrating misuses this principle.

As already pointed out, naiveté can be a positive factor in the context of this law. It can, however, also be a detriment that prevents us from benefiting from it. Naiveté can also mean gullibility and, in this sense, we take at face value whatever we are told. We could base major decisions on an unrealistic assessment of something or someone and be very disappointed or misled as a result.

Gullibility can lead to unrealistic expectations or the adoption of a viewpoint so limited that disappointment and disillusionment are the inevitable results. For example, imagining that a certain person is perfect can have disappointing consequences. Whether that person is a partner, a teacher, or a friend, we could perceive and relate to him through the filter of our naiveté, rather that the objectivity of who he is. This would lead to feeling let down and then possibly blaming the other person who doesn't live up to expectations. Conveniently avoiding our own part in the situation, we can criticize the other person or the nature of the situation as being the cause of the problem. Not only are we being naïve in what we expected, but we also assume a posture of innocence that doesn't allow us to realize that the problem was of our own creation.

Naiveté can also lead to our being too open or accommodating. If we are so eager to serve or please that we accept whatever anyone else asks us to do or tells us is so, we leave ourselves open to being limited or drained by the other person. This is one reason why working within a clearly defined context or system maximizes the potential of being of service. It helps to maintain appropriate boundaries. Not including the spontaneous selfless service that one might perform when confronted with an unexpected emergency, service is usually best performed within a defined context that has limits and boundaries. Even the soldier who puts his life on the line functions within the clearly demarcated strictures of the military. The idealistic teacher works within the academic framework in order to impart knowledge. The healer works within the system of healing that she has studied. Such professionals could be idealistic in their motivations, but by working within the context of their systems they avoid the pitfalls of excessive idealism and meet success in their service.

Service can require attention to detail. If we are serious in our desire to improve a situation, we have to make sure that everything within that context is addressed. In this respect, no stone is too small to be turned over and considered. For this reason we should seek to establish or follow existing parameters. The framework enables us to remain focused on the task at hand and to perform it effectively. It helps us not be distracted by having to make judgment calls or perform extraneous tasks. The structure could also be an external one with which we connect, such as a recipe while cooking. It could also be something that we create ourselves, such as a business that we initiate and run. The system might be an external one that we adapt to our own personal needs, such as spiritual teachings that we integrate into an eclectic blend of philosophies and techniques to help us awaken our higher self.

Sometimes, however, that context can become a trap, limiting us to whatever the system is designed to assist. Our focus becomes myopically tied to the system, and our experience is restricted. We could be so focused on performing the function that our attention to detail takes on a higher priority than the service itself. However successful or effective we are in our helpfulness, our overall awareness still might be limited. This is the pitfall of using a sense of duty to avoid considering the bigger picture and working within a greater context.

One such form of over-attention to detail is micromanagement, or excessive analysis. This is another type of idealism that borders on perfectionism. We might ask perfection of ourselves, of other people, of a relationship, or even of an external situation. We might expect ourselves to have perfect knowledge of a subject or to execute something perfectly. This type of striving has several potential drawbacks. One is the tendency to prohibit ourselves from risking anything that might reveal a flaw or imperfection in our thinking, awareness, or behavior. Another is the tendency to be critical of anyone or anything, ourselves included, that does not embody and express perfection. And most consistent and undermining of all is the tendency to be plagued with worry. Worrying is a state of mind that affirms the probability that something happening now or that will happen in the future will be less than desirable, less than acceptable—in fact, imperfect. When we worry, we forget the Principle of the Eternal Present. We create a condition in our mind that may not ever come to pass. Of course, the more we affirm the possibility we are worrying about in our mind, the more likely we are to create it.

The body is another arena of potential misuse of the Principle of Service. We could become compulsive about our health maintenance program, micromanaging our diet or being so strict with our workout program that higher priorities are left unattended. At the other extreme, we could be so lazy about focusing on the body that health issues compromise our ability to think clearly and function well. When we don't serve our bodies and work to maintain the quality of our health, we wind up limiting the service we can offer.

If we are overly focused on health maintenance, we might overlook the well-being of our inner self. Our unresolved emotional or psychological issues can be root causes of physical problems. Focusing on the body to the exclusion of the psyche and spirit can lead to nonphysical issues becoming physical problems.

Vanity also can be an obstacle to a balanced service to one's body. If we are a clotheshorse whose priority is to keep up with fashion, or if we compare our body to an idealized image, we serve a relatively lower-octave aspect of who we are. We relate to the body as a commodity to be observed and admired, an instrument that helps us to receive recognition, approval, and acceptance from others, rather than as a vehicle for personal growth and consciousness development.

We can also misuse the Principle of Service by using service as a means to an end. Instead of helping someone or improving a situation for its own sake, we might do something for someone else as a way of indebting them to us, ensuring that they will try meet our needs at a later date.

The challenge of the Principle of Service is to give of ourselves with no hidden agenda and to do this in a way that prevents anyone from taking advantage of us. Altruism with a healthy dose of discrimination is a combination that can enable us to help others in appropriate and realistic ways.

Spiritual Opportunity

The novel *Catch-22*, by Joseph Heller, focuses on the military during the Korean War. Big-shot officers walk with swagger, and talk about the big important stuff. They have medals and brocade on their uniform and are either revered or reviled by others. But basically, none of them really has much power because they actually don't know what's going on. The real power is held by the one with the most information about the entire operation. He happens to be a lowly private. It is his assignment to be of assistance to everybody else, but in fulfilling his role, he realizes that it is he, not the officers, who is really in charge. This is an illustration of not only the Law of Service but also the potential influence that one can have as a result of being supportive to others.

Spiritual masters of the Far East have noted that the two most effective ways to enhance spiritual growth are meditation and service. Through meditation we refine the vibration of our own being by attuning it to cosmic harmony. In service we honor Oneness within all things and connect with Source as the vital life force that creates everything we can see, hear, feel, taste, or touch.

Vajrayana Buddhism teaches the importance of the Four Thoughts. The first of these is to be aware of the blessing of human incarnation, for it is only in human form that one can experience the enlightened state.

The second Thought is the reality of impermanence. Briefly, this principle states that everything is in constant motion and continually changing, continuously flowing into new combinations. If we become too attached to what is or too expectant of what can be, we wind up trying to control the experience, rather than living, learning, and growing through it. (See chapter 11 for a more complete examination of this concept.)

The third Thought is the realization that our condition at any given time, the circumstances of our lives, are a direct result of our karma: the results of thoughts, feelings, and actions that we perpetrated in the past. (This topic will be addressed further in chapter 10.) For now, suffice it to say that much of our work is to resolve past karma, freeing us to make new choices in the present.

The fourth Thought is to work for the liberation of all sentient beings. This is the path of selfless service. We learned through the Principle of Both/And that duality is an illusion. All that exists is a part and an expression of Oneness. Service is a way of living that truth. Through Oneness, we perceive others as different aspects of who we are, different forms of the same Source. The point of liberation is the realization of our connection, not only to each other but to the Creative Spirit that gives us life. The purest and most complete way to realize that connection is by awakening to the divine consciousness that exists inherently within us. To serve others to the point of that awakening is the most spiritual expression of who we are.

The spiritual quality associated with the Law of Service is *humility*. When we are humble, thoughts of our own needs or desires rarely enter our consciousness. Our point of attention is on others, and we see their needs as our own. Humility enables us to act in service as a conduit of divine life force and love. Mother Teresa was questioned about her ability to live amid so much poverty and sickness. Why did she choose that lifestyle? Did she ever yearn for a more comfortable existence? Her answer was to note that she was unaware of her physical surroundings. She claimed that doing her work permitted her to remain in "constant communion with [her] husband." Her "husband" was Jesus Christ, the spiritual spouse of Christian monastics.

The Principle of Service enables us to remain in a state of purity. We don't have hidden agendas; we don't attempt to manipulate others for our benefit; we are content to allow the pure love of Divine Spirit to flow through us and out to others. We maintain our spiritual connection and feel uplifted by our efforts to assist others.

Regardless of one's spiritual affiliation or path, the surest way to access Spirit through service is to allow our consciousness to rest in Oneness. From this perspective, service is not self-destructive. It doesn't mean going without. On the contrary, we derive something most precious from our efforts when we serve with this awareness. We allow our consciousness to reside within the One.

When we serve within a system, there are rules to be followed. Being compliant to those rules frees us from needing to figure out all aspects of what to do and how to do it. Much of it is spelled out in the blueprint. The mind is thus freed to focus on what it will. If we choose to allow the mind to rest in the eternal presence of the Divine, we experience the peace and love of that presence, even as our efforts benefit others. If the system we are functioning within provides useful, needed service, we essentially serve Spirit by working within the system.

Spirit serves all life by providing the various qualities and resources needed for survival and well-being. To be of humble service—to provide others with the assistance they need within a context that is available and appropriate to us—is to act as an extension of Spirit. "From each according to their ability to each according to their need."

One aspect of humility is modesty. Modesty pertains to how we demonstrate our gifts, whether in the form of physical beauty, creative inspiration, intellectual brilliance, or even spiritual radiance. We share only in ways and at times that benefit others and not so that attention can be drawn to ourselves. The *I Ching* states: "When a person holds a high position and is nevertheless modest, he shines with the light of wisdom; if he is in a lowly position and is modest, he cannot be passed by. Thus, the superior person can carry out his work to the end without boasting of what has been achieved" (Hexagram 15. Wilhelm translation).

The Bottom Line

The universal Principle of Service enables us to assist with and possibly improve a condition, situation, or relationship. It offers the opportunity to be discerning and motivates us to develop our skill so we can be most effective and efficient in our efforts.

This principle works closely with the Principle of Survival and the Principle of the Eternal Present. Like the Principle of Survival, the Principle of Service is oriented to the physical plane. Both emphasize relating to life in meticulous, thorough ways in order to create a safe and stable reality for ourselves and to help others. Like the Principle of the Eternal Present, the Principle of Service enables us to focus on what's taking place in our immediate circumstances, so that we can help others without crossing any unhealthy boundaries.

The Principle of Service is quite different, however, from the Principle of Creativity. Unlike the latter, which prioritizes instinct and initiative, the Principle of Service stresses deliberation and discipline. This is not to suggest that we should choose one over the other. The challenge is to be aware of the situation at hand and discern what best fits the needs of that situation. Ideally, we can implement both by being creative in our service. Integrating these two principles can involve seeing something that needs doing and just doing it, using the courage of creativity in the act of service, or alteringpreexisting system to fit the needs of a new situation.

The Principle of Service enables us to be helpful to others even as we maintain a self-contained attitude within ourselves. Our satisfaction comes from the knowledge that we are improving a situation—and not from external recognition.

Affirmation: "I express Divine Will by doing things that are helpful to others."

The Law of Service

If a person would rule he first must learn how to serve, for only in this way does he secure from those below him the joyous assent that is necessary if they are to follow him.

—The *I Ching*, Hexagram 17, Wilhelm translation

Chapter 7: The Law of Harmony

Harmony is the manifesting expression of the Will of the eternal Good.

—Manley Palmer Hall

Group Mind

My friend Paul is a professor at the University of British Columbia. His field of study, as well as his passion, is killer whales. The Canadian government has provided him with a small island off the coast from which to do his research. He has tried many innovative ways to learn about these animals, such as putting microphones in the water to record their communication with each other, and putting speakers in the water to record the type of music that attracts or repels them. Classical music and certain types of jazz are turn-ons; rock and roll is definitely a turn-off. Evidently, they prefer music that is more harmonious.

The area in which Paul works is called Blackfish Sound. The local indigenous people refer to the killer whales, or orcas, as blackfish and revere them as manifestations of divine power. The killer whale has no predators. They are the top of the food chain in the ocean. Over the years Paul has gathered many stories about killer whales from local fishermen who have had contact with them in a variety of ways. Most of the stories extol the intelligence of the animals, especially their ability to function in social units called pods. One such story is about a young orca who was captured by a company who wanted it for a Marine World exhibit. They kept the whale in a cage made from logs that had been sunk deeply into the bottom of the bay. There was no gate, no way for the whale to escape or to be rescued. However, after a few weeks of captivity, his pod came to his rescue. They joined together and, as a unit, rammed the logs repeatedly until they had been loosened to the point that the young whale could swim to freedom. Killer whales are smaller than blue or humpback whales. One big bull alone could not have broken through the barricade. They had to unite and work as a team in order to liberate their family member. Cooperation, of course, is another form of harmony.

Harmony exists when a combination of parts functions as an orderly whole. When all the parts of an organism, social order, ecosystem, or work of art fit together proportionally, then harmony is achieved. This is the nature of life and is expressed in the universal Law of Harmony.

Harmony is about the relationship of one thing to another. It could be whales acting collectively in order to accomplish something important for the whole pod. It could be a husband interacting with his wife. It could be an individual's striving to create a harmonious relationship between her body, mind, and soul. Harmony is created when all parts of an equation coalesce, supporting each other and helping to create a more cohesive and stronger dynamic.

Harmony is something that we feel. When there is harmony in a family or a society, the members' sense of well-being is increased. They can feel it in their bodies. One reason that harmony can connect us in mystical communion with Divine Spirit is that the underlying structure and flow of the universe is harmonious. So when our environment in any way reflects this principle, we feel more connected and more at one.

We can also sense harmony when we hear a piece of music or experience it in art. A painting might strike us as beautiful because of its harmonious color choices. I remember a college professor talking about the architectural beauty of a building as something "that provides delight," and she didn't mean only delight to the eye. A building exists in three dimensions, so the delight must be experienced and felt as well as seen in order for it to truly be delightful.

Different parts of a unit have unique functions. Simultaneously, all parts of the unit reflect each other. The Hindu affirmation *Tat Twam Asi* means "that's me, too." In other words, whoever we are observing or relating to is a mirror of ourselves. This suggests that life itself is a hologram in which everything is a reflection of everything else. At the spiritual level, the One represents the whole universe. At the mental level, it represents our wholeness with society. At the physical level, it represents our wholeness with ourselves.

The Koran states that "God loves the equitable." It exhorts us to relate to each other as children of the same source, implying that we are all equal in the eyes of the Creator. Indeed, we all have a lot more in common than we have differences. All people everywhere are striving for happiness, security, and a sense of well-being and peace of mind. All people want to be liked, loved, approved of, and appreciated. The challenge faced by humanity is to create a social order that reflects our equality and hence, flows in harmony with the universe. Failing to create this equitable harmony can lead to the establishment of hierarchies in which some people are seen—or see themselves—as being better or more important than others. By observing others as reflecting aspects of ourselves and realizing that we are their mirror as well, we can avoid any tendencies to put people into hierarchies and viewing them as greater or less than ourselves.

The Principle of Harmony frees us from this false duality and enables us to work toward wholeness through the process of mirroring. This means recognizing that the qualities of others that we admire are the parts of ourselves that we need to enhance. The aspects of others of which we are contemptuous are parts of ourselves to work on and change. Sometimes we can become invested in seeing someone else as being wrong or bad as a way to avoid acknowledging the behavior in ourselves. Relationship provides a valuable mirror through which we see ourselves more clearly and as such, it can provide fertile ground for self-awareness and personal growth.

Astrological Correlation

The signs of the zodiac are placed on a wheel called a horoscope. There are twelve signs, so when viewed on the wheel there is a natural polarity between each pair of opposite signs that share a common axis. One way to understand the nature of any such polarity is to see the opposite signs as mirrors for each other, as opposite sides of the same coin. So they are working toward the same end but differ in their points of view. As mirror images, the two signs offer each other feedback that provides a clearer sense of self for both. The integration of each pair of polar signs, and ultimately the integration of all six polar opposites, is the mystical path to Oneness. For example, the Principle of Creativity is oriented toward personal development and expression. Who I am and what I am creating my life to be are prime points of focus in order to flow with that principle. Its opposite, the Principle of Harmony, however, is based on sharing the basic self and the life we generate for ourselves with others. Thus, we see how the signs that oppose each other on the wheel, as well as the universal laws they represent, create an interactive dynamic. How we relate to that dynamic will determine our success in consciously working with both principles.

There are three ways that we can benefit by integrating the principles connected by polarity. The first is in developing more self-awareness. As we interact with others, we learn about who we are. The second is through developing perspective on ourselves, based on the feedback we get from others. The third is through integrating opposing principles. That integration is, in turn, suggestive of something we need to do, a direction to pursue, in order to blend the oppositions. Each of the principles on any axis is dissimilar to its opposite, so we are challenged to resolve the inherent tension between them in order to grow in a centered way.

Integrating the laws in this manner promotes growth. If we fail to integrate them, we are left to deal with the inherent conflicts of that axis, which may prevent our using either principle in a positive way. Both ends of the axis are available to us to be manifested as we choose, but both must be manifested, or we cannot take advantage of the potential of the principle. If we don't, if we only express the influence of one but not the other, we tend to project the law we that we aren't owning onto someone or something external. By owning half and projecting half, we allow someone else to decide how we are going to experience that energy. Even if we flip back and forth between the two ends, we don't achieve wholeness because we never use all the energy available to us. This can lead to projection, judgment, and a lack of empowerment.

The astrological sign that correlates with the Law of Harmony is Libra. Opposite Libra on the wheel is Aries, which corresponds to the Principle of Creativity. While Aries (creativity) is about self, Libra (harmony) is about relationship between self and others; specifically, a one-to-one relationship. We can experience that as a primary spousal union or one with a good friend, business partner, counselor, teacher, or even spiritual master. With this as the focus, the priority is to keep the relationships positive for all concerned. But Libra doesn't necessarily have an innate sense of how to create quality relationships based on harmony. This is the lesson to be learned, both by Librans and the rest of us who seek mystical communion through the universal laws.

How to Align with This Law

In Greek mythology the goddess Harmonia was the daughter of the god Ares. Since Aries is about creation, it is implied that harmony is a quality that is created; it is something that requires clarity of thought and intention. By choosing to create harmony, we work within the context of the universal pan.

The Law of Creativity provides the energy and means to generate an identity and a reality that provide us with a clear sense of our self and our creative potential. The Law of Harmony challenges us to create ourselves in ways that integrate all aspects of who we are so that our lives flow synchronously and congenially toward others. It also challenges us to see others as we see ourselves. Regardless of visual or cultural differences, we are all one people. The Law of Harmony is the first law that is specifically concerned with socialization. Good relations with others start with the work we do on ourselves. As we continuously work at becoming and remaining centered (see chapter 5), our self-esteem will improve. This in turn will determine the degree of our acceptance of others. If our relationship with ourselves is healthy, honest, and growing, our relationships with others will reflect that. Once we feel strong, centered, and integrated with the many aspects of who we are, we are more able to give the support to others that is the basis of all loving relationships. This creates a pattern of mutual support. The mirroring involved can inspire us to see in others qualities we want to incorporate into ourselves.

As we become more comfortable with who we are, it becomes easier to integrate ourselves into a greater social whole in pleasant ways. When we realize that everyone reflects everyone else, we can relate to others and ourselves in a more balanced way. To develop a sense of balance in relationship, we work on monitoring the interactions between ourselves and others. If someone continually gives more than he receives, he will feel drained and resentful in the long run. To avoid this dynamic, we strive to see that the energy shared between ourselves and others is equal.

We don't always have to be satisfied with ourselves in order to be open to a relationship. We merely need to have a positive sense of self and an awareness that we are progressing. In Goethe's *Faust*, an aged professor makes a pact with the devil. The professor, Faust, agrees to give his soul to the devil in return for eternal youth. The devil receives Faust's soul when Faust becomes "satisfied." As an academic, Faust had spent his lifetime learning and developing his mind, but in the process he had failed to grow socially, so his personal life had grown stale and boring. He knew that intellectual growth never ceased, so he had assumed that social development wouldn't either. He assumed that his intellectual curiosity would be matched by his desire for pleasurable experiences. As long as he wasn't satisfied, his soul remained his. But once he was satisfied, he stopped striving, and his soul became the devil's. This is true for everyone. As long as we are on the path, the progress continues. But until we reach enlightenment itself—complete union with Spirit— we shouldn't expect to feel satisfied because there is still work to be done. Of course, if our goal is enlightenment, we wouldn't consider selling our soul in the first place. One problem with Faust was that he prioritized re-experiencing the lost time of youth on the physical plane over the ultimate liberation of enlightenment. We don't have to make the same mistake in order to affirm our continued growth.

One way to jumpstart our growth is to see ourselves as the person we are striving to become. This helps to break old patterns that may be self-limiting or unnecessarily self-critical. Of course, we have to back up this affirmative viewpoint by continually doing the inner work, so that the new external paradigm is matched by a new internal architecture. To do this in terms of integrating with life, we start by getting to know ourselves, then seeking someone or something that complements who we are. When we are with that person or are engaged in that activity, our sense of fullness is enhanced but not altered. The key is to establish our own center first, to develop the relationship with our own core being and to feel comfortable with ourselves and our own patterns and rhythms of growth. Only in this way can we then find a person or situation that is our true complement.

We can also provide others with support in their process by relating to them as if they already are who they are striving to become. This can get tricky. We might relate to them based on who we want them to be, rather than who they actually are. Or we could put out lots of quality energy to someone who doesn't return it. This would be a good time to implement the quality of discrimination inherent in the Principle of Service. Is that person making the changes or not? Is she returning the energy by being openly, generously supportive of you? If so, keep up the positive, open attitude toward her. If not, cut back on your involvement. There are three benefits to being open in anticipation of others' changes. First, we give them room to grow and change. We don't hold them to their old self but as someone who is striving to be different. Second, we create a path through which they can relate to us. Third, we stay out of the line of fire if someone uses us as a scapegoat, saying we are the problem or the cause of his unhappiness, rather than simply seeing us as the mirror of his own dysfunction.

The Mirror of Relationship

Relationship can take many forms. It can involve a superficial acquaintance, a colleague, relative, neighbor, dear friend, lover, or a primary partner. All of the dynamics previously discussed can pertain to any or all of these relationships. But one quality that pertains only to a primary, or spousal, relationship is intimacy. A good definition for intimacy is voluntary vulnerability. Some people equate intimacy with sexual contact, but I think it has more to do with revealing ourselves in a deep way. This enables us to express our true feelings, including sensitivities, shadows, and other things we may feel are awkward or that we may be ashamed of. When we do this, we let the partner know that which we otherwise would keep secret. If we refrain from revealing our deeper self, it is because we either do not trust the other person, or we fear that person will reject us if he or she knows certain things about us. As we reveal these things, we are freed from having to carry them entirely within us, and we build trust that the partner will not reject us when we take the leap and open up in a deep, emotional way. For a harmonious relationship, this process of sharing needs to go in both directions, so that one partner is not responsible for taking all the risks. If both partners accept the risk of revealing, the openness and honesty leads to personal transformation for each. However, if we are open but our partner is not, it might be that he or she does not value intimate relationship or is unwilling or incapable of getting in touch with such profound realizations about himself or herself.

One image to keep in mind as we approach the depths of a relationship is the "staircase of intimacy." We can visualize ourselves as a very small child, holding hands with another very small child, who is our partner. We are both standing at the top of a long, narrow, steep, dark staircase. No lights, no railings. Our intention is to descend the stairs together, and as we do, we will grow closer, creating a meaningful emotional bond. But it's pretty scary. After all, little kids don't know how to do a lot of things. So we proceed very slowly. We swing our right foot out over the first step, but don't actually put our weight down on that next step until we see our partner is ready. This is all risky stuff. So we take our time. We don't want to pull the other person down too fast, because we could both lose our balance and fall all the way down the stairs. We don't want to put up too much resistance because then we won't go anywhere. Assuming we both intend to descend the stairs and can find a rate that is mutually safe and workable, then gradually we can both descend together and in the process become more emotionally open and bonded to each other.

By being open with a partner about sensitive or challenging parts of ourselves, as well as being open to his or her vulnerability, we create a deep connection of emotional honesty upon which to build an intimate relationship. And through this bond we can see deeper parts of ourselves in the mirror of our partner who is sharing the deeper parts of himself or herself with us.

Another vehicle through which we can experience mirroring is the arts. Whatever the creative medium, what we create can provide instant feedback about who we are and possibly about the society in which we live as well. Experiencing someone else's creative expression can also provide a useful mirror. Painting, music, words, movements can all serve as windows for seeing ourselves more clearly. What is most significant in the artistic process is the emotional response, mental clarity, or spiritual inspiration that provides access to a deeper level of ourselves.

Parenting also can be a mirror, though at times hard to look at. If our children are "acting out" and are generally difficult to relate to at home, in school, or in the community, we must look to ourselves as the source of the problem. Our children are merely acting in accordance with the patterns we have set up in our family dynamic. Sometimes children might be acting out unresolved issues of the parent. To get them to change their behaviors, we, as the parents, need to become aware of and deal with those aspects of ourselves that have not yet been worked out. Then we can work at changing the family dynamic and watch what happens. There are exceptions, of course. Sometimes the energies of the parents and the child just don't mesh easily. Children might come in with a lot of anger or with trust issues that require an immense amount of love, patience, and understanding on the parents' part in order to support them to work through and change their patterns. Sometimes the problem requires an objective perspective from outside the family to act as a catalyst for change.

Justice and Retribution

Two primary qualities associated with the Principle of Harmony are justice and retribution. Justice is important because in order to live in harmony, there must be certain standards, such as laws and values, that are agreed upon by the people involved in a social group. This is one way that organized religions can be useful, as they provide a framework of morals and ethics that support a harmonious social order as well as individual direction and growth. By living in accordance with those ethics, we connect with life in mystical communion. From this point it is easy to see the importance of relating to others with kindness.

Sometimes we, or society as a whole, are challenged by people who live by a different set of values and behaviors than we do. The problem is how to respond to them. If these people are sincere, we can at least be open to discussing our differences. In order for a culture to continue growing and to remain viable, it must integrate new ideas and behaviors periodically. If, however, the challenges to the social order come from people or groups whose intention is antagonistic and who seek to disrupt the social harmony without offering a viable alternative, it's a different story. Society needs to protect its members and respond to its challenges in a manner consistent with its laws and mores. This helps the group, as it maintains the stability of the social order and allows people to dialogue in ways that are not threatening to the established order. Justice implies commitment to equality and respect for the other, reminding us that we are all in this together and might as well work toward the common good.

Retribution implies revenge. Revenge implies punishment. You hurt me; I hurt you. An eye for an eye. This pattern actually subverts access to the Law of Harmony and illustrates how it functions when off-center. One steps outside the accepted order to achieve personal satisfaction. This is the fundamental problem with capital punishment.

We espouse the belief that it's wrong to kill (as established in the Ten Commandments, a standard to which Western cultures claim to agree and uphold) and then justify murdering the killer as an act of retribution. When we kill a killer, it reduces the community to the same act of destruction. We become killers. This removes the group from the path of mystical communion with the Divine, and each member becomes complicit in deliberate, premeditated killing. This is forbidden by the very law we claim to uphold.

An example of retribution that is justifiable, however, comes from the pod of killer whales I mentioned earlier. It is a story that illustrates the intelligent cooperation among the whales, and it involves two loggers who habitually took a small boat out every day to a little island where they logged the trees. The loggers would roll the trees to the edge of a cliff, where large stakes prevented the logs from rolling into the water. When the pile of logs was big enough, the loggers would pull the stakes, the logs would roll down the cliff and into the water, and the current would take them to the mill. One day after rolling a log to the pile, they noticed a pod of killer whales swimming below the cliff. One logger suggested pulling the stakes to see if they could "nail a whale." The other logger said no, but the first logger persisted and pulled the stakes. The logs rolled down the cliff and hit and killed a whale. When the loggers took their boat across the sound that evening, the whales returned. The whales knocked the boat over, and the logger who had pulled the stakes was never seen again. The other one lived to tell the tale.

Not Aligning with This Law

One danger of the Principle of Harmony comes when we focus too much on the outer world, when we live our lives "outside in." Everyone wants to be liked by others, but sometimes our need for external support is more than just positive mirroring. It can extend to the point where we depend on others' feedback in order to see ourselves. This allows others to define, validate, or justify our life; their opinion of us becomes more important than our opinion of ourselves. This is another form of judgment, although instead of our being critical of others, we allow them to be critical of us. We "senior" the other person to us, giving them our power. Some people go through life with a collection of externally designated authority figures. They give their power away to these people and then desperately try to get it back by placating them. If, however, we use the mirror of someone else's life as an inspiration for how to grow and improve our own life, this promotes self-awareness and personal growth. We focus on becoming aware of our personal blind spots, and then we do something about them. If instead we get stuck in behaviors that satisfy only others, regardless of what we really want to do or say, the price we pay for positive feedback is self-betrayal. Without being honest and real with ourselves, we severely limit our ability to connect with Divine Self.

Another version of imbalance occurs when we try to find that one person with whom we are in complete harmony, the person who will provide positive feedback at all times. This desire can lead to a lifetime of disappointing relationships, both with ourselves and with others. Or we might try to find a partner who can satisfy a specific need; for example, someone who can provide economic security or sexual gratification or some other form of material-plane protection or fulfillment. Others might look to relationship to satisfy an intellectual need, an opportunity to converse and share ideas and information. Some people look for a partner to improve their public image. Or they might simply want to get together with someone in order to play, laugh, and have a good time. These are all realistic, common social drives and needs, and these types of alliances work to a certain extent, if we like the people who fulfill our expectations. Somewhere along the way, however, if we stop enjoying the encounter, we could blame our partner for failing to meet our needs. Ultimately, the dynamic fails because we perceive them as our source of satisfaction and ourselves as a passive participant. We project our hopes and desires onto them instead of working to fulfill them ourselves. We want others to complete us, to fill in and compensate for the empty places within us, instead of using the mirror they offer to see what we need to work on and complete within ourselves.

With all the give-and-take interaction that this principle addresses, it is easy to lose the self and feel as if we are merging with the other person. The point of balance between ourselves and other becomes blurred. To avoid this pattern, we need to locate our "internal fulcrum" to find the point of balance that lies within each of us. We can then integrate the body/mind/soul trinity without the need for feedback from or interaction with anyone.

By being considerate of others' state of being, by being thoughtful of their needs, and by being cooperative in our dealings with others, we effectively use this law. In learning to relate to others with diplomacy and tact, we create a social environment within which everyone is acknowledged. We do our part in allowing others to see who they are. This enables them to do the work they need to do on themselves to feel whole within, as well as a sense of unity with us.

Instead of seeking completion through relationship, we need to try living "inside out." Establish the relationship with ourselves first. Getting ourselves centered will always precede a meaningful relationship with another.

Judgment and Prejudice

A common way to block the flow of the Principle of Harmony is through judgment. The state of judgment comes from the perception of life as duality, in which everything is seen as opposing something else. It is bigger or smaller, more or less, lovable or worthy, etc. Judgment overlooks the Principle of Both/And, which states that all things and people contain all the possibilities for manifestation. Judging a person restricts our experience of them by the limits of our own experience and consciousness. We judge them as being either better or in some way inferior. In this respect, judging another actually reflects how we feel about some part of ourselves. Ultimately, judgment is a self-limiting behavior. We limit both our relationship and the other person because of our judgment of who he is, what he does, and why he does it.

Judgment can also be based on an attachment to a situation's being a certain way. Rather than accepting it for what it is, adapting to or learning from it, we assume that the cause of our discomfort is someone else.

Negatively judging someone else or blaming something external for our own disharmony are ways of projecting parts of ourselves that we don't like, don't know, or aren't comfortable with. This, in effect, makes an excuse for something about ourselves that we are unable or unwilling to address and resolve. This is another example of living "outside in," but it is different from seeing others as a mirror of ourselves. When we see ourselves mirrored by the behavior of others, we use that relationship as a vehicle for self-awareness and self-development. Judgment, on the other hand, is about projection. Instead of using other people as a mirror, we put the spotlight on them. We focus on their mistakes, problems, or limitations as a convenient way to avoid working on our own. We could also blame others for creating our problems, rather than owning them as something we had an active role in creating. Projection creates limited relationships, but more important, it limits our potential for personal growth.

One of the ironies of judgment is that it can lead to the assumption that others are judging us as well. It's possible that this assumption is correct, and that we are both relating through projection. After a while there is no relating going on at all, just people relating to the images they project onto each other. When this occurs, we could feel compelled to judge and project as a means of self-defense, to protect ourselves from everyone else who socializes in that way.

Prejudice is another form of judgment. It involves a negative opinion about an entire group of people. Prejudice extends beyond personal relationship. It reflects a belief system that is limited in both scope and experience. In chapter 6, discrimination was defined as the process of making subtle distinctions between similar conditions. The implication is that after a period of review and contemplation, conclusions are drawn that help to define a reality. This type of analysis will usually preclude prejudice. But without such detailed analysis, discrimination is simply one person's opinion based on limited information and experience. This, then, becomes prejudice. A person who doesn't want to take responsibility for his life or his condition places the blame for his misery on an entire class of people or an entire set of conditions outside of himself and his control. It's easier to point the finger at someone else than at ourselves. Or, as my friend the late Betty Bethards used to say, "When you point one finger at someone else, there are three more pointing back at you."

If we manifest these patterns, and we know it and don't like it, there are a couple of things we can do. We can try to be conscious, working to change our behaviors, then see how others respond. Some people will follow our lead, and our relationships will then gradually improve. Others, however, might respond to our unspoken changes by accelerating their own bad behaviors. This leads to another option: end our involvement with these people.

One reason why we project and judge is due to our attachment to harmony. In this scenario, our goal in any social situation is to create and maintain harmony at any cost. We are willing to accept peace without the clarity of what the problems are or how to resolve them. We don't want anything to be other than enjoyable. Our assumption is that harmony is black or white. Either we create and maintain it, or we disturb and destroy it. We are not aware that the harmony in a relationship can be temporarily set aside while we and our partner acknowledge our problems and work out our differences. Thus, harmony can be used as a tool to help resolve issues. As a result, unsatisfying behaviors or qualities persist in the relationship.

We may be delightful, congenial, friendly, and thoughtful. There are, however, other aspects of our nature, both in terms of how we relate to others and how we relate to ourselves, that could use improvement. Projection, judgment, and attachment all prevent those conditions from improving.

Marriage

These misuses of the Principle of Harmony can especially manifest in romantic relationships. We may have an ideal of what a relationship is supposed to be, regardless of who we are, what our partner needs, or what the actual dynamic between us is. These idealized expectations and the romanticizing of our partner (or even placing him or her on a pedestal) are ways of avoiding what's really going on. Human relationships can be tricky, especially in a marital situation.

Throughout history, and from culture to culture, people have chosen different ways to unite. In contemporary society, primary relationships are monogamous. Some animal societies, such as that of the wolf, the great ape, and the eagle, reflect this concept of commitment. But some cultures have preferred free and indiscriminate relationships. The indigenous peoples of Russia and certain African tribes had no concept of the institution of marriage. Relationships were based on the temporary sexual drives of the males, who were allowed to exercise their animal instincts without restraint. Women were related to communally, as was the land and the food. In some tribes, such as the Malaccan people of Malaysia, women were passed from man to man. Certain tribes in Australia allowed women to leave a union any time they chose. The original word for marriage in Hawaiian meant "to try." The Hawaiian culture, along with those in Siberia, South Africa, and Tibet, believed that marriage was an experiment and could be ended by either partner at any time.

Group marriages have also been accepted in some parts of the world. In Tibet, for example, it was the custom for a group of brothers to marry a group of sisters. Each of the brothers would take turns cohabiting with each of the women. The Jews and Muslims practice a custom called "levirate," in which a man is obligated to marry his brother's widow.

Arranged marriages commonly took place in Europe during the Middle Ages. The upper castes of India arranged marriages that were based on compatible connections between the individuals and were oriented toward strengthening the family and community. Compatibility was usually established by astrologers. The parents of a newborn would take the infant's chart to the family astrologer, who would compare it to other horoscopes available to him. Based on his analysis, the child would be betrothed to someone who offered the best possibility for an auspicious union. Arranged marriages in Europe, on the other hand, were a way of strengthening the economic or political power of the aristocratic families entering into the arrangement. The focus was on increasing the power and land-holding of a man or a family. In more modern times, aristocratic social orders have been replaced by those based on social equality. Marriages among all classes in industrialized societies throughout the world have tended to be based on mutual economic need, rather than on patriarchal power. However, in a contemporary society, men tend to earn more money than women, even when doing the same work. Therefore, women often still rely on the economic power of men to provide security for themselves and their children.

The practices of polygamy (one man, more than one woman) and polyandry (one woman, more than one man) have been popular in different parts of the world. In hunter/gatherer tribes, men would lead violent and dangerous lives, often dying in the hunt and leaving a disproportionate number of women to men. So it made sense for several women to be connected to one man. Women have found polygamy acceptable as a vehicle for sharing the labor of child-rearing and food gathering. If the men were absent frequently or for long periods, the sisterhood of the extended polygamous family also offered social interaction and comfort. At times when the men were present, a variety of potential sexual partners would limit the demands on any one wife. This resulted in fewer pregnancies for each woman. It also allowed for longer periods of nursing the children already born. Similarly, in societies where men grossly outnumber women, polyandry has been accepted and practiced. The rationale in both situations is the same: security for the individual and survival for the tribe.

Although still practiced in some indigenous cultures, several factors contributed to the decline of either casual or multiple relationships and the development of monogamous marriage. One has been lifestyle change. Approximately ten thousand years ago, humans started to become agrarian. The cultivation of food and the domestication of animals replaced hunting and gathering. As cultures became more sedentary, the genders gradually became more equal in number. Another factor has been economic. Planting and harvesting crops put a premium on land and eventually, the concept of private property developed. The physical strength of men was directed more toward protecting their gardens and fields than toward hunting. The institution of private property brought with it the patriarchal society. The Principle of Survival was manifested differently as men sought to avoid bequeathing their property to other men's children. Rather, they sought to ensure the survival of their own lineage. Relationships involving multiple wives evolved into those with a wife and a series of concubines. Men invested in women in order to draw children from them, as if they were interest on an economic venture. The first step in this process was to procure a wife. In some cultures, women were stolen from their own tribes and essentially became slaves to their husbands. As the culture became more established and secure, wealth grew, a man owning the most property were also the strongest economically. They were seen as desirable husbands, men who would provide a woman and her children with the greatest degree of security. Thus a father would offer a substantial present to a potential son-in-law, called a dowry. This could be livestock or a sum of money for the right to transfer "ownership" of a young woman from father to husband. In none of these situations was marriage entered upon for romantic reasons, let alone those of equality and personal choice. Marriage as an institution was a contract that hopefully led to a profitable arrangement, but it was not one of equals.

Children came to be seen as a workforce and thus became economic assets, as well as a group who could care for their aged parents. The greater the number of his children, the more wealthy a man was perceived to be. As the Hindu society of India developed, marriage became almost compulsory. Unmarried men had no status; unmarried women were disgraced. Marriage was considered the cornerstone of both family and society. It was so important that it couldn't be left to chance, to passion, or to the romantic ideal. Marriages were arranged, and the relationships were based on loyalty, endurability, and compatibility of the horoscopes of the individuals. The karma of each child was addressed so that it could be acknowledged and expressed through the union.

The Jews, Muslims, and Chinese also allowed either the parents or marriage brokers to determine mates for their children. Often, the matrimonial ceremony was held during childhood, although consummation took place after the children reached puberty.

Some cultures saw this as a way of minimizing the effect of passion and sexuality on relationship. For others, it was a way for women to be perceived as equal to men in their needs or their rights.

Even with marital vows and commitment, adultery was common, especially among the nobility in Western Europe during the Middle Ages. Although women could be punished severely for this, being condemned to anything from disfigurement to death, men could get off with merely a monetary fine. Theologian St. Thomas Aquinas defined what was to become the acceptable role for women in the Western Christian belief system when he wrote: "The woman is subject to the man on account of the weakness of her nature, both of mind and of body. ...Woman is in subjection according to the law of nature, but a slave is not. ... Children ought to love their father more than their mother." Not much harmony there. And the price for breaking this universal law is still exacted both in Western culture and on our environment and its resources.

The universal Principle of Harmony is based on equality. Men and women have different but equal strengths that they offer to the family and society, enabling both to function effectively. The values and priorities of the genders also tend to be different. Unfortunately, by subjugating one-half of the human race based on the ignorant prejudices of philosophers or antiquated traditions, our ability to survive and the quality of our experience during incarnation has been compromised. Fortunately for many women of the Middle Ages, in the middle, artisan, and noble classes, the dictates of the monks of the church often went unheeded in the secular parts of society. There was thus more freedom and acceptance of women, especially at court, than would have been expected or acceptable to the church.

Romantic Love

Romantic love became popular in the Middle Ages, but it rarely led to or was found in marriage. The concept of romantic love was, at that time, revolutionary. It was created by the poets and troubadours of the day. Romantic love consisted of a man idealizing a woman and the potential she offered in satisfying his physical desires. Through the rosy lens of romanticism, the embodiment of the perfect woman was the Virgin Mary incarnate. The ideal woman was defined as being sweet, submissive, and vulnerable; someone who needed to be "saved" by a man from living a lifetime of boredom, insecurity, or debasement. She, in turn, could use his desires to require him to serve her in a variety of ways, from providing physical protection to providing her with rare and desirable possessions or tokens of affection. It was the sexual possibilities, fueled by the tension between desire and the unattainable, that produced and fostered the romantic love ideal, not the consummation of an actual relationship. Romantic love was unique to the aristocracy at a time when the increase of wealth had led to an increase in idleness. The lower classes could afford neither the time nor energy to pursue such things. They were, however, also freed from the excessively restrictive demands of the church and the court to do as they pleased.

The concept of romantic love marked the beginning of a paradigm shift in which women were beginning to be seen and related to less as property and more as people. In and of itself, this was a primitive—or at least unsophisticated—way of changing the social dynamic between men and women. But it was a start. Romantic love does not always ensure security for the woman or children, and it isn't necessarily fair. Yet the balance between the sexes is better than it was, because women have attained more professional and economic options than they had traditionally. The primary relationship between men and women seems to be headed in a more equitable direction. In the beginning of patriarchal times, women and children were valued as economic assets by men, because women, through their procreative power, supplied the man with a labor force. Now, things have reversed and men, through their ability to generate greater financial resources, are seen as economic assets to women and children. In none of the above scenarios, however, has relationship been defined, perceived, or experienced as a union of equals. Whether on economic, social, or even sexual terms, it has generally remained an institution between people with an unequal degree of power.

In more recent times, and especially in industrialized countries, women have been afforded more freedom of choice in their professional experience and consequently have risen up the ladder of socio-economic equality. The invention of reliable forms of birth control has accelerated this freedom and led to changes in relationship dynamics. The old reasons for marriage no longer need to apply. The contemporary social structure, political climate, and economic realities place emphasis on different values and priorities in personal relationship. Romance and physical affection are certainly in higher focus than they had been traditionally, and they are often the reason why people decide to commit to each other. These are, however, still less than ideal bases for a healthy, enduring primary relationship. The mass media has prioritized these qualities by providing images of beautiful people having fun, as if to suggest that only by being young and sexy do we have the potential to have fulfilling relationships. This inevitably influences many people's relationship choices and desires. Whether or not this is a good idea, we do at least have the freedom to choose.

These days, relationships are based more on personal proclivity than ever before. We have the potential to be with someone because we want to be, not because we have to be. With this freedom of choice also comes the necessity of working on the relationship. Arranged marriages were based on duty and strict family structure. If love evolved, fine. If not, at least both persons knew what was expected of them, and it was hoped that at least fondness and mutual respect would develop.

When a relationship is based on personal choice, if one or both partners are unwilling to process and work on the relationship, it will become stagnant. The romance fades, and the physical attraction of the partner fades with it. We could opt to stay in this type of relationship, settling for comfort and security. Or we could place a higher priority on personal growth and fulfillment in a changing, vibrant, honest relationship. If these are not present, our unhappiness can be a wake-up call to leave the relationship. Potentially, we are less bound by family demands, economic necessities, or political pressures, so we can afford to be a cocreator of our primary relationship. We all have personal needs, feelings, and desires, and it is natural to expect that our partner is interested in and cares enough about us to help us satisfy them. Similarly, we should become aware of our partner's needs and feelings and seek to accommodate him or her as best we can.

There are still the potential traps of projecting an idealized, romanticized image onto our partner, and of relating to that person as we want him to be, rather than as who he is. We are not, however, unalterably bound to a person or relational patterns for life. If both parties are process-oriented, their issues can be resolved, and a deeper quality of love can develop. Sensual gratification and physical or emotional security become less important than the emerging bond of deep emotional connectedness. The emotional investment made by both people makes the relationship more enjoyable.

What, then, is the basis for a healthy, growth-oriented, mutually fulfilling, committed relationship in today's world? Women are experiencing greater economic autonomy, and men are realizing the benefit of being in touch with their inner being. Realistic relationships, freed from the external constraints of the past, need to be based on individuality. Who are we, and what do we need in relationship? In talking to clients over the years, the biggest blind spot among people that I've seen is the lack of awareness of what they need in a relationship. Once we have a handle on this, we can proceed to work on developing a friendship with someone who shares common interests and values and with whom we sense that our needs can be met. If we both feel a connection to each other and feel as if we are "seen" by that person, the relationship can proceed from a friendship to something more singular. One of the important ingredients in creating a realistic, fulfilling relationship is the degree to which the other person accepts us. If we can just show up, be who we are in the process of relating (and in turn, be sensitive to the other person's needs), and feel accepted, we may be on our way to a long-term union.

The essence of compatibility is based on three factors. First is our degree of love for each other. Second is our degree of commitment. Third is our shared willingness to do the work necessary to stay together in a harmonious, egalitarian relationship. These are not factors that can be determined simply through questioning each other; rather, they must be answered through internal dialogue. Periodically, we can confer with each other to compare the results of this inquiry. Assuming our findings are similar, the relationship is working, and a commitment is realistic and, quite possibly, enduring.

Projecting the Past

Another potential pitfall when trying to work with the Principle of Harmony is labeling. In labeling we define, in logical and conscious terms, everything and everyone around us. These labels are often based on past experiences. Whether or not we enjoyed the previous relationships, we project them onto our present and send it out into our future. Attachments, limitations, and expectations from previous experiences wind up limiting us in terms of what we can create in the present. Labeling is limiting. It prevents us from being open to the opportunities that are available in a new situation. Instead of using these variables to create a fulfilling relationship, we perceive and define what *is* in terms of what *was*. This may seem to give us a sense of controlling the unknowns of a new relationship, but it also limits our potential to respond to situations in ways that are appropriate and healthy, let alone inspired and creative. This is in direct conflict with the universal Law of the Eternal Present. Not being aware of what is taking place around us, let alone how we are responding to these events, compromises our ability to flow harmoniously in the here and now. We experience the present in terms of our past.

However, there are also certain similarities between these two principles Remember that one of the tenets of the Law of the Eternal Present is that our here-and-now experience is based in our past. In order to effectively and successfully be here now, we must acknowledge and work through what we previously experienced. We have to know where we've been in order to see, clearly and accurately, where we are and where to go from here. If we don't acknowledge our past, and work through and resolve the issues generated from our history, we cannot truly be present, and our relationships suffer accordingly.

The universe always provides what we need. It offers us the potential to cocreate with it, as an equal. It provides the raw material and the inspiration; we provide the time and energy to manifest it. But we need to be willing to work with these energies and concepts in order to benefit from them. Although these qualities exist as potential for everyone, they need to be consciously worked with so that they can help to manifest healthy and fulfilling relationships.

Spiritual Opportunity

In chapter 46 of the *Tao Te Ching*, Lao Tzu says, "A person can achieve his own happiness only by pursuing the happiness of others, because it is only by forgetting about his own happiness that he can become happy." By being caring and thoughtful of others, not only can we become happy and feel good about ourselves, but we can establish relationships based on a heart connection. Since we tend to attract those with similar styles and patterns of relating, if we relate to others with heart, we will receive in our heart as well. Like attracts like.

However, if we try to thoughtfully put others before ourselves and relate from the heart, relationships can be a challenging aspect of our pursuit of a mystical connection to Oneness. It's one thing to be aware of ways we can connect with Spirit, but unless we are living a monastic lifestyle, we will be involved with people every day. Developing relational skills within a spiritual framework includes recognizing others as manifestations of the same spiritual Source from which we issue. They, too, are expressions of the Divine.

The Hindu social greeting *namaste* translates as "I acknowledge the Light within you." This begins an encounter at a refined level of interaction. By perceiving the Divine in others, we are more likely to relate to them with kindness and respect. They are, in turn, more likely to return the favor, so that a profound sense of harmony is established. It is best if we frame an interaction at all times as a spiritual act and an opportunity to enhance our mystical attunement to Divine Oneness. Through such interactive sharing, harmony expands in all directions.

As the Beatles pointed out, "The love you take is equal to the love you make." This is another way of saying that we are mirrors of each other. The quality of energy exchange between us is determined by what we choose to create and by the response from the other person. Note the complementary interaction between creativity (Aries) and harmony (Libra). We can learn a great deal about ourselves through conscious relating and by remaining open to receiving honest, objective feedback from others. How we want to be perceived and related to will determine how we share with others and, in turn, how they will relate back to us. Others see themselves in the mirror of our honest and objective feedback to them. In this way, we can consciously create pleasant, enjoyable, and fulfilling relationships.

Another contemporary aphorism that pertains to relating is "What goes around comes around." This reminds us that the energy we put out will ultimately come back to us. This is a simple reference to the concept of karma, which is fully delineated in chapter 10.

Balance

The spiritual quality associated with harmony is *balance*. We establish balance in our life by making sure that what we receive is matched by what we give. Similarly, we usually give what we want to receive. I remember playing gin rummy with my grandmother when I was a child. She always suggested that I pay attention to what my opponent was discarding, because it provided insight into what he was looking to receive. In relationship, as mentioned earlier, one of the keys to fulfillment is knowing what we need. When we know what our needs are, we increase the potential for fulfillment in relationship.

Furthermore, we create harmony in our life when we refrain from offering more than can be appreciated or returned. It's important to remain balanced in our relating. For example, it is important to be

The Law of Harmony

cooperative and considerate of others and of the wider environment around us. Being peaceful will likely promote peace in our life, but there are times and situations when the appearance of being peaceful is actually a form of being passive and can lead to feeling drained. We might even put ourselves in jeopardy by being too nice. There's an old story about a tiger that was terrorizing a village and threatening to eat the people. The citizens went to a holy man who lived nearby and told him of their fears and concerns about this animal. He promised to intercede. He found the tiger and told him to be nice to the people, to not threaten their security and well-being. The tiger promised he would change his ways. A few days later the tiger appeared before the holy man. The poor cat was bleeding and bruised from a beating he had received at the hands of the suddenly courageous people. The tiger said that once the people realized he was peaceful and harmless, they had their way with him. The holy man looked at the tiger, shook his head, and said, "I told you not to bite and kill. I didn't tell you not to growl." The lesson here is that peacefulness needs to be balanced with self-affirmation.

Balance also pertains to the spiritual light that resides in everyone. We all have the opportunity to make endless choices every day: what we eat, with whom we speak, what we say, what we read, and how we respond to the weather. The choices we make differentiate us. The underlying, unifying truth for everyone—and ultimately, all of life—is that the energy that creates the essence of who we are by those choices is the same for all. We all share equally in that divine energy.

The Principle of Harmony takes into consideration our relationship with all that transpires around us. In striving to live a balanced life, we should take into consideration the continuous cycles, laws, and patterns of nature, as well as the features of our immediate social environment. Hexagram 15 of the *I Ching* says: "It is the law of nature to make fullness empty and to make full what is empty ... high mountains are worn down by the waters and the valleys are filled up ... the superior person does the same thing when he establishes order in the world; he equalizes the extremes that are the source of social discontent and thereby creates just and equitable conditions."

To live in harmony within a social context requires not only that we are considerate and cooperative but also that we work with others to create a society within which the universal principles of harmony, justice, and equality are acknowledged foundations of society. Social justice implies a balanced use and allocation of resources among all members of society. In the 1960s, Eldridge Cleaver, a leader of the Black Panther Party, commented on the plight of the poor in the United States, stating, "We don't have economic problems in our country; we have distribution problems." This statement applies to this day and to the international community as well. When the situation is remedied even within one nation, its culture remains strong because it functions in conjunction with the greater, ongoing laws of life.

Harmony must first be established within ourselves, separate from other people and external events, by uniting the fundamental dualities within—the receptive yin with the expressive yang. This inner marriage of opposite forces enables us to realize that we are the embodiment of Oneness. There are times in our lives when it is acceptable, appropriate, and healthy to manifest more of the yin qualities and behaviors and less of the yang, and vice versa. Maintaining these two elements in conscious balance enables us to cocreate and maintain amicable relationships. If we meet with resistance to our expression and desire for harmony and justice, we can still hold to our inner fulcrum and produce a different but appropriate response. Often, the unpleasant feedback we receive from others is simply a mirror to our own patterns. We can respond either in an equally unpleasant way, or we can use the dissonant interaction as an opportunity to get more centered and from that point, alter our behavior. We can refrain from judging the actions or labeling the motivations of others. We can stay centered and realize that "they" are providing us with insight into ourselves. By working to remain balanced and centered in relationship to others, we have a greater opportunity to perceive ourselves, as well as everything and everyone outside of us, as manifestations of the same Divine Light. From this point of recognition we perceive and relate to everything as Oneness. We realize that all life is in interconnected harmony, pulsing and radiating the light and love of Source itself.

The Bottom Line

The universal Law of Harmony posits that everything that exists is an interconnected manifestation of the Source of life. We successfully engage this principle when we respond to our experiences and relationships with harmony and equanimity. When we perceive everything and everyone around us as embodiments of light and reflections of the beauty and radiance of our own being, we are in sync with the Principle of Harmony.

This principle's polar opposite, the universal Principle of Creation establishes us as links in the never-ending chain of manifestation. Working with this law helps us to feel potent, self-affirming, and full. Different cultures throughout history have evolved varying strategies for creating meaning and fulfillment for their people, with greater or lesser degrees of success.

In order to establish our own sense of well-being and happiness in our life, we need to develop a clear sense of what we need from the universe as well as from other people. Then we can put out to the universe, as well as to others, the energy that will enable our needs to be fulfilled. We must relate to others the way we want and need them to relate to us. If we share ourselves in ways that reflect the higher, lighter aspects of ourselves, others will respond in kind. And in the process, everyone in the situation will feel loved, safe, and full. The more we feel the light and love, the more we have to share. And the more we share it, the more there is for us to receive. In the process, we feel the Oneness that flows through all that has been created.

Affirmation: "I do for others what I would have them do for me."

Give full measure, when you measure, and weigh with even scales. That is better and fairer in the end.

—The Koran

Chapter 8: The Law of Eternal Life

Except a man be born again he cannot see the Kingdom of God.

—John 3:3

Life after Death

My father was a good man. He was kind and loving to his family, supporting us with his spirit and sense of humor as much as through his hard work. He was a good role model. It was a shock when he was diagnosed with cancer. The surgeons were unable to remove all the cells of the tumor during the operation. Even after radiation treatment, we knew his time remaining with us was growing short. It was devastating to see this happy, upbeat man fading into a mass of pain in his last few weeks of life. Our family was gathered around his bed when he died. He knew he was loved and cared for by those he cherished the most, and it was a relief to know that his suffering had ended.

Since that time I have had several dreams about my father. In each one he has become progressively more present, culminating in one particular dream. In this dream I am sitting at the desk in my office when suddenly the door swings open, and my father enters the room. He is smiling as he usually did, but what is striking about him is his body. It is iridescent! Normally, color is not a significant feature of my dream life, but in this dream, the radiant, flowing cascade of color is unmistakable and powerful. At first I am startled and even a little afraid of what is happening. But as this image becomes clear, I think, "Hey, there's my dad!" My second thought is that he has died. But as I sit there gazing at this very real, very dynamic person, my third thought is "He's not dead; that's him right there. He's as alive as I am right now and as alive as he's ever been!" This dream left me feeling exhilarated, knowing that my father still existed. Our means of contact are obviously diminished, but that he is still an extant being suggests that somewhere, somehow we can be together again.

The concept of life after death was not new to me. It was something I had read about, contemplated, and even taught and discussed for decades. But never before had I experienced something so immediate and personal that it surpassed any need for logical explication. My father had checked in to say hi, to reassure me that he was fine. By extension, he also helped to validate for me the Principle of Eternal Life beyond any doubt. And in my mind, this dream raised reincarnation from a possibility to a probability.

My friend Betty Bethards, author of *The Dream Book*, spent decades lecturing about the importance of dreams. She teaches that our dream images can teach us about ourselves, especially about hidden or unacknowledged parts of who we are. By working with our dreams we can gain valuable insights that can be applied to the process of personal growth. In her opinion, everything in a dream—every person, every object, every action—is a reflection of the dreamer and an image to contemplate and learn from. The only exception to that is if the dream is of a loved one who has left the earth plane and passed over. Under those conditions, she maintains that often that person has literally come to us in the dream state. From my experience of a series of dreams about my father, culminating with this luminescent vision in my office, I concur with her precept. If this is an accurate interpretation of those dreams, then my father is still alive, in spirit if not in body.

The Law of Eternal Life and its accompanying principle of reincarnation, appears in cultures and religious traditions from every corner of the world. As far back as seventy thousand years ago, both Neanderthal and early *Homo sapiens* buried their dead with objects and food to accompany them into the next realm of life. The Oglala Lakota shaman Black Elk said, "The power of the world works in circles. Even the seasons form a great circle in their changing and always come back to where they were. The life of a man is a circle from childhood to childhood, and so it is in everything where power moves."

The Druids of Great Britain also maintained a system of relating to and worshipping life that included reincarnation. Geography, physical science, natural theology, and astrology were their favorite studies. They also had fundamental knowledge of herbal medicines. Their scope was such that they held political dominion over the people to the point that no activity was started without consulting them. They taught the people of both Britain and Gaul about the immortality of the soul and reincarnation. They believed that if you borrowed something in this life, you could pay it back in the next.

The indigenous people of Australia believe that the souls of their ancestors reincarnate but always in the same clans into which they were originally born.

Verse 22 of the Bhagavad-Gita says: "Just as an individual forsaking dilapidated raiment dons new clothes, so the body-encased soul, relinquishing decayed bodily habitations, enters others that are new." Your body is like clothing (as noted previously, Betty Bethards would refer to the human body as the "earth suit"). From this perspective, it needs to be repaired or replaced from time to time. The body is discarded when it no longer serves as a viable vehicle to enhance the learning and growth process of the being within it.

The Hindu concept of the deity is a trinity: Brahma the Creator, Vishnu the Sustainer, and Shiva the Destroyer. Shiva is considered the most powerful energy form in the Hindu tradition, and some scholars believe him to be the oldest god in the history of deity worship. To limit his domain to "the Destroyer" is misleading. His powers of destruction are not deemed negative but are actually part of a process of annihilation that leads to the emergence of new, healthier energies and patterns. A better word to describe Shiva, therefore, would be the Regenerator. He symbolizes the eternal process of death that always leads to another rebirth.

In the third century, the early Christian theologian Origen wrote "Each soul comes to this world reinforced by the victories or enfeebled by the defeats of its previous lives."

In the New Testament, Revelations 21:3 says: "God is with men and He will dwell with them ... and there shall be no more death." This offers an affirmation of the eternal presence of Spirit, implying that we are on a path of liberation that ultimately will enable us to exist in eternal communion with Spirit. The degree to which an individual soul awakens and connects to this presence in a given lifetime determines the next step on his or her evolutionary journey. We might reincarnate on earth, or we might remain in a higher realm of creation and consciousness, existing unindividuated in Divine Oneness.

Upon experiencing the enlightened state, Buddha related, "I remembered many, many former existences I had passed through: one, two, three ... fifty, one hundred ... a hundred thousand in various world periods."

The Greek philosopher and mathematician Pythagoras, who lived in the sixth century BC, was an initiate in the Egyptian, Chaldean, and Babylonian mysteries. He taught that the individual soul "transmigrates" into successive bodies. To transmigrate means to pass from one state or condition to another. The key question therefore becomes: What determines the quality and circumstance of one's next life?

Astrological Correlation

The astrological sign associated with the Principle of Eternal Life is Scorpio. As is appropriate with something as primal and intense as birth and death, Scorpio is the most complex and passionate of the twelve signs. Most of the other signs are associated with an animal totem. Scorpio has four. Each one refers to a different state of consciousness or behavior that is fundamental to the Scorpionic nature. Each is important and displays a significant aspect that reveals the nature of this archetype. The first is the scorpion, an animal that is very private and prefers to live in places that are damp, dark, and cold. Scorpions also are belligerent, unpleasant creatures. The female will often devour her mate upon completion of mating, and if she's around when her eggs hatch she is liable to eat her young. This part of Scorpio consciousness is beneficial, however, in two ways. Each of the twelve signs of the zodiac partake of one of four elements: fire, earth, air, or water. Scorpio is a water sign. Water implies depth, sensitivity, intuitive awareness, and the need for security. The scorpion is a positive image because it demonstrates that Scorpio is a very private sign, usually avoiding attention and the potential for emotionally painful situations whenever possible. It also points out that as the sign of death and rebirth, Scorpio can be self-protective. At times the drive to survive can impel a volatile or explosive action that demands others to leave them alone. The Scorpionic nature is such that caution and care are required of those who seek a significant relationship with a Scorpio.

A more pleasant totem for Scorpio is a human being. This references Scorpio's orientation to home, family, and security. This is a sign that feels things at the deepest level of human potential and that can offer safety, security, and powerful nurturing to those closest to them. The potential drawback to this largesse is a tendency to make others' needs, feelings, and values their own. Thus, Scorpionic individuals can lose track of who they are in their attempt to provide for others.

The third Scorpionic totem is the serpent eating its tail, which is an ancient symbol that refers to the pursuit of knowledge, wisdom, and consciousness. This implies that the Scorpionic mind is vast and fertile. It can be comfortable studying science, metaphysics, the occult, and even the arts. Any subject that provides information about the nature of life can be of interest. Scorpio is the sign that is most curious about reality and asks the big questions "Why are we here, and what is the meaning of life?" In this sense, Scorpio is one of the most mystical of the twelve signs. It wants to go beneath façades and superficiality in order to know the truth. Scorpio's polar opposite sign, Taurus, focuses on the bottom line of physical survival: food, clothing, and shelter. Scorpio focuses on the bottom line of life itself: birth, sex, and death. The downside of this aspect of Scorpio is the tendency to stay in the laboratory or the library, learning valuable lessons about the nature of life but failing to get out and share that information with others. Scorpio is not necessarily antisocial, but it can often feel awkward and uncomfortable in social situations.

The fourth image for Scorpio is the eagle or the phoenix. The phoenix is a mythical bird that is said to rise from the ashes of something destroyed and bring new life through regeneration. This is the essence of Scorpio—a sign that deals with life from a mystical point of view, focusing primarily on transformation and rebirth. In this sense Scorpio is also the most regenerative of the twelve signs, implying the ability to heal the self as well as others. The healing could be physical, psychological, or a combination of the two through shamanic intervention.

The eagle is known to be the only creature that can look directly into the sun without going blind. Its correlation with Scorpio implies that through a series of tests and challenges and by processing the intimate experiences in life, the Scorpionic experience provides the opportunity to evolve from sensitivity and secrecy, through deep emotional bonds with family and friends, to a universal understanding of life and actual enlightenment.

How to Align with This Law

Cycles occur throughout life. There is the daily cycle of the sun rising in the east and setting in the west. There is the cycle of the seasons, as the spring weather warms and we plant crops and then harvest them as the sun's warmth starts to wane. Likewise, there is the season of a human being, lasting from the bloom of youth to the winter of old age. Cycles are everywhere, a part of life. So, too, the concept of eternal life pertains to a continuous cycle of death and rebirth in which we sequentially enter a series of human forms, interspersed with existence in a nonphysical condition. This Law of Eternal Life is not limited to the continuity of human life; it is a process at work in many contexts, large and small. In fact, we apply this principle when we throw out the garbage every day, discarding something no longer needed, something that has outlived its usefulness or functionality. But this principle is not limited to physical plane awareness alone. Its potential for transformation challenges us to penetrate all aspects and phases of life. Whatever has become stagnant or dysfunctional—the garbage of who we are and what we are doing—needs to be either discarded or altered so that it can once again serve a useful purpose.

Inquiry

This principle confronts us with the need to be continually updating our awareness of who we are, what we are doing, and why and how we are doing it. This can pertain to obvious things such as attitudes, priorities, or social behaviors. It can also pertain to things that are more subtle, such as assumptions about the nature of life and our place in it. Examining values—whatever we define as important and meaningful—can enable us to realize which parts of our life have become insignificant. Whatever is exposed through introspective review and self-analysis as old and outmoded, decayed, boring, or toxic must be released. This is an example of the healing power of this law. In this sense, healing manifests through the elimination of anything toxic in our system, be it physical, emotional, psychological, spiritual, or behavioral. Through this process we might realize that our previous value system is one of the parts of our life that needs revision. We may have outgrown certain values or have been basing our lives and decisions on someone else's values. If there are values that don't conform to our experience and perceptions of ourselves and our life in present time, they need to die so a rebirth can take place.

Exploring assumptions is a very important part of this process. Assumptions can be formed at any time and in any area of life. When we make an assumption about something, we presume that what appears real to us is a fundamental truth about life. Some of our most important assumptions are made in early childhood when we are not objectively aware of our environment and when we also lack the analytical and verbal skills to question our experience. As we observe our family members relate to themselves, each other, and us, we assume that those patterns are reflective of how everyone functions. For example, we might take for granted that extreme behaviors are commonplace. Many of our choices and decisions, both in childhood and in adulthood, can be based on those assumptions. This can cause us to confuse a personal experience we had from a preverbal, preconscious time with a universal law. For example, as a child we assume that our parents love us. If our parents fight between themselves or are hostile and abusive to us, we could assume that cruelty is a viable, acceptable expression of love. We not only grow up accepting that behavior from others, but we could also be aggressive toward others.

When a relationship doesn't last or feel good to us or the other person, we are left with the pain of loss as well as confusion about what happened. We could question behaviors, values, or contentious issues that arose between us, involving everything from money to sex. But unless we penetrate deeper and examine the core assumptions we have about life and relationship, we won't really know why things didn't work out. Regardless of any superficial changes we make, unless we analyze and update these assumptions the next relationship will probably have the same result. By looking at the basic elements of our life regarding such things as self-image, self-esteem, relationship needs, and behavioral patterns, it can become clear what we need to change. Which assumptions no longer accurately define who we are, and which ones no longer work and perhaps never did? Through this process we can let go of the outmoded patterns and create new ones. We can start having healthier experiences in life.

Programming

Another way to work with the process of death and rebirth in one's life is by reprogramming fundamental imprints that were internalized in childhood. This is another example of the healing potential of this principle. This could encompass subtle things that affect us emotionally and psychologically or things of a more obvious and overt nature, such as social behaviors or self-esteem. Reprogramming is a transformational process that enables us to break old patterns. Transformation eliminates stagnation, replacing it with new life. Defining the areas of life that require attention is one step in the process. We also need the courage to face the results of our internal research honestly and take whatever steps are appropriate to alter the situation.

Reprogramming can facilitate profound change that deals with primal elements of who were are. It isn't done easily, lightly, or quickly. It involves a deep penetration into our core self and the kind of life we are creating. Often such analysis will reveal something that has been an important part of our life but that now must be released. "Out with the old" frees up time, energy, and resources to create the new. But the letting go can be a painful purge. The emotional attachment to whatever needs to be replaced may be as hard to let go of as the physical attachment to a possession, the social attachment to a person, or the attachment to and comfort level with a habit. Such attachments help create a sense of security, and letting go of them might make us feel as if our security is being undermined. It may seem as if maintaining the attachments, even to something broken or unfulfilling, is preferable to the process of purgation.

The most important transformations will often be challenging at the deepest levels of emotional experience and cause us to feel vulnerable. Dealing directly with the feelings and the issues they embrace can be so uncomfortable as to cause us to overlook or be in denial about their very existence in the first place. Letting them go and replacing them may feel scary as well as painful. Rather than just going through the transformation mentally and having to confront our fears and insecurities in our mind, we might be more successful if we approach the situation in a physical or emotional way. Physically, transformation can occur with intense exercise. The exercise needs to be so demanding that it enables us to release emotions and the behaviors or attitudes to which they are attached. This may be through mountain biking in steep terrain, or swimming dozens of laps in an Olympic-sized pool, or pounding nails for hours a day. It could be through martial arts classes or working out intensely and consistently in a gym. By doing any of these activities we can purge some old, stagnant patterns and tendencies. As we recuperate from the ordeal we can experience a rebirth, an opportunity to create a new aspect of ourselves.

Emotional outlets can also be useful in this overhaul process, especially if they involve external events that evoke an emotional catharsis; for example, going to an athletic event and pouring our passion into cheering for our favorite team or player. This is relatively simple and impersonal but it can provide a viable opportunity for emotional release and renewal. In a more personal and profound sense, weddings, bar mitzvahs, funerals, or other types of meaningful yet rare family gatherings provide a means to open our deepest levels of emotional experience and express them exuberantly. Movies and plays also can provide impetus for emotional release. When I go to a film, one of the factors that determines the degree to which I enjoy it is the emotional catharsis I experience.

Creative expression, with all its potential for raw, intimate exposure of the inner self, is one of the most personal opportunities for a sense of renewal. But it can also leave one feeling quite vulnerable. This could happen if our creativity is public, such as an actor giving a tour de force performance, or a singer putting his or her soul into a moving song in front of an audience of strangers. But it can also be experienced in the privacy of one's own home by writing a poem in which the words evoke just the right sentiment, or by painting a picture whose colors and forms induce a certain internal response.

Transformation and Relationship

The most personal way to create a fundamental conversion of who and how you are, and the way in which this experience can be most profound, is through primary relationship. As with other aspects of life, we might create a union with someone that starts out with love and commitment and devolves into boredom and stagnation. To alleviate this, it's imperative that periodically we and our partner get clear with each other. Keeping each other updated about our respective life experiences is an important part of maintaining the relationship. This can involve sharing our feelings, fears, or vulnerabilities. Exposing our innermost thoughts and emotions, things that we share with no one else, is especially significant in this process. It can entail sharing feelings of shame or those shadowy parts of who we are that we'd rather keep hidden and are not easy to examine, let alone expose. By sharing them, we create a deeper, emotionally honest connection with each other. As a result, the relationship becomes a safer, more secure environment within which to continue our own growth and transformation.

We may be afraid that by opening the door to our own private Pandora's Box that we are giving the partner ammunition that he or she can use later to hurt or reject us. In this case, we need to tune in to our inner being. Do we feel safe with this other person? If not, it's not the right time to be too open. In a good, healthy relationship, one in which we feel safe and in which we love and care about each other, the more we let the partner know who we are, the more of us there is for them to love.

One way to create a loving, emotionally honest relationship is to visualize and work with the image of "the staircase of intimacy" discussed in chapter 7. Remember that the process of sharing ourselves needs to be reciprocal. If we find our partner understanding and supporting us in our openness, we gain the confidence to proceed. Assuming that our partner also opens up and trusts us with his or her vulnerability, the relationship will get deep, emotionally bonded, and intimate. If we truly love someone, that love will increase when we find out more of who that person really is. An additional benefit to this process of opening and deepening is that it offers another vehicle that will take us down the road to rebirth.

When we reveal ourselves, we also become free from the burden of carrying and hiding parts of ourselves, hoping that no one else notices all the baggage we're dragging around with us. We are free to be who we are. As noted when discussing the Law of Creativity, if we don't like something about ourselves we are free to change it. Failing to acknowledge our inner truth, even to ourselves, limits the creative process.

Physical Intimacy

One of the most profound ways of sharing our depth is through physical intimacy. There is a long tradition that stretches back to the Isis cult in ancient Egypt that posits sexuality as a vehicle that creates a significant bond between lovers. Obviously, this can enhance the sense of emotional closeness, not to mention the sense of physical satisfaction. But the Egyptians and countless generations of ensuing practitioners used sex as a means of experiencing a state of transformation as well. The ritual within which the emotional/physical becomes the spiritual is called sacred sexuality. In the Egyptian Isis cult, the prime deity, Isis, was revered as the supreme goddess. This cult maintained that through all women, dating back to the Divine Mother herself, men could experience transformation. It is as if the woman guides the man to the state of primal being through sacred sexuality. The basis of this belief system is reverence for the sacred feminine. Called *horasis*, it denotes the experience of enlightenment through transcendental sex with a priestess. Women are not seen as sex objects, however, nor used by men for carnal gratification. They are seen as manifestations of the divine feminine, the source of life, the closest men can come to a connection with the Divine. In this sense, to have sex with a woman in a clearly defined, ritual context is to experience transformation.

Traditions such as Tantra yoga and sex magic have developed specific techniques that lovers can use to achieve the state of consciousness transformation. They take time and clear intention to master, and certainly, the woman is not just leading the man but is a complementary cocreator of the experience. She tastes the transformation even as her partner does.

It's interesting to note the differences between the Principle of Eternal Life and the Principle of Love with respect to sex. The latter values sex as a vehicle for expressing and sharing love. Sex, being the vehicle for procreation, creates the physical manifestation of that love in the form of a child. The Principle of Eternal Life, on the other hand, relates to sex both as a vehicle for personal transformation and as a tool to connect two lovers in a deeply bonded emotional embrace. Although these two principles are not necessarily in conflict, they place a different value on the same experience. The challenge is to integrate both laws (a good opportunity to employ the universal Law of Both/And) and find within ourselves the ability and drive to be physically intimate in a way that combines both love and transformation.

Ritual and Initiation

Transformation can be a peak experience. It is an experience that can never be repeated and that changes us forever. In the process of conscious death and rebirth, today's peak becomes the foundation for tomorrow's reality. Thus, another path to personal rebirth is any type of ritual that is consciously designed to provide a peak experience. A ritual can be something we do on a regular basis, like a daily meditation or a monthly observance of the full moon. Or it could be something done once as a means of bringing about a specific end. For example, if we've recently broken off a relationship as a result of having been betrayed or abused, we could create a ritual that involves burning the photos or possessions that remind us of our connection to that person. This may not create a clean slate, purging all the memories and feelings, but it serves as an affirmation of our intention. Such a ritual will help us break not only our bonds to the other person but also to the patterns we engaged in that eventually led to the conclusion of the relationship.

We can create rituals on our own, performed in exact accordance with our needs, or we could join with others in a group ritual, such as a march or meditation for world peace. Funerals and wakes are other examples of this type of ritual. Sometimes wakes become raucous affairs. Through consumption of alcohol, the mourners' inhibitions are released and they feel free to intensely, passionately express their feelings about the departed or about life. In some cultures this could continue for a day or two. Most of the funeral practices in the Western cultures tend to be somewhat tame or controlled affairs, done in a certain way and for a particular period of time. In other places, however, the wailing and crying can go on indefinitely. In some cultures it is even customary to hire "wailers," whose job it is to cry and carry on in order to evoke deep grief in the hearts of the mourners. In the Australian Aboriginal culture, funeral rituals can go on for weeks or months, depending on the status of the departed. These are grand affairs in which the cultural aspects of dancing, chanting, playing didgeridoo, and painting on the chest or coffin of the departed engage the men of the clan. Traditionally, this was the purview of men, although in modern times women are also allowed to perform some of these functions.

One way to have a peak experience of personal transformation is through spiritual initiation. An initiation is a method of creating a transition from one state of being to another. Sometimes this takes place through a rite of passage, as when a young person begins to apprehend the spiritual context and belief system of the culture within which he or she is living. After such a passage, initiated youths are charged with certain responsibilities as they learn to take their place within the tribal context. Another type of initiation can involve a shift in consciousness. Here we identify less with ourselves as a limited, ego-based entity and more with the experience and perception of ourselves as a manifestation of the Divine, part of the never-ending chain of creation. An initiation is something we must prove worthy of, as we let go of identification and attachment to self and replace it with awareness of Self. Some types of initiations can involve life and death situations. One either passes the rigors of the test, or one might not physically survive the challenges presented.

When we make a commitment to change, when we continuously seek to eliminate parts of ourselves and our past that have outlived their usefulness, when we are willing to risk vulnerability and the insecurity of change, we embrace transformation as a priority in our life. As a result, we are constantly engaged in death and rebirth. We learn to be unafraid of death, because we realize death is not a final ending.

It is said that when we die we will be asked to review our life—to assess our thoughts, feelings, actions, and choices. We will judge those things in relationship to how they furthered the development of the wholeness of our being—and that of others—and the extent to which they allowed more awareness of and access to Divine Spirit. The more we hide from the internal process of transformation, the more we will have to deal with at death. The more we embrace conscious renewal, the less encumbered we will be and the easier it will be for us to identify with and reside in the light of Oneness.

Not Aligning with This Law

The key to working with this principle is to remember that eternal life combines the experiences of birth and death. One is the obverse of the other. When we die in one context, we are born into the other. When we die in another situation, we are born into yet another. Another way to define the Principle of Eternal Life is as the Principle of Eternal Rebirth. In a sense, this principle expands on the Principle of Both/And. The unity that the Law of Eternal Life offers functions both on the material plane and through the interplay between different dimensions of consciousness. When we prevent ourselves from experiencing this law in its cyclical form or when utilize only part of the law, we are unable to access its full potential. This could be an obsession wherein we become so attached to one part of the cycle that we never access the rest of it at all.

Death is a major issue for most people. The very idea that someday our body will cease to exist is at once obvious and terrifying. Death can be equated with annihilation; with no body, it would seem that we simply cease to exist. We can put up many types of resistance to this inevitability. Denial is the choice of many. Seeking to postpone death, or even aging, is another popular notion that appeals to many in our youth-oriented culture. Cosmetic products that promise removal of aging signs, the use of synthetic or organic hormones that offer the hope of literally extending life, and plastic surgery are all methods of denial that are in high demand. Some people get stuck hanging on to the body long after any quality of life has disappeared. The fear of death is so strong, especially in the Western world, that it has become institutionalized. When a family member becomes terminally ill, people are sworn to secrecy. It's as if it's a taboo subject, not to be discussed with anyone, especially the one who is dying. The patient is given over to the doctors to "save." A dying person is often shunted off to the hospital. Is this to increase the likelihood of continued life, or to prevent the family from having to minister to and deal with their ill relative or friend? The medical establishment, in general, supports this tradition. An ill person is often given little support to being able to die at home, surrounded by loved ones, even if it is requested by family and friends.

At the collective level, the fear and denial of death also leads to ruinous environmental policies. Modern civilization is set up to grasp and use as many of the earth's resources as it can for as long as it can. The daily destruction of our environment in the name of "progress" is cashing in long-term sustainability for short-term gain. Because the thought of not being here in the future is so overwhelming, most people don't strive to maintain and ensure the beauty, diversity, and strength of our physical surroundings. They want to maximize their comforts now and conform to the "I want it all" philosophy, with little or no thought to subsequent generations. What will be left for our great-great-grandchildren in terms of clean air, water, and soil? How viable will the biodiversity be in terms of being able to sustain human life?

The denial of death also has led to the obsessive youth culture, as well as a turning away from those who are closer to the end of life. Those who are no longer attractive and productive tend to be shunned. In the process, all their wisdom and understanding of life—what it is and how to cope with it effectively—is lost. What is more tragic (yet symptomatic of the modern world) than the reality of elderly people, homeless and hungry, living out their days abandoned and in squalor?

The fear and denial of death can alternatively manifest as a morbid fascination with it. Years ago I was friends with a young woman. I was visiting with her on a particularly hot summer day and noticed that she had several dozen scars running perpendicularly along her veins from wrists to elbows on both arms. Quite shocked, I asked if she had ever tried to commit suicide. Seemingly surprised, she looked at me and said, "No. However, whenever I'm bored or lonely, I take a razor blade and play with my veins." This is called "cutting" and is recognized as a psychological disorder. It's also a way of playing with death.

Because birth and death are such primal experiences, we might develop a desire for these events that is so strong, it becomes an unquenchable longing. We might thus engage in behaviors that are high risk—physically, socially, or emotionally—in order to create an inevitable crisis point. We become willing to live on the edge in the hopes that the exhilaration will produce—or approximate—a death/rebirth experience. The more we relate to such an experience in external, physical ways only, the farther we are from realizing what it really is. For beyond the obvious physical birth or death, the reprogramming and rebirth that this law implies is something that transpires internally in a very deep, profound way.

Activities that bring a person close to the edge in one way or another—including such things as racing cars at high speeds or engaging in unprotected sexual encounters—suggest a death wish, or at least an attitude of casual connection to the body. Thumbing one's nose in the face of death is indicative of a lack of regard for the sacredness of life. Those who do this don't really value the blessing and the opportunity that having a physical body provides. They might prefer immediate physical gratification instead of being more conservative in protecting and taking care of their body. Or they might assume that leaving the body is a finality, that after life there is only oblivion. In the context of that way of thinking, it makes sense that one would want to eat, drink, and be merry to the maximum degree for as long as he can, regardless of the consequences or the resources that will be depleted in the future. "Once we're gone, we're gone." That way of thinking runs counter to the Principle of Eternal Life.

While we don't have to joyfully embrace our physical death, there is no avoiding it when our time comes. There's an old folk tale about a man walking through a bazaar. At one booth he notices a hooded figure sitting off to the side, staring intently at him. The man suddenly realizes that this is Death and that it has come to get him! Undaunted by the inevitable, the man runs out of the bazaar, jumps on his horse, and gallops away, saying that he will "run so far and so fast that death won't find me." But as the man approaches a steep, narrow ravine, a hooded figure stands at the top of the hill with his foot on a large boulder, poised to push it down onto the fleeing man. Moral of the story: we can recognize when death is coming and it's our time to go, but we can't outrun it.

Being caught in denial about the nature of life and death, whether by tempting death or trying to escape it, limits the possibility of maximizing our potential. Truly accepting the inevitability of death while also embracing life can ultimately free us to live a more meaningful and growth-oriented life. It's been said that we can't really love life until we love death. Letting go of what we have, including our body, is a way of making room for something new. If we don't let go, eventually what we have stagnates. Ironically, it is the very act of letting go that establishes a flow of energy that brings new possibilities into our life. It is hard to let go. It might generate a deep sense of loss or exacerbate a sense of insecurity. It may feel better to maintain whatever we have or feel or how we behave than to let it go and possibly have nothing at all. Ultimately, this attachment is to the ego and to all the experiences and memories from our past that combine to form who we are in the present. The way out is to work with the process, to ask ourselves what we are so afraid of. How can we create a happier, more fulfilling life and a deeper, more lasting sense of security for ourselves? What is it that we would actually lose by letting go? If we discover this still has value, it isn't time to release it. But if it is time, we need to trust the process. After the letting go comes the renewal. After the death comes the rebirth. This is how the Law of Eternal Life works.

Getting trapped in the fear of our own death is one way of misunderstanding the nature of an experience of loss. Another way is by becoming attached to the emotional aftershock of the loss. Mourning and grieving are natural facets of this dynamic, and everyone grieves in his own way for as long as he needs to. To get stuck in this phase, however, is to avoid dealing with the inevitability of life's perpetuity. Attachment to loss also prevents us from re-creating our lives in ways that enable us to acknowledge and experience the blessings of being here now.

We might also err on the other side with this principle. Instead of focusing only on the death part of the cycle, we could become obsessed with the birth part. We might endlessly change superficial aspects of our life, such as friends, job, living situation, or physical appearance in the unending quest for "a new me." I knew a women who was so attached to changing her living environment that she would continuously move the furniture around the room or from room to room. If she couldn't actually change her residence, at least she could have the visual experience of seeing a new environment every day. Some people also express attachment to birth by continuously being pregnant. They may be unable to effectively care for all of their children once they're here, but the birth is such a peak experience that they find it hard to stop.

Getting emotionally attached to others is another way we could misuse this law. This is especially true in a primary relationship or extended family context. We could care so much about others' well-being that we sacrifice our own in order to benefit them. This can lead to merging with them to the point where their needs become our needs, and their values or lifestyle become ours. Even if our intention is clear and well-meaning, it leads to stagnation for all concerned. Being that attached can lead to the need to control. If our sense of security is based on our ability to provide security for others, our security-producing behaviors could lead to dependency as well as emotional stagnation for all concerned.

Another misuse of this principle comes from trying to force others to transform. We might be motivated from a sincere desire to help others change from stagnation to growth. But we could also attempt to force others to change in ways that benefit us more than it does them. In either case, the other people could resist our efforts. They could perceive us as being manipulative, invasive, or intimidating. Ultimately, this leads to power struggles in the relationship—complete domination by one person or complete rejection by the other. Demanding that others do something, regardless of how beneficial we think that change might be for them, is not an experience that leads to rebirth for anyone, let alone a closer connection to Divine Spirit.

Transformation can also apply to our understanding of something. For example, a scientist may spend years of his career researching a certain topic. He will formulate distinct conclusions based on that research. But as time goes by, he needs to update his own work or be open to the conclusions of others in his field and change his opinions accordingly. Without this openness, his development of understanding in his field will remain limited, as will his own perspective on that aspect of life.

Spiritual Opportunity

As mentioned earlier, one of the images associated with this principle's astrological correlate, Scorpio, is the serpent. The serpent has played a fundamental role in the cosmologies of cultures around the world and throughout history. As mentioned in chapter 2, the Australian Aborigines refer to the rainbow serpent as a symbol of the prime deity, the origin of life. In Central and South America there are snakes carved in stone in the temples. In Ohio there are burial mounds in the form of a serpent. These were built by the Adena people who lived in that area from the sixth century BC until the first century AD. They curve and meander through the countryside, so that the serpent's head and tail line up with the summer and winter solstices, respectively. The coils pertain to the equinoxes. The creators of these mounds could have been trying to relate the concept of death to the four directions, which, in turn, reflect Oneness. The serpent is represented prominently as a hooded cobra in India, and as the sacred serpent of the Greek god Hermes, who is often depicted holding a staff intertwined with serpents. This staff, the *caduceus*, and is regarded as the emblem of healing by the medical profession.

In the Garden of Eden the serpent is the catalyst for Adam and Eve's expulsion from paradise. The traditional interpretation of this narrative is that the serpent manipulated Eve into eating the apple, which represents the forbidden fruit of knowledge. For this transgression, Adam and Eve were expelled from the Garden and forced out into the world to suffer, instead of remaining safe and comfortable in paradise. But there are alternative ways to interpret this story in which both the serpent and the Garden take on a totally different meaning. In the Gnostic tradition, the serpent was seen as a hero, a teacher imploring Eve to open her mind and become conscious. The tree that the serpent was coiled around represents the human spine. The etheric spine is said to be the repository of Kundalini energy, the vital life force within the human body, like the caduceus mentioned above. Thus, the tree/spine/caduceus brings the message of consciousness and the unlimited potential for healing and creativity that lies with each of us. Whether consciousness is defined as sinful or as liberation is a question we have to decide for ourselves.

The serpent as a symbol of evil temptation is valid only if we see consciousness as limited to the physical body. Attachment to one's body or to the material plane will, of course, limit one's consciousness. But seen from the point of view of so many other cultures, the snake is an archetype of the process of learning the fundamental truth of life, the experience of consciousness development. The molting process that the serpent experiences is a symbol of transformation.

The spiritual quality associated with this principle is *transformation*. Like the snake eating its tail, developing consciousness leads to transformation, and transformation leads to evolving consciousness. In this context the snake is a symbol of immortality or reincarnation. As it sheds its skin, it re-emerges in a seemingly new body. There is an ancient superstition that snakes never die unless by violence. Left to themselves, they would live forever.

In contemplating eternal life, what, in fact, does exist continuously? It certainly is not the physical form. The gift symbolized by the serpent is one of awareness and eternal life. The serpent represents Kundalini energy—the vital life force contained in the human spine. As we develop our consciousness, the Kundalini is raised from the base of the spine to the crown of the head. When that happens we become enlightened. We have access to the omniscient awareness of Divine Spirit itself. To access that limitless consciousness is to be at one, a state that once experienced can always be re-accessed. We can live eternally in that state if we can master ourselves and mystically attune ourselves to our divine nature.

The serpent symbolizes living in perpetuity through the shedding of its skin. This molting process is a catharsis, the ending of who we have been and the beginning of who we are. The process never ends. As long as we seek to develop our consciousness, the means to do so will be provided and the results of the process will continue to propel us into new states of awareness. When we engage in this, we realize that there is something greater than ourselves that flows ceaselessly. We have the means and the freedom to tap into that force, awaken to its presence, and discover the key to eternal life.

The vehicle that enables us to be conscious of this process is our soul. As discussed in chapter 4, "The Law of the Eternal Present," our soul describes the essence of our being. Our soul carries the initial imprint of our creation and the karmic vibrations that are the result of the thoughts, words, feelings, and actions we have manifested since the beginning of our human incarnations. Our soul is immortal. It is that part of us that is preserved from lifetime to lifetime. It remains even in the discarnate state, awaiting the next incarnation, the next opportunity to explore and create our being, to satisfy our desires, and to resolve karmic issues from our past. A positive, harmonious dynamic exists when the soul, living in the eternal present, displays its willingness to let go and evolve into new realities and dimensions of consciousness.

Becoming aware of our condition in life is a step on the path of consciousness. This path will take us to the awareness of our intentions and motivations, as well as their outcomes, realized or potential. It will also enable us to see beyond our specific drives and their results to larger patterns that are the building blocks and touchstones of our life. This process of awakening will ultimately take us to the threshold of Spirit, to the point of origin of our soul itself. Beyond all the specific features of any incarnation, what remains from lifetime to lifetime is the consciousness of self in relationship to Spirit. The Dalai Lama has said "the concept of rebirth is principally the continuity of consciousness."

Ultimately, transformation pertains to developing our consciousness so that we perceive life from the perspective of Oneness. We identify as being one with Spirit, not as an ego being, separate from all that surrounds us. It is this process of awakening that the prophets referred to as salvation. Through salvation we are saved from the pain and suffering that all beings experience when they perceive through the lens of separateness. Salvation ultimately implies knowing that our potential is to be reborn in Spirit. We are redeemed from the pain of isolation and alienation when we are reborn in consciousness and can live continuously in the context of Oneness.

The Bottom Line

On the astrological wheel, the sign opposite Scorpio is Taurus, which in turn embodies the Principle of Survival. As mentioned previously, oppositions can provide us with perspective on the nature of each end of the axis. The Taurean perspective is that while we are incarnate, we have the spiritual right to be here and to put time and resources into maintaining a safe, secure, reliable, comfortable, material reality. Taurus is inherently self-reliant. Its job is to help us preserve and protect our being during incarnation.

The Scorpionic perspective is that eventually we will pass from this plane and move on to other states of being. Provided that we use the body and other material resources with consciousness, physical reality is a blessing, providing a profound opportunity to learn how to live within divine consciousness. If we become too attached to this plane, however, we become limited by it. It is imperative that we embrace the Principle of Eternal Life in order to take advantage of the opportunity that having a body gives us. We do this while simultaneously remaining ready and willing to let go of that body, our ego, and all the trappings that accompany it.

In addition, Scorpio adds to the concern with survival the concept of sharing.

Whereas Taurus values autonomy, Scorpio is more oriented to the give-and-take of relationship. It wants to feel safe enough to share its resources with a partner and needs to be open to receiving energy from the partner as well. This process circulates the energy between the partners and mirrors the process of death and rebirth. As with all oppositions, balance is the key, and balancing our self-reliance with our intimacy is the secret to this one.

Secrecy is another fundamental aspect of this principle. On a personal level, we instinctively withhold the more sensitive parts of ourselves until we feel safe enough with someone to open up. On a metaphysical level, this is the principle that seeks to understand the mystery of the universe. Secrecy is beneficial even in this context because knowledge is power. The more we understand about the nature of life, the more powerful we are. In addition to the potential to misuse that power, we could be attacked by others who are afraid it. Understanding the endless cycle of birth, death, and rebirth is a profound part of the quest for truth. The ultimate goal of that quest is the enlightenment of Christ consciousness. In modern times the concept of rebirth has been popularized and simplified to the point that we are led to believe that if we are merely immersed in water, thereby duplicating the external experience of Jesus being baptized by John, we will be reborn through a connection to Jesus. In reality, being reborn does not necessarily have anything to do with water or Jesus. We don't duplicate Jesus's experience as a way to get closer to him but rather to awaken the Christ consciousness within ourselves.

There is also a significant connection between the Principle of Eternal Life and the Principle of the Eternal Present. The latter deals with our connection to our roots, our family and tribal ancestors. One way to honor these forebears is to be as present to our immediate experience as we can. The Law of Eternal Life makes a connection between sex and personal transformation through deep interactive relationship. The connection between those two laws is defined by contemporary scientists who posit that once we begin to have sex (whether or not as a vehicle for reproduction), the genes that control longevity begin to shut down. In his book *Healthy Aging*, Dr Andrew Weil states that "nature is very much concerned with perpetuation of life at the species level but cares little for individuals once they have passed on their genes. It is the trade-off between sex and death. By choosing a reproductive strategy that increases the likelihood of the survival of the species, nature commits to the death of individuals."

The essence of the Principle of Eternal Life is expressed through the polarity of life and death. If we adopt a cavalier attitude toward death, have a death wish, or deny that we will ever leave this body, we remain ignorant of this law and are not engaged in the process of consciously and fearlessly creating our reality. We remain stuck in habits, stagnant emotional states, and unhealthy behavioral patterns. We live an unexamined life.

On the other hand, by developing a love for life and a true understanding of how magical it is and what we can do within it, we change that dynamic and embrace our experience in a powerful, transformed way. If we truly understand the polarity, we are able to conceive of existence beyond the body, and even while incarnate we can perceive the material plane as the dream that it is. Seeing through the illusion can awaken us in consciousness to the realm of the Divine. This part of our journey is actually a process, something we engage in consistently throughout our life. By paying attention to the little, immediate elements of life and making sure that they fit into the bigger picture of our lives, we can eventually learn to see and examine larger and more eternal areas of reality. Death is part of life. Each inhalation of breath represents a new life, each exhalation a new death. Transformation is a process of consciousness development through which we gradually come to see ourselves not as one who is continually affected by these immediate ebbs and flows but as one who identifies with being.

Affirmation: "I reclaim my divine, eternal nature by flowing consciously through the illusion of endless cycles of death and rebirth"

> *And death shall have no dominion.*
> *Dead men naked they shall be one*
> *With the man in the wind and the west moon,*
> *When their bones are picked clean and the clean bones gone,*
> *They shall have stars at elbow and foot;*
> *Though they go mad they shall be sane,*
> *Though they sink through the sea they shall rise again;*
> *Though lovers be lost love shall not;*
> *And death shall have no dominion.*
>
> —Dylan Thomas

Chapter 9: The Law of Abundance

> We have given you abundance.
>
> —The Koran, 1:108

My wife owns a store. It's unique in that its stock ranges from toys to collectibles to high-quality used clothes. There's something for everybody, from tourists to locals, to people buying gift items for birthdays and Christmas. Because her store is in a resort town, she does most of her business in the summer, when the tourists flock to this quaint area on a river in Northern California. Some customers come back year after year and tell her that they look forward to shopping in her store when they're in town. Others have jokingly complained that there are so many interesting things of such a varied nature that they get lost for hours, browsing and buying. After getting established over a number of years, business became so good that my wife expanded by moving to a larger building. When she first opened the new space, her main problem was finding enough things to stock the larger area. She scoured flea markets, yard sales, and thrift stores. She researched catalogues and went to gift shows. As her customer base expanded, she continued to look for new things to stock. At first she was concerned about not finding enough items to satisfy her customers and to keep them coming back. But as time went by, she realized that regardless of the season, the size of the facility, the requests and desires of the marketplace, or the variety of goods that she stocked, there was always enough. This understanding provided the mantra that has carried her to success for many years: there's always more.

Abundance pertains to the limitless expanse of what exists and what is being created every day. The manifestation of the Law of Creativity generates this abundance. On the material plane, we are given an abundance of resources that enables us to be everything from an individual merchant stocking a store to a species surviving indefinitely. The fruit of every tree contains at least one seed that is designed to grow an entirely new tree. Some of the fruit will be eaten; some of the seeds won't germinate. Enough do, however, that the continued propagation of that tree is guaranteed. When fish spawn, they can lay millions of eggs. Most won't hatch. Some that do will be consumed by predators or eliminated by other environmental factors before they reach maturity. But enough will reach maturity that the continuation of the species is guaranteed. Out in space, the Hubble telescope has revealed a physical universe that is seemingly without end. When focused on what was previously thought to be a dark part of the sky, the super-power telescope has discovered literally millions of star clusters and solar systems that were never known to exist. Some of them may even be able to support life as we know it. Like the spawning fish and the tree seeds, the universe creates far more than is needed in order that it may continue to exist. Abundance is the principle that allows the universe to perpetuate itself.

Beyond the material plane, what is available to us in terms of energy and creative potential is truly limitless as well. In the book of Exodus, Moses is told, "The Lord God is merciful and gracious and abundant in goodness and truth." The Law of Abundance also applies to consciousness and the limitless potential we have to experience life in a direct, mystical way. For example, the supply of spiritual energy is boundless. The profusion of life forms is a reminder, on the physical plane, of what Source is able to generate on every plane of consciousness. It suggests that there may be other life-generating planets in other solar systems. There may even be other dimensions of reality that are nonphysical as well. One of the more compelling qualities of the universal laws is that they apply to everything and everyone—everywhere. These are the rules by which the cosmos continues to abide every minute of every day.

Multiple Belief Systems

Because abundance is a universal law, it operates in all forms of physical and nonphysical manifestation. It is at work in the variety of ways that people interpret their relationship to life. The nature of this relationship reflects the consciousness of those defining it. In other words, our personal concepts of the spiritual world reflect the connection we feel to our physical and nonphysical environments. Throughout history, people's concepts of the spiritual realm have taken the form of belief systems, cosmologies, and religions. Within the context of religion, the elemental forces of nature have been conceptualized through deities and philosophies. Through these creations people have sought connection with nature through either direct, mystical interaction or the myths and ritual ceremonies that eventually became formulated into religions. The abundance of these systems reflects the abundant spiritual forces that surround us, seen and unseen, that can both help and hinder the quality of our lives. These systems have provided ways for their creators to feel more in control of the elemental forces surrounding and affecting them. They also offer ways for individuals to expand their consciousness and ultimately integrate their own personal awareness with the Divine.

Philosophy provides an intellectual definition of what the Divine is or isn't, and it is one method through which humans can relate to it. Philosophy provides the basis for religion. In keeping with the nature of the Law of Abundance, a plethora of religious traditions have evolved over the past three thousand years. Although some of these traditions support the seeker in mystical quest, most do not. One of the problems with some traditional organized religions is that over time, they have become politicized. The essence of the teachings has become sublimated to political power or job security for the religious officials involved. Instead of seeking to emulate the original teacher, who was usually a mystic, these people seek to have their congregants conform to certain standards of behavior and lifestyle. There may be nothing wrong with those behaviors per se, but they usually do not connect the person to the awareness and experience of the Divine in a direct, mystical way.

One of the most primitive spiritual belief systems engages the immediate and personal connection people have to their environment. *Animism* is a worldview in which natural phenomena are alive and have souls. These could include plants, minerals, the wind, or bodies of water. The Aboriginal people of Australia believe that although there is a prime deity from which all manifestation emanates, there are also different spiritual beings who created each animal, plant, mountain, and all other physical phenomena. They take this idea a step further by assuming that the deity who created each thing is still alive in that form. They refer to the place where humans can connect with spiritual beings as "Dreamtime." This is a place of transcendent consciousness, a place where human ancestors as well as archetypal beings live. It can be accessed in both the sleeping state and the waking state. Dreamtime is a place of spiritual and creative inspiration and guidance.

The Kwakiutl Indians of the Pacific Northwest affirm their connection to nature by carving totem poles with images of animals that they consider to have certain powers. During their ritual dances, the people wear the mask of an animal with which they identify. By wearing that mask, the dancers assume that animal's identity as well as its power.

Similarly, the Celtic tradition honors the Green Man, the embodiment of nature. He is the consort of the great goddess, the source of life. He serves creation through preserving and working with the natural elements of soil, water, plants, and animals.

One of the opportunities that an animistic culture offers is of making significant, personal connection to the elements of nature in ways that can spiritually and medicinally benefit the entire tribe. The person who can access and work with this connection is the shaman. He or she has the ability to make direct contact with animal spirits and have a special relationship to them. The shaman experiences abundance through his ability to connect with nonphysical beings and share the information gained in order to heal or spiritually inspire individuals within his community.

The Law of Abundance

When Charles Darwin made his journey on his ship, the *Beagle*, he was accompanied by a Catholic priest named Martin Gusinde. Gusinde made the following notes while observing a shaman there in trance:

The man was strolling along, [appearing] lost in dreamland, without thought or purpose, when he suddenly found himself in the midst of visionary apparitions. Around him were crowds of herrings, whales, swordfish, vultures, cormorants, gulls, and other creatures. All were addressing him respectfully, and he was beside himself. His whole body was numb, and he dropped to the ground and lay there without moving. His soul was consorting with the spirits, and feeling, while among them, an inordinate joy.

How Gusinde knew what the shaman was experiencing is puzzling, but nonetheless, this is a perfect description of the mystical state.

The religion of paganism is similar to animism in that it perceives the Divine in nature. In pagan tradition, observation of nature, such as the changing of the seasons, provides an understanding of Source and of how life works. Being aware of one's physical body and its interactions with the environment offers a way of being in touch with the universe and, as such, becomes a form of worship.

The Ancient Greeks were a polytheistic culture. In polytheism there are numerous gods and goddesses, each one having his or her own role to play in maintaining peace and harmony. The Greeks' primary gods and goddesses were said to live on Mt. Olympus. The Greeks also believed in a sky god, Uranus. Uranus was depicted as a detached patriarchal figure, somewhat threatening but otherwise divorced from human affairs. Aristotle refined this concept by writing of the Unmoved Mover. This archetype was less intimidating but no less removed. This concept reflected the Greeks' perception of a large chasm between the prime deity and humanity. Another polytheistic culture that predated the Greeks and which provided the intellectual and philosophical basis of Western culture was the Egyptian. Egyptian spirituality emphasized the mystery of life and was shrouded in layers of myth and ritual. Much of their belief system focused on death and the desire to avoid damnation in the afterlife. The Romans are also part of our philosophical heritage, although they copied and co-opted much of their cosmology from the Egyptians and the Greeks, adapting it to the needs of their culture.

The religious traditions of the Far East offer and teach mystical techniques as ways of becoming aware of the Divine. Taoism is a tradition that originated in China approximately 2,500 years ago. It advocates that humanity strive to create its relationships and social institutions in ways that reflect the harmony of nature. Its two best known books are the *Tao Te Ching* and the *I Ching*, or Book of Changes. Taoism poetically attempts to put the mystery of life into words, to define that which cannot be defined. Chapter 25 of the *Tao Te Ching* says, "There exists something formlessly fashioned, that existed before heaven and earth; without sound, without substance, dependent on nothing, unchanging, all pervading, unfailing. One may think of it as the mother of all things under heaven. Its true name we do not know; Way is the by-name that we give it." An interesting facet of the concept of the Way is that it is a manner of describing Source as being non-anthropomorphic.

Hinduism is the oldest of the five major religions, with its origin in India being sometime between 2500 and 1500 BC. The word Hindu is derived from Indus, the river valley where it began. The foundations of Hinduism were recorded in early Sanskrit texts called the Vedas, which present poems and mantras as vehicles for connecting with the Divine. The science and practice of yoga emerged from the Hindu tradition as well. Yoga is a system that enables a person to make direct connection with the Divine, and many types and forms of yoga have been developed. The most well known is hatha yoga, which consists of a series of body postures. Other forms of yoga develop the control of the mind and the will (raja yoga), intellectual and philosophical understanding (jnana yoga), devotional love (bhakti yoga), or service (karma yoga; see chapter 6, "The Law of Service"). Yoga practices also involve pranayama, the practice of working with the breath in order to bring vital life force into the body. All forms of yoga are designed to help us integrate parts of ourselves in harmonious ways and ultimately to integrate our individuality into the Oneness.

The origin of Buddhism, the other prominent world religion that took root in India and spread throughout Asia, can be traced to Siddhartha Gautama, who lived in India in the fifth century BC. Like Taoism, Buddhism seeks to provide a clear framework for a philosophical understanding of the universe and the nature of life. Also, like Taoism, in Buddhism there is no deity. But Buddhism goes beyond the mystical poetry and evocative imagery of the Taoist and Hindu traditions to provide the seeker with specific techniques of meditation that offer a more immediate and personal connection to Oneness. Like yoga, Buddhism doesn't simply offer ideas about consciousness development; it suggests concrete methods to attain it. Through various meditation disciplines, the yogis and the Buddhists have evolved systems that enable individuals to alter their consciousness and perceive reality from the point of Oneness, rather than merely the point of their individuality. The emphasis is on direct, personal experience. Thus, Buddhism offers a mystical approach to divine connection, in addition to one based on philosophical understanding.

One significant change in the development of consciousness and the ensuing religions that evolved from it took place in the West and the Middle East. It was the concept of monotheism, the belief that there is a prime deity (Yahweh), who is not in any of the forces of nature but beyond it, in a realm apart. The Greek concept of the sky god was a precursor to this, but Abraham is considered the father of monotheism. He lived sometime between 2000 and 1500 BC. The Bible tells us that he was the first person to have direct contact with the one God. In this sense, we could consider Abraham the first mystic of a Western spiritual tradition. To the early Israelites, adhering to a religion with one God meant being loyal to only one deity instead of the multiplicity of gods and goddesses that were common among the various pagan tribes of the Middle East at that time. The original meaning of Yahweh, or Jehovah, the One God, was that of a tribal deity. It took centuries for this concept to evolve to include all beings and everything that exists. As mentioned earlier, the concept and definition of a deity is a reflection of the consciousness of the people at the time that concept became popular. Thus, as human consciousness continues to evolve, our sense of a deity evolves as well.

It is ironic that the progenitors of the three main Western religious traditions—Judaism, Christianity, and Islam—were mystics. We can assume that Abraham was a mystic because the Bible tells us that he had direct, personal connection with Yahweh. The next and most famous and popular Western mystic was Jesus. Assuming that he was born into a Jewish family, he would have learned the tenets of Judaism of his time, which would have included the extensive laws governing every aspect of life. The Jewish philosophy was that if one followed those laws, one could come to know God. During his life Jesus was able to connect with Divine Source by attaining the mystical state of Christ consciousness. But he was not content to merely understand the teachings and follow the laws that they embody. From the point of Christ consciousness, Jesus claimed that he "came not to change the laws, but to complete them with love." Thus, one of his greatest gifts to humanity was to reveal the power and fundamental importance of the universal Principle of Love. Jesus's life symbolizes the ultimate potential of human experience. He taught that the primal connection to Source is available to all and already exists within us. To become aware of and live within that connection is the definition of Christ consciousness, where there is no separation between the Divine and humanity.

The third great Western mystic was Mohammed, who lived in the fourteenth century AD. While on spiritual retreat, Mohammed was awakened by a being he called an angel. The angel enveloped Mohammed in an overpowering embrace and commanded the confused and illiterate man to "recite." The outcome of this recitation is the Qur'an, which literally means "the recitation." The words that spontaneously sprang from Mohammed while he was in divine communion with the angel enabled the listeners and readers of those words to have a clearer, deeper understanding of the nature of the Divine.

Over time Judaism, Christianity, and Islam have evolved into more philosophical and doctrinaire (and less mystical) approaches to the teachings of the words of their great masters. Within these traditions, however, mystical schools have evolved. Sufism is an esoteric spiritual system most often connected to Islam. Although Sufis go back as far as the early Christian Gnostics, Sufism flourished under Islam, particularly in the eighth century AD. Sufi initiates were taught to be receptive to the esoteric or inner spiritual understanding, to look within to find a direct personal experience of the Divine. It is this intimate relationship that is, according to the Sufis, the very purpose of life. The prime vehicle through which this connection is made is love. The experience of joyful ecstasy, a state of consciousness always available to all people, draws one to the Divine Beloved. The modern Sufi avatar, or God-realized master, is Meher Baba. He taught "Don't worry, be happy" as a mindful, mantra-like path of obtaining the state of divine consciousness.

The Sufis employ two techniques as a means of attaining this state. One is simple awareness in the present, the "be here now" also taught by yogis and Buddhists, discussed at length in chapter 3, "The Law of Both/And," and chapter 4, "The Law of the Eternal Present." Using the word Al-lah, or God, as a mantra assists in this process. The second technique involves music, chant, and dance. By moving the body or using the voice in a rhythmic manner, we can access a trancelike state and transcend self-awareness. We feel the joyful ecstasy and are pulled into loving communion with the One. To the Sufi, or to mystics of any tradition, God is the only reality. Nothing exists but God, thus the world is Divine. The Sufi Gulshan-Raz said, "Every man whose heart is no longer shaken by any doubt knows with certainty that there is no being save only One. ... In his Divine Majesty the *me*, and *we*, the *thou*, are not found, for in the One there can be no distinction."

Kabala is the esoteric, mystical branch of the Jewish tradition, first recorded in the thirteenth century. This system evolved a mythology that became a method for exploring and expanding consciousness. The Kabalists described a process whereby God made himself known to humanity in different ways. Each of the ways, or steps, is complete in itself and contains the entire mystery of the Divine. Hence, each of the steps (called Sefiroth) is both one of the many and the totality. Each word of the Old Testament refers to one of the Sefiroth, and accordingly each verse of the Bible describes an event or phenomenon that had its counterpart in the inner life of God himself. However, the Kabalists believe that before one can benefit from the Sefiroth, one must be in a peaceful state of mind. Reflecting the ideas of the Sufis, the Kabalists sought to feel joy and happiness and to eschew remorse and anxiety. Isaac Luria, a major proponent of Kabalism in the sixteenth century, taught that "God can only be found in joy and tranquility." How different from the theology of Martin Luther, who taught that "God can only be found in suffering and the Cross." As mentioned in the introduction of this book, the mystical path can involve much suffering as one journeys on the road to enlightenment. Yet not all philosophers and theologians espouse suffering as the only way. The renegade Catholic priest Matthew Fox calls for an end to the doctrine of original sin and a replacement with a belief in original blessing. We might characterize the difference between him and Martin Luther as the distinction between a mystic and a philosopher. Fox refers to life as a journey that leads to direct connection and the realization of the truth of life. Luther sought to reduce life to a system of rules that describes the Divine as "out there," something to please in an attempt to feel good about our life here on earth.

Astrological Correlation

The astrological sign associated with the Law of Abundance is Sagittarius. Sagittarius's nature is to be expansive. It the sign that is most oriented toward tasting life from the broadest range of perspectives and experiences. Sagittarius can apply its expansive abilities in many ways, one of which is attitudinal. It is possibly the most positive, optimistic, and joyful of all the signs. This orientation enables Sagittarius to create positive and desirable situations for itself, as everyone likes and wants to be around positive people. Like attracts like.

Sagittarius is the sign of the higher mind, that part of us that is continuously involved in the development of consciousness. To the Sagittarian, every experience and situation in life provides the opportunity for a lesson. I've had many Sagittarian clients over the years who have shared with me that their only fear was realizing that they aren't learning anything new. Sagittarians can be drawn to any type of academic study and will often remain in the academic realm professionally. As one of the most independent signs, however, Sagittarius also enjoys learning about something that may not have any professional application but that is nonetheless enjoyable to learn and helps to expand the mind.

Knowledge is freedom. The more we know, the more awareness we have; the more conscious we are of ourselves, the freer we are. This is true at both the individual and collective levels. Collectively, this principle can manifest as new or evolving philosophies and spiritual paths. The more abundant they are, the more we, as individuals, have to choose from. One may be striving for the "one perfect path," one that, when followed with consciousness and commitment, will take us to the light of Oneness. Realistically, however, there are as many paths as there are seekers. Achieving the state of Christ consciousness is more about the intention and commitment than it is about any specific path or system.

The Sagittarian focus on consciousness development can, at best, lead to the understanding of a broad range of metaphysical perspectives for developing a higher-minded understanding of life. At worst, it can lead to a narrow-minded, dogmatic, know-it-all attitude that stifles further learning for the individual and tries to limit others from expanding their awareness. The difference is based on the individual's commitment to the process of learning and developing consciousness. The greater the commitment, the more open-minded the seeker is to all paths and perspectives. The more closed, the more that person may demand that others accept his or her personal experience or belief as being universal.

Sagittarius is the sign of the prophet, the teacher, and the guru; one who is honest in seeing the truth and open in the communication of it. A prophet is a type of mystic who seeks to integrate his personal perspective with his principles in order to point others in a direction that can enhance the well-being, freedom, and joy for all beings. One type of prophet is a visionary. A visionary is one who shows the way, a kind of human map, who intuitively "sees" a higher path of action. The visionary's focus is more on the future than the past or present. Both the prophet and the visionary provide a clear perspective of where we need to go, either individually or collectively, in order to continue—in a conscious, deliberate way—the process of growth and evolution. Sometimes prophets can be outspoken about their perspective and experience. They serve to warn others about the traps and pitfalls that await if their current behavior is maintained. Some are prophets of doom who focus on calamity. Others offer a dream of a better way and a better world, something that can be achieved by persevering in our current patterns or by changing what we have been doing and pursuing a new direction. In either case, prophets seek to expand people's awareness. Their teachings broaden their students' perspective about what they are doing, the ramifications of their actions, and the available alternatives.

Sharing the good-naturedness of the Sagittarius archetype, people often find the true teacher appealing because of his or her positive attitude. The positive attitude can be expressed through humor and storytelling. The latter can take the form of regaling an audience with tales or stories that carry some form of message or teaching. Humor can be an important component of those stories, but it can also stand on its own. The Sagittarian can use his or her expansive perspective to find the irony or other forms of humor in anything. Humor can be used as a tool to educate or entertain and as a means of helping others to expand their minds into the universal understanding that is fundamental to the Sagittarian.

Sagittarius is adventurous by nature. It is the sign of long-distance travel, which can be another way to be expansive. By broadening our physical horizons we can also broaden our mind. Sagittarius is also a sign of service. It provides support to others through sharing of knowledge and wisdom or in areas of the community that have a charitable focus. Fund-raising for the Girls Clubs or Boys Clubs or being active in the town library, the PTA, or as a museum docent are all activities that the Sag can embrace enthusiastically and joyfully.

How to Align with This Law

The key to knowing and tapping into abundance is consciousness. Taking advantage of this law has a lot to do with attitude. By this I mean being committed to the process of developing consciousness. To do so requires that we remain open-minded at all times. There is always more information to take in and from which we can learn. What may appear to be just another ho-hum day filled with the routines of our life could, in fact, offer an opportunity to experience something new, something from which we can learn and grow. The "lesson of the moment" enables us to continue to learn more about what life is and has to offer. An open-minded attitude is best applied to everyday activities and by noticing the connections that take place within situations or environments. We can learn a lot by paying attention to how people function in different situations. What is the difference in the way people behave when they are comfortable and safe as opposed to when they feel threatened? Why do they act as they do, and are those behaviors effective? How are the people and phenomena in a specific context connected? What do they have in common? When we seek answers to these types of questions, our consciousness expands.

Consciousness also expands when we are attentive to nature. Birds, animals, and insects can inform us about life in any situation. We can also feel a connection to Divine Spirit by feeling the wind, observing the clouds, or noticing fluctuations in air temperature. Abundance exists not only in the plethora of phenomena, but also in perceiving and understanding how everything is interconnected.

Learning can also take place within the context of specific subjects, whether we take a class or undertake an entire course of study. By being open to taking in new information, we access the Principle of Abundance. There is always more information that can teach us about the meaning of life and our place in it.

Note the similarity between this and the Principle of the Eternal Present, which also reminds us of the importance of attention. One difference between these laws, however, is that the Principle of the Eternal Present is grounded in a personal, emotional experience; the Law of Abundance provides the opportunity for a much more objective range of perception and understanding.

Higher Learning

Attitude also influences how we learn. If we look forward to eagerly pursuing new information or embracing the adventure of each day, we will learn more and enjoy the process. This enjoyment, in turn, will provide the stimulus for more learning. The point is to cultivate an attitude of enthusiasm in welcoming life and its endless, abundant possibilities. This attitude, combined with positive encounters, generates the appetite for more exploration. Even when situations are stressful, challenging, or painful, with the right attitude we can see that they offer opportunities for expanding awareness. Something as seemingly simply as undertaking the study of a subject that takes our mind into a new realm of perception can be an adventure. Study can also involve job training, learning more about ourselves or the world around us, or about how each reflects the other, thus offering new possibilities for understanding our potential in the world.

Over time, a positive attitude toward learning will expand our experiences as well as our consciousness. The idea of expansion is central to this principle because the more we experience and learn, the more we realize there is no end to this process.

Travel

Being adventurous is another way to access this law. The word "adventure" usually conjures up the sense of doing something exciting, something brand new and out of the realm of past experience. Traveling to foreign countries or even to different landscapes and cultures of our native land can evoke this sense. In the United States, for example, if we grew up in an urban area on the East Coast, traveling to the Bible Belt in the South, a rural area in the

Southwest, or a farming community in the Midwest would provide an opportunity to explore life in a context different from the one in which we grew up. We can shake up some of our basic assumptions about what life is by simply paying attention to what other people are doing and how they relate to each other.

We can also seek to understand the spiritual or religious attitudes of the cultures we visit. How do they experience a transcendent reality? This question becomes even more striking when we realize that every culture has such a concept. Yet even though they might verbalize or intellectualize about it, they might not prioritize it highly enough for it to provide any real benefit to the citizenry. Examples can be found in most industrialized Western cultures. Time, energy, and resources are given to more mundane activities that provide physical comfort, pleasure, and social status. This, however, provides no real emotional or spiritual sustenance. In the so-called "developed" countries or "first-world cultures," the emphasis is on commodification. "Things" are seen as ends in themselves. Possessions have value because of what they can do to help us feel safer or more comfortable or because they reflect status. For many, there is little awareness of the real cost of those material goods. An open-minded, curious person might be concerned about the cost in natural resources and human exploitation required in the creation of a certain object. One might want to question the legacy we are leaving to future generations in terms of financial debt and misuse of resources. These questions can lead to an understanding of how we can make the best use of the limited resources still available to us. They can also precipitate a shift in priorities so that fulfillment and well-being are sought more through consciousness development and less through attachment to objects.

By contrast, when we travel to a culture that emphasizes the transcendent qualities and possibilities of life, we can discover a different perspective and value system. Those cultures that prioritize the transcendent experience seek to deepen and honor their connection to their ancestors and to their spiritual guides and teachers. How they relate to the natural elements and how they employ those elements in the creation of objects reflect an alternative approach to reality. In 2000 I was invited to participate in an Aboriginal festival in Australia—the Garma Festival, which means "healing" in the local language. Black and white people got together to share their philosophies, knowledge, and experience in areas ranging from education to healing to music. With open-minded and open-hearted interest, we exchanged information, both academic and experiential, that was designed to further the cause of human welfare and well-being. My purpose in being there was to learn more about Aboriginal music, specifically the didgeridoo. I learned how it can be used in spiritual ceremony for healing and for the purpose of entertainment and personal enjoyment.

The purpose of the observant traveler isn't necessarily to make value judgment as much as it is to learn about the diversity of the human experience. The more varied our travels, the more we expose ourselves to different contexts and value systems, and the more we will see that the creative potential of human communities is virtually limitless. In this respect, we could even say that the Law of Abundance is also operative in the way that people create culture and community.

If we combine study with our travel, we can broaden our perspective about why people and cultures have evolved as they have. Modern life shows the diversity as well as the homogeneity of human culture, but it is beneficial to study both a country's history and cosmology before traveling there, in order to understand its fundamental nature. Sometimes, the original state of a people is buried under generations of new growth. By studying the origins of that group, we can gain a clearer understanding of who they are and how they got to where they are. The more we understand the past, the more we can understand the present, and the clearer will be our vision for the future.

Gratitude and Altruism

Another method for tuning in to the flow of the Principle of Abundance is to notice all the ways in which we are blessed. One such method is through reciting gratitude prayers. We can do this throughout the day, expressing our thanks for even simple and mundane things, such as being able to see or hear or walk up a flight of stairs. Gratitude can also include singular things that may have meaning only to ourselves, such as our family, our partner, our job, or our health. When we become aware of all the ways in which Spirit gifts us, it is natural to want to share our abundance with others.

One quality that accompanies this principle is generosity. We usually think of generosity in a material or financial context, when we share what we have with someone who has less than we do. But generosity can also include providing an abundance of information to a seeker or an abundance of support to someone in need. What are the limits of our generosity? When and how do we decide that we have given enough?

One way is by clearly delineating our morals and ethics. The difference between these two concepts is that one pertains to the collective experience, the other to the personal. Morals are behaviors by which a society defines what is acceptable or unacceptable. They are principles of right and wrong that a body of people agrees to uphold and on which they base their cultural and social interaction. Morals define standards of conduct that are considered virtuous. Ethics define the degree to which a person chooses to conform to the collective moral customs. In a healthy, conscious society, the two would blend most of the time. But there are situations where an individual cannot accept and follow the norms established by the many. They may be too extreme, one way or another, or contrary to what a person decides is or is not acceptable behavior. A person who chooses to ignore a commonly accepted moral precept in favor of an alternate behavior may be judged as immoral or unethical by others, and in an objective sense, he could be. But he could also be a visionary, maverick, or iconoclast acting outside the boundaries of a defined reality and, in so doing, awakening or inspiring the consciousness of the masses.

The difference between a rebel and an eccentric involves attitude and intention. If one acts outside the mainstream but is centered and acts with the intention of being honest and doing something that is beneficial to others, he or she may be rebelling from restrictive and unnecessary social constraints. If the person is off-center, however, he may be acting out of self-interest only. He would not only be outside the mainstream but would act in ways that disrespect and subvert abundance for the group.

By clearly defining our personal behavioral ethics and being consistent within that framework, we can determine how much of anything—time, money, attention, etc.--is appropriate to share with or give to others. Many Native American peoples, such as the Lakota of the upper Midwest and the Kwakiutl of the Northwest, include giving as a main part of their ceremonial celebrations. It is felt that giving was a way to reward people for heroic acts, for taking care of the less fortunate members of the tribe, or as a way of congratulating someone on their marriage or birth of a child.

Gratefulness is linked to altruism by tuning in to the bounty and blessings that we receive. It is a natural response to feeling grateful when recognizing our good fortune that we would want to share it with others in an altruistic fashion. A benefit of altruism is that it keeps things flowing. Whether in the form of material resources, time, or physical activity, being generous with others creates more abundance for all concerned. This principle is enhanced when utilized in combination with the Principle of Service. In terms of the Principle of Abundance, service involves providing others with what we know or have—with an attitude of generosity. Sharing can inspire others, awakening them to new possibilities of experience and understanding, especially when done with an open mind and open heart. When the purpose is to benefit others, not ourselves, we benefit by learning how to create a more enlightened environment that offers more opportunities for learning and self-development for ourselves and for others. Practical examples of service in this context often involve volunteering. Being an athletic coach to a group of boys or girls, occupying a seat on the city council or the PTA, or teaching literacy to adults in the local library are concrete ways of contributing our time, energy, and experience in a way that directly and immediately benefits others. Those who benefit from our efforts will then make greater contributions back to the community that includes us.

Humor

Another aspect of the Law of Abundance is that it stimulates our ability to see a situation from a variety of perspectives. One possible perspective is irony. To see the ironic or the absurd in a situation is a form of humor, which is another way to access this law. Prophets and teachers can use humor to make a concept easier to understand or as a way to make a painful point easier to accept. Sometimes humor can emanate from storytelling or yarn-spinning. With humor we relate an incident so that the listener sees the situation in an unexpected way, while also learning from the tale itself. We add an element to the process of education that makes it enjoyable to learn.

There is a limitless variety of philosophies and spiritual paths, any one of which can provide the framework and tools for consciousness expansion. Exploring the ones that seem interesting can lead to the one that is most inspirational. Perhaps we might even prefer an eclectic blend of several traditions. Whatever our path of choice, when we develop our consciousness within the context of philosophy or spiritual practice, it will always enable access to the Law of Abundance.

Not Aligning with This Law

The biggest problem that can accompany the Principle of Abundance is excess. Too much abundance can be too much. This can occur in several ways. One is in planning or promising to do something that is unrealistic and beyond the scope of our ability or resources. On paper, an idea may look great, but practically speaking, it is not feasible. We become disappointed because our perspective and expectations were expanded beyond the point of the possible. Similarly, we could have an unrealistic expectation about others assuming they are capable of doing something that, in fact, they are not. We could also relate to something or someone based on an idealized projection and ultimately feel drained or disillusioned by the process. Another type of excessive idealism is to have an unrealistic standard of ethics. Philosophically, it may seem like the right way to be, but practically, it may be hard even for a saint or bodhisattva to conform to it. So even though we may be trying to do the right thing, we may end up feeling self-critical or embarrassed. A third scenario of excess is in being overly generous and overextended. We promise more than we can deliver. We give of ourselves based on desire, rather than on ability. We lead people to believe that we are capable, and they rely on us to follow through, but then they become disappointed, disillusioned, or even angry when we don't provide as promised.

The main problem with all these scenarios is lack of perspective. We observed how the issue of poor perspective can also arise in misusing the Law of Service. But in that case, the problem is an overly limited point of focus. In the Law of Abundance, the problem stems from an overly expanded point of focus. Again, notice the importance of the interplay between the laws. The antidote to the excessive expansion or idealism is the discrimination offered by the Law of Service. Being meticulous in our self-awareness and selective in what we offer can counter any tendency to overextend. So by applying the Law of Service, we can overcome some of the potential pitfalls of the Law of Abundance. Inherent within the Law of Service, however, is the tendency to become overly focused on the details of a project or situation. By applying the Law of Abundance, with its expanded perspective, we can short-circuit that possible problem. Through the integration of these two laws, we can develop a clear overview of a state of affairs and function effectively within it by paying attention to the details of how to make it work. We can see both the forest and the trees.

Excess can also involve overindulgence. One glass of wine tastes so good, a second must taste even better, a third better yet. One portion of food is so satisfying, a second would surely be even more so. Whatever we value, wherever we find personal gratification, if we "let ourselves go" to experience it to excess, we get a sense of immediate gratification followed by a more extended period of regret. If we indulge our love of reading excessively, we may never have the time for social experiences that could serve to validate the truth of what we are studying. Not only would we limit our social life, we might sublimate feelings of fear and awkwardness as well.

Another potential misuse of this law involves waste. Indulging in petty pastimes might waste time that could otherwise be used productively. This would be trading long-range fulfillment or growth for immediate gratification. Waste can also be a by-product of excessive indulgence. For example, restaurants in the United States throw out huge amounts of food daily. They entice customers by offering a vast array of items on the menu. Most people have come to expect this. Realistically, however, most of the food offered will not be ordered and, as the food needs to be fresh, it must be discarded at the end of the day. The more expensive the restaurant, the more extensive the pattern.

Many years ago I worked for the United States Forest Service, where one of my jobs was to fight forest fires. Fighting a forest fire is like a military mission. A main camp is set up where the firefighters eat and sleep. They march or are flown by helicopter into the fire area to do battle with the enemy. One fire I fought was very extensive, requiring hundreds of men and women and almost two weeks of work to finally control and stamp it out. During that time, a steady stream of food and equipment was trucked or flown into the encampment. There was enough food to satisfy a small army and enough tools and machinery to successfully do our job. When the fire was out and the battle ended, there was enough food left over for at least two more days. There were also crates of unopened, brand new chainsaws, shovels, and rakes. As the firefighters were leaving, all these supplies were destroyed or buried by bulldozers. We couldn't take the food home to our families, nor could it be donated to hungry people. The rationale behind this waste was that the Forest Service could report that all the money spent on the fire had been spent. This would ensure that next year, this agency could request even more funding from Congress. After all, there could be an even bigger fire next year and without the increase, the resources to fight it wouldn't be available—no matter the waste of resources that produced the food and machinery, as well as the taxpayers' money that paid for it.

It is ironic that the abundance of our planet's natural resources can be as destructive as it is useful. For example, water is the basis of life. Without water we couldn't survive. But water can manifest in myriad ways—some beneficial to humans, some not so beneficial. It can come as gentle rain that fertilizes crops, as excessive rain that brings flooding, or no rain at all, as drought. Fire is another basic element available here on earth. It can be beneficial to us as a means of cooking our food and keeping us warm. It can also manifest as a forest fire generated by lightning or a volcano. For tens of thousands of years, humans must have felt threatened by these awesome elements of life. One strategy designed to help humans feel more in control was to create a harmonious relationship with these elements. We have learned through the centuries to, at best, bring those forces into greater, more consistent alignment with human needs and, at worst, keep them at bay and limit their destructive power. Nevertheless, the devastating power of the elements does still overwhelm us at times—witness Hurricane Katrina or the decades-long drought in Sub-Saharan Africa. Moreover, environmental scientists are warning that dramatic and extreme changes in climate are imminent and will increase the intensity and frequency of hurricanes, tsunamis, floods, droughts, and forest fires. These manifestations are responses from Mother Nature to our excessive pillaging and wanton destruction of the earth's natural resources. This is a good and instructive lesson about the consequences of misusing one of the universal principles that governs our physical universe.

The resources that we need to survive are abundant but also limited. When we mine, log, drill, or fish at will and with no long-range plan or vision, we foolishly and needlessly squander precious resources. When we pollute the soil, water, and air indiscriminately, we eliminate the very resources that could keep humanity existing indefinitely. Humanity is moving in the direction of marginalizing itself by destroying its own habitat. This is not only self-destructive and self-serving, for both corporate interests and consumers, but also a misguided response to a material reality that can seem confusing and terrifying. If, on the other hand, humanity starts prioritizing the spiritual quality of discrimination inherent in the universal Law of Service, we will be able to be more selective in our use of resources and to limit ruthless exploitation. By taking further advantage of the universal Law of Survival, we will prioritize preservation over exploitation.

Another misuse of the Principle of Abundance can happen through bias and dogma. We are guilty of bias when we assume that our cultural norms must be the "right" ones and that those people who do things differently are "wrong." This attitude denies the open-minded perspective that is the potential of this principle. With a biased attitude, we do not seek to expand our awareness by learning from others but instead, we concern ourselves with validating our own limited point of view and experience. Often, this point of view is defined within a cultural context. "Those people" are different from us in some obvious yet superficial way. And, of course, we assume that our way is better or preferable.

One quality of the Principle of Abundance is that everyone is entitled to be themselves. Abundance implies diversity. This manifests in the human family through different racial groups and ethnicities, and in individuals through freedom of opinion or perspective. Certain Native American tribes, such as the aforementioned Lakota, created their society so that everyone, regardless of their interests, tendencies, or predilections, was accepted within the social context of the tribe. When we fail to embrace all people as family, equal in their right to fulfill the same needs that we all have, we sacrifice the birthright of all on the altar of personal bias. We allow a "group mind" definition of reality or our own limited knowledge and understanding to color our experience.

A personal dogma is more philosophically based than a bias. Philosophers attempt to understand reality by defining it in a mental construct. To synthesize and promote their perceptions, they create a doctrine that upholds their point of view. Sometimes that doctrine is a methodology for examining and understanding the truth, and it can boil down to dogma if the original spirit of truth becomes obscured. Of course, not all philosophers and philosophies are guilty of being dogmatic; some are open to being questioned. For example, Socrates was a great philosopher and teacher in ancient Greece, whose method of instruction has become known as the Socratic method. Instead of telling the student what the answer was to a question, Socrates asked his students to look within themselves and their own perceptions and experiences to find the answers to major questions.

This reminds me of a great professor I had in college, Ernest Becker. Becker's lectures rambled in many directions. The students wanted to record his every word, hoping to connect the themes after class. But Becker refused to allow the students to take any notes at all. If he noticed a student defying his edict, he would tell him to put down the pen or leave the class, permanently. He wanted us to think for ourselves, not merely memorize and regurgitate his thoughts. He wanted to challenge us to teach him what he didn't know by sharing our perceptions and knowledge with him. Dr. Becker's lectures were the antithesis of dogma. He cultivated our creative mind and our own understanding, rather than indoctrinating us with his points of view.

The Socratic method is also reminiscent of conversations I had with our children when they were in school. Instead of asking what they had learned each day, I inquired about whether they had asked any good questions.

Other philosophers and their doctrines are more limited by their own perceptions and conclusions. They pass their precepts off as truth, with the expectation that other people will conform to their belief system. Rather than focus on principles of behavior as the basis for social interaction, they extol us to relate to others based on the rules of a preconceived, arbitrarily defined standard. The more such information is rendered as absolute, without proof or by decree, the more it will tend to be used as a political tool that enables one group to benefit in same way at the expense of another. The more this type of dogma is invoked, the more beneficial it would be to respond to with a heavy dose of the quality of discrimination accessed through the universal Law of Service.

Judgment can also be an impediment to benefiting from the Principle of Abundance (as it is with the Law of Harmony). In this case, judgment can limit our perspective and understanding of a reality, situation, or experience. More important than judging a situation, however, is learning from it. Sometimes a person can be guilty of being judgmental when his or her limited personal perceptions and relationships dominate a philosophy that is based on openness and equality. Sometimes judgment is an extension of a blind belief in narrow, prejudicial dogma.

Another misuse of this law takes place when we confuse it with "luck." The concept of luck assumes that good things happen to people by chance. I once had a landlord who marveled, with a mix of jealousy and admiration, that I was able to make a living as a professional astrologer. Each month when he came to collect the rent, he would shake his head and say, "Thank your lucky stars!" In addition to being an outmoded cliché—and quite annoying to hear monthly—it did disservice to what I was doing. There was nothing lucky about my work or my success. It was a combination of skills, integrity, hard work, and patience. Luck assumes that things happen accidentally, that there is no plan or strategy that created the experience at hand. If the universe is based on abundance, then each of us has opportunities to create the types and quality of experiences that we choose. We can each use the tools and support available to us to create the types of experiences that most benefit us.

The universal Principle of Abundance is about positivity. Instead of viewing desirable or beneficial outcomes as luck, it is more valuable and honest to accept the good things in our life as being the result of two attitudes. One attitude is positive thinking, which utilizes the Law of Creativity. This involves conceiving of a plan or a goal and visualizing it as if it were already happening. In so doing, we create a thought form and send it out into the ether, where it can take root and eventually manifest. This is similar to affirmation and prayer. Affirmation is a technique through which we can access the creative principle and manifest a certain condition ourselves. Prayer is a way of focusing our intention so that our actions lead to a specific beneficial result for self or others. Regardless of whom it benefits, it is a way to solicit the support of external forces, such as spirit guides, saints, or ascended masters, the gods or goddess of a metaphysical path, or the Supreme Being itself. We must be cautious, however, when supplicating external forces, because this could be based on the assumption that the help we need is outside ourselves or that without external intervention, we won't achieve our goals.

We have learned, for example, that the creative power of the universe lies within each of us. It is one thing to want assistance but another to assume that only that assistance will guarantee our success. Certain indigenous tribes traditionally performed a rain dance. This was not only an appeal to a higher deity to bring rain, but also a way of focusing the people's consciousness and energy to envision the rain. They created an environment through their thoughts and actions that led to precipitation. There was nothing lucky about it. It wasn't based on some external force being pleased enough to satisfy the desires of the tribe. It was the people themselves who created the conditions that led to the realization of the desire. Prayer can be powerful, and enlisting the support of higher beings can help any endeavor. But it doesn't take the place of our own abilities or the application of hard work.

The other attitude that can help lead us to beneficial outcomes is meeting opportunity with preparedness. Sometimes this technique involves working with the practical and concrete. For example, the due diligence of thorough research is a way to enhance the quality of our experience. Spending time contemplating the nature of a situation and defining an outcome that would be beneficial to us enables us to both know what we want and recognize the desirable goal when it becomes available to us. Again, there is no luck involved. It may appear to an external observer that we happened to be in the right place at the right time and just "lucked out." But the work and preparation we undertook, quiet and internal though it may have been, is what created the advantageous outcome.

Spiritual Opportunity

The key to working effectively with the Principle of Abundance starts with defining what parts of the abundant universe we want to take advantage of. For some, the need is for greater material sustenance or comfort. For others, abundance implies limitless emotional fulfillment. There are those who seek to satisfy a never-ending curiosity about the nature of things through lifelong learning, while others seek constant stimulation through physical adventure. Whatever form of abundance attracts us, the spiritual quality associated with this law is *joy*. Joy is an ever-renewing quality of life available to all people at all times. Sometimes it is easy to feel joy. Our life experience is gratifying because we have achieved what we have been working for; our primary relationship has reached a new level of intimacy; our young children are growing up happy and healthy or our adult children are making good choices and thriving. Joy also exists without any kind of external context whatsoever. We can feel joy even if there is little in our external reality to feel good about.

Even in times of great challenge or stress, the potential to tap into and feel joy is there. This can be hard to acknowledge; I know this because of the times that have been hard in my life, when I've been frustrated by everything and felt abandoned by the universe. At these times, the one thought that engendered the greatest amount of resentment within me is that "joy is always available." In a state like that, I don't want to feel joy; I want to revel in my misery, luxuriate in my victimization, and feel justified in my anger at life! In reality, I am preventing myself from feeling joy because I deny its presence. If I want to cling to my unhappiness, that's okay. But if I want to acknowledge my despair and work to overcome the challenges at hand, that's okay, too. If I choose the latter, I can apply myself to these challenges and might even feel joy in the process. I am free to choose what I do and the attitude and quality with which I do it.

One of the keys to feeling joy is acting in accordance with our ethics, our sense of right and wrong. Doing things in a conscientious way can bring a deeply felt sense of inner joy. Yogananda said, "Righteousness is the crucible for joy." Another expression of joy is laughter. Yogananda suggests we all become "smile millionaires." The simple act of smiling at another person, or smiling because it's a beautiful day, or because we are affirming our gratitude prayers connects us to joy. It can even lead to a spontaneous outbreak of laughter and thus, to the flow of ever-present joy.

Freedom is another spiritual quality associated with this law; specifically, the freedom of thought, the freedom to develop the mind as we choose. We are free to create or adhere to any belief system, philosophy of life, or ethical mode of relating to others; the freedom to learn about what life has to offer and what it means. Some societies are created so that individuals are free to be themselves and to gather with others to create the kinds of laws they choose to live by; others are not. The latter are dictatorial or fascist and base their consensus reality on bias and dogma. The former more fully take advantage of the Law of Abundance.

The Law of Abundance provides us with the support to become our own prophet, teacher, or source of guidance. We become so by being true to ourselves in all our thoughts, words, and actions, emphasizing personal authority. One way to do this is by developing a personal system of ethics. This involves deciding at all times how to behave, how to influence others, and how to respond to them. Our individual ethics determine how much freedom we have and how much joy we can experience. The more we accept and embrace the diversity of life—in terms of the human family and culture—the closer we are to forming a mystical connection to Divine Spirit. We become those who show the way by demonstrating through action, attitude, and honesty what life means to us and what we, as unlimited beings who are part of an abundant universe, can create it to be.

The Bottom Line

If we list the laws in a circular format, the Law of Abundance would be opposite to the Law of Both/And. Because oppositions can act as mirrors and provide perspective, the Law of Both/And serves to remind us that regardless of the abundance of spiritual paths or religions, they are all reflective of the same quest: the desire to experience life through mystical communion. Depending on the intention and dedication of the seeker, any or all of those paths can lead us to the same destination of Oneness.

The Law of Abundance

Contemporary journalist and humorist Wes "Scoop" Nisker defines DNA as Divine Natural Abundance. The Law of Creativity teaches that life is continually renewing and recreating itself in limitless ways, patterns, and forms. The Law of Abundance adds to this the concept that there is always more. Whatever we enjoy, whatever brings satisfaction in any area of life at any time, is available to us in a never-ending supply. Similarly, whatever we fear and whatever brings sorrow is also potentially ever-present. Whichever reality we choose to create, whatever mind stream we tap into is where we are. The freedom of choice is ours. And no one can prevent us from splashing around in the context that offers the greatest meaning and fulfillment for us. We actualize and embody abundance when we identify with Spirit and realize that this source of satisfaction is ourselves. Nisker was a radio newscaster on an alternative FM station in the early 1970s. He used to end every broadcast by saying, "That's the news. If you don't like it, go out and make some of your own."

Affirmation: "Abundant joy and gratitude are my guides and my companions."

> *Anoint and cheer our soiled face*
> *With the abundance of thy grace,*
> *Keep far our foes, give peace at home;*
> *Where thou art guide, no ill can come.*
>
> —The Book of Common Prayer

Chapter 10: The Law of Karma

> *The Cosmic Vibration that causes the birth and sustenance and dissolution of beings and their various natures is termed Karma.*
>
> The Bhagavad-Gita, VIII: 3

Responsible Action

One of the most important jobs that parents have is to teach their children independence and self-reliance. One of the most important aspects of this lesson is teaching children to be responsible for what they do. When my children were young they would often come to me, complaining that one of their siblings did this or that to them. Sometimes it would be obvious that the older one was taking advantage of the younger. But just as frequently, it would be a situation where the elder was goaded by the younger, in which case the elder's behavior was at least understandable. There would, of course, be the requisite lecture to the elder child about not taking advantage of age or size. But I would also ask the younger child what he had said or done that generated the response from his big brother or sister. In the early years, the stock answer was, of course, "Nothing." As the years progressed this same discussion ensued when my children would complain about something that happened at school or in the neighborhood. After expressing my compassion for their misery, I would follow with the inevitable question about their part in the scenario. For many years, the stock answer was at

The Law of Karma

the ready. Even as they grew older and the discussion became more detailed, they would not own up to being anything but the passive and wronged one. Imagine my pleasant surprise when my youngest, at the age of fifteen, came home with a tale about how his friend's big brother had hit him and been mean to him, followed immediately with what my son had done to perpetrate such a response. There was no breath, no pause, just a continuation of the story. He wasn't looking for pity or even exoneration. He seemed to just want to vent, to get his pain and suffering off his chest to a safe and loving ear. There was nothing I could think of to say. I was not only proud that he was owning his part in the scuffle but pleased that all the seemingly fruitless discussions over the years were finally paying off. He had been listening all along and comprehending more of what I had been saying as he grew, unbeknownst to me. He was indeed realizing the connection between what he did and what happened to him. It was at that time that I introduced the concept of karma to my rapidly maturing son.

Karma is the law of action. The initial action of the universe was the big bang, which began the creation of the material world. This was the first karmic manifestation generated by Divine Spirit. Its primal expression was and still is sound, specifically in the vibration *om*, as noted in chapter 1. In that primal state, everything is pure, emanating directly from Spirit and radiating throughout the universe. What motivates the creative impulse is love (see chapter 5), the divine intention and spark that exists within all matter and forms of life. When we are in tune with this primal force, our resultant expressions reflect its purity, and the ramifications of our actions reflect its goodness. But if we are not connected to Source, our intention will tend to be more self-serving, and the resulting responses will reflect that as well.

To understand and deal most effectively with the Law of Karma, we need to realize that action not only includes what we intend (cause) but also what we create through it (effect). Karma is not the "Law of Bad" or the embodiment of the Grim Reaper. Action alone does not necessarily lead to recrimination or punishment. The purpose and plan behind the action is key. If we do something with altruistic intention that leads to pain and suffering, the karmic consequence is different than if we act out of self-interest and inflict a similar degree of pain and suffering.

The karma of our actions is not limited to physical manifestation. Anything we put out into the world generates karma. Conversing with a friend generates karma. If words are intended to inspire or bring clarity to someone else, this generates a similar response from the universe. But if we are gossiping or sharing unpleasant information about a person or an incident, this will generate a totally different response. It was noted in chapter 1 that all action originates in emotion, moves into thought, and eventually reaches outward expression. Even if we don't share our feelings or thoughts with anyone else, the fact that we are entertaining them generates karma. Betty Bethards was fond of saying, "Thoughts are things." By simply conceiving of a thought-form and entertaining it in our mind, the energy generating that thought creates ramifications.

Continuing to feel, think, or act in certain ways increases the likelihood that these expressions become habits. Over time, these habits become deeper and more affirmed, as if we were scoring a groove in our being through which energy will flow. The deeper the groove, the easier it is for the energy to run there, and the harder it is to redirect the stream. The more we allow the energy to move along the course of least resistance, the more ingrained the patterns and behaviors become—and the more likely they are to continue. The nature and quality of those energy patterns will determine our karma and, ultimately, the nature and quality of our life.

Karma can also be a collective phenomena. All of us alive today are currently reaping the results of past actions taken within our family, ethnic group, and country. Collective karma envelops everyone, within any social or ethnic context. There is an old saying, "May we be blessed to live in a time of tumultuous change." This may seem like an oxymoron. How could it be a blessing to live in chaos? Turmoil provides an opportunity to exercise our personal creativity in a way that, combined with others' creative efforts, can generate a healthier, more enlightened collective reality. When forced to respond to turmoil, we also participate in the creation of new karma that will involve and circulate throughout each person in the collective. In a more stable time, the necessity, the opportunity, and the will required to create new dynamics would not be present.

In our own personal experience we have complete control over how we respond to past karma and the karma we create in the future. We are ultimately responsible for balancing our own karmic ledger. In the bigger picture, we also share the karma of what has already taken place with thousands or even tens of thousands of people. For example, racism in the United States is a shameful scourge that permeates all of society. No doubt, in the case of African Americans, it stems from the kidnapping and enslavement of their ancestors, dating to a time prior to the American Revolution. As someone born in the mid-twentieth century with European ancestors, I can claim no connection to that. I didn't create slavery, and had I been alive at that time, I would not have condoned slavery or owned any slaves. Therefore, racism toward African Americans in the United States is not my issue. I live in this society, however, and its cultural ethos affects me. Certainly my interaction with other people, not to mention the political climate in which I am living, is influenced by slavery-based racism. To claim that it is not my concern is either ignorance or denial. I have to deal with this whether I want to or not. By acknowledging the existence of racism, I can be more conscious in the creation of new social patterns and behavioral norms that will permeate the culture of the future.

Astrological Correlation

The astrological sign that embodies the Law of Karma is Capricorn. Capricorn is an earth sign. Consequently, its orientation is to be traditional, cautious, and conservative. It wants to do what is commonly acceptable, so it prioritizes knowing the rules and then endeavors to function within the context of those rules.

Capricorn is ambitious and competitive. It will either create a structure through which to achieve its goals or choose to function within a previously created framework that will enable it to achieve its objectives.

Capricorn can be group-oriented. This can manifest as being good leaders and organizers. It can also allow the Capricorn to feel comfortable on stage, enjoying the attention and appreciation of an audience.

Capricorn is concerned with authority. The question is, whose authority? If Capricorns are centered, they view themselves as the prime authority figure in their life. They strive to act within a clearly defined framework that enables them to be productive within a self-defined context of integrity and personal honor. The person they are trying to impress with their actions is themselves. If Capricorns are off-center, however, they will tend to try to impress external authorities from whom they seek recognition and approval.

The higher octave of this sign is activated through personal responsibility. When we strive for total responsibility for all our feelings, thoughts, and actions, we are clear in our intentions and the ways in which we strive to implement them. Self-control and self-discipline are key allies in this quest. The lower-octave manifestation of the Capricorn leads him to be controlling in situations and to try to control the others involved. The off-center Capricorn can strive to take responsibility for things that do not pertain to her. Whether we seek to control others or allow ourselves to be controlled by their issues, the result is limitation. Although it is obvious that off-center choices and actions limit others, what might not be so clear is that in so doing, we also limit ourselves. This restriction comes from being focused on controlling others or by demanding what others should do for us or for themselves.

While the concept of limitation is central to this sign, it is not always a negative one. The primary orientation of Capricorn is to be productive, but if we do not define restrictive parameters on our actions, our productivity diminishes. If, however, we limit ourselves to a specific point of focus, to a particular goal we are striving to achieve, we can allocate all our resources in that direction, and our chances for success are increased. Similarly, by consciously and deliberately choosing the ways in which we are limited, we conserve energy that we can apply to other areas of life. For example, if we work hard in our youth, we ensure a more prosperous retirement. If, on the other hand, we extend our adolescence and avoid taking our adult self seriously, we may feel free in youth but become severely restricted in old age.

The centered Capricorn is responsible, hard-working, and honorable in its actions. The off-centered Capricorn will tend to be inhibited, fearful, and manipulative. In either case, Capricorn is action-oriented—a perfect sign to represent the Law of Karma.

How to Align with This Law

Understanding and working effectively with the Law of Karma requires acceptance of personal responsibility. Ultimately, this means learning how to accept total responsibility for all feelings, thoughts, and actions. Each of us has work to do in this respect. We may be a housewife, doctor, teacher, carpenter, chef, gardener, or entrepreneur. We might be a parent, a poet, or a politician. In addition to our roles and professions, we also have another job: taking responsibility for the energy we generate in all situations and at all times. Our manifestations, as well as the intentions behind them, will create the degree to which we are limited or liberated in our life.

Our current condition is a direct result of what we generated in the past. As discussed in chapter 4, "The Law of the Eternal Present," our experience in childhood was a direct result of the karma we created in past lives. Similarly, whatever we are experiencing as an adult is a result of what we've felt, thought, and done since childhood. There are no victims. Nobody "does" anything to us that we have not set up ourselves. The Hermeticists of the Middle Ages were disciples of the Greek teacher Hermes Trismegistus, who shared his knowledge of alchemy and high magic with his students. He himself gained his knowledge from the god Hermes. The twentieth-century scholar Walter Scott wrote: "Hermes was a traveling god [of the Greeks] who taught people to revere and worship one God." He lived a life of intellectual contemplation and gave little thought to the material world. His disciple was called Hermes Trismegistus, meaning three times the power and knowledge of Hermes.

In their search for divine connection, which was the ultimate purpose of alchemy, the Hermeticists taught that the fourth cause of disease was what they called the Law of Compensation. This required that a person pay for their past "indiscretions and delinquencies." Depressing thought—or liberating reality? The bottom line is that our current situation isn't new. It has been in existence, in some respect, for some time. But whatever our degree of suffering, it is something we can change. Nothing is irremediable. Ultimately, the Law of Karma provides the means of freeing self from confusion, dysfunction, despair, poverty, or illness.

If we can accept the fact that our past choices and actions are the primary causes of our problems, then it is easy to realize that different choices and actions taken in the present are the way out. We are our own savior. Remember that we are a manifestation of the Divine Source. We have all the creative potential of Source. The light that is the spark of our being is a fragment of Oneness. All the purity with which life began remains in our soul. By tapping into that divine birthright, we have access to the energy, clarity, and motivation to alter previous patterns and generate ones that will eventually lead to a lifetime of health, harmony, and happiness.

The first step in this direction is to feel empowered. Are we in control of our life? Do we feel that we are capable of changing our life? If not, why not? Are there areas of life in which we feel stuck or inhibited? We begin by examining our childhood experience. Note any voices that spoke to us in a restrictive, repressive, or dismissive tone and continually reminded us that we were not or could not do this or that. Those voices may still be lurking in our mind and may now be internalized messages that continue to define us. Sometimes those messages were personally directed at us by parents or teachers; sometimes they were part of our family legacy or social context. An example of the former is being told by a jealous or competitive parent that we weren't very pretty, intelligent, or talented.

When children are not offered realistic, healthy choices, they grow up without a sense of personal empowerment. They don't feel as if they have control over their lives. The "family legacy" can be specific to our clan, but it can also apply to all other families of our ethnicity or economic status. Perhaps the programming is a way to cover a racial or ethnic inferiority complex following generations of exploitation or servitude. The family ethos keeps us tied to a certain belief system or mode of behavior. Collective karmic restrictions could be more of a general social stricture, such as "Don't climb trees; it's not ladylike," or "If you're too smart, independent, or assertive, you'll never get a husband." This way of thinking defines the value of a girl, based on her ability to attract a man and fulfill her biological function as a mother, sending an underlying message that the value of a female is dependent on being married. Boys are told, "Be a man; don't show your feelings," or "Make a lot of money in order to support our family." Again, the programming is predicated on living a traditional lifestyle, with no other choices allowed within the cultural context.

Not only can these messages be restrictive, but they may have nothing to do with who we are or what we are meant to do with our life. Timothy Leary was famous for advocating that we all "turn on, tune in, and drop out." His idea was that we should align ourselves with the truth as we perceive it, and eschew the restricted reality defined by our cultural history. He encouraged us to look beyond the traditional social paradigm that places conformity above all other choices or values. The idea was to be one's self and do what we wanted before someone told us to "grow up and get a job." With this in mind, we should first affirm ourselves as the prime source of permission, approval, and recognition. If we go along with other people's ideas and expectations, they will approve of us, giving us strokes and support. But if the expectations don't reflect who we are, we will probably feel dissatisfied, unfulfilled, or resentful. Regardless of how successful we are in conforming to cultural or familial expectations, we are essentially living someone else's reality. Even if we're good at it, it might not fit us. Our parents may relate to us in ways that reveal their own insecurities or their concern for our well-being and happiness. But if these don't reflect our truth, accommodating them will not generate happiness.

One simple way to test our degree of empowerment is to ask ourselves, "Who validates my reality?" There is only one correct answer to this question. By taking the responsibility to affirm that we are the prime authority figure in our life, the one who defines what happiness means as well as how to go about achieving it, we become empowered.

Personal Tools for Altering Karma

Once we are on the path or have achieved personal empowerment, we can access our toolbox. These are the resources and assets available to us that will enable us to change our lives and to alter our karma. The first tool is taking personal responsibility, in terms of self-awareness and personal growth. The next is clarification of goals. Without a clearly defined goal, if we do arrive somewhere the obvious question would be "Where am I, and why am I here?" We may have expended a lot of energy doing something that is only marginally useful or fulfilling. We may have simply perpetrated the negative habits and patterns that created our suffering in the first place. To make sure we are employing self-awareness and setting goals, we need to take a realistic assessment of who and where we are. What do we like about our condition, and what don't we like? When we acknowledge that we created the experiences we are having, even if unconsciously, we start to use our sense of empowerment to create a new reality.

We may have numerous goals. These could include career, financial, social, or relationship issues. Internal goals also need to be on the list. What are we seeking to manifest in terms of peace of mind or relationship to Spirit? A concept that I introduced in my book *Astrology and Consciousness* is "the myth of myself." This is a projected thought-form of who we would like to become. The existence of this person begins as an ideal, a vision of someone we would like to be but at present are not. We begin by defining this person in all ways and areas of life. Each aspect of this image could represent parts of ourselves that we like and want to expand upon or enhance. Other elements could reflect our heroes and heroines or role models from real life, books, or movies. By gathering all the qualities, attitudes, and behaviors of these models and putting them into one context, we define the myth of ourselves. Then we have to do whatever is necessary to become as much like that person as we can, to evolve from myth to manifestation.

One of the qualities necessary for making our myth of self a reality is self-discipline. In his book *Whispers from Eternity*, Paramahansa Yogananda wrote: "The kingdom of my mind is begrimed with ignorance. By steady rains of diligence and self-discipline may I remove from my cities of spiritual carelessness the ancient debris of delusion." It is not an easy process to change the karmic patterns present in our lives. The more focused we are on the goal, however, the faster the change. The key ingredient is self-discipline. Some of our friends and family members may support us in our process; others may not. Those who don't support us probably prefer relating to us in the way we have been because it is comfortable for them. Perhaps the way that the relationship has been enabled them to overlook their own dysfunction and negative karmic patterns. If we change, they are challenged to do the same. They may feel threatened by the forced abandonment of their security system and hence, resent us for creating a life that works for us.

Once our goals are established, we must commit to working diligently and tirelessly until we are who and where we want to be, regardless of feedback or support. Sticking to the path may require letting go of certain things that have brought satisfaction in the past but at the expense of real freedom and happiness. These things can only be accomplished by staying on point and not letting ourselves get distracted by someone else's fears or our own need for security.

To support the development of this discipline, we need to get organized. This process begins by eliminating extraneous activities—things that are not supporting us on our path. On a material level, I try to arrange my physical space so that everything in it reflects my goals in some way. The objects around me support my discipline by being visual reminders of what I am trying to achieve in my life, providing little lifts through my day that enhance my commitment to my goals.

Some of us might resist becoming more organized and remain attached to old and restrictive karmic patterns. For example, one might want to be free to be however or to do whatever seems interesting or fun in the moment. This seeming sense of freedom can actually lead to lack of a big-picture or long-range goal. Therefore, this pattern reflects lack of organization and can prove to be limiting in providing an ongoing and deepening sense of fulfillment or accomplishment.

Developing structure might make us more visible, either to ourselves or to others. Fearful of what might be revealed, we remain absorbed in the chaos. We may feel safe but in fact remain stagnant. We need to find the courage to risk putting forth a new image.

Organization also implies efficiency—learning how to work smarter, not harder. This can be done by doing something quickly, without sacrificing quality. This maximizes our time for doing things that really feed us and enables us to break old, restrictive karmic patterns. By becoming more aware of the logistics of our time and activities, we can change a karmic pattern. Developing a sense of empowerment, becoming self-disciplined, and getting organized can lead to creating positive karma, providing the basis of what will eventually be a happy life.

A final component in consciously creating our own karma involves time. As said before, an understanding of what we are experiencing in our life right now is a culmination of previous feelings, thoughts, and actions. These are not going to change quickly. Certainly, patterns that we have recently created will leave soon and can be replaced quickly. But most of the more serious issues have evolved to a deep, even primal level of our being. They will need to be extricated with diligence, discipline, and patience. Time is an aspect of existence that is unique to human beings. The only thing that resembles what we call time are the cycles of heavenly bodies that move through space in definable orbits. Events such as the annual solar cycle, highlighted by the solstices and equinoxes, or the monthly lunar cycle, highlighted by the new and full moons every fourteen days, create a temporal environment that provides a context for human activities.

Human beings developed the concept of time to mark their temporary stay on this plane of being. Ultimately, however, time is an illusion. Beyond the observable, predictable cycles, time is a human-made construct that helps to provide us with a sense of control. The more specific and minute the time measurement, the more illusory it is. The concepts of hours, days of the week, or months of the year are helpful in broad contexts only. The notion of time helps us deal with what might otherwise be fear and awe at the overwhelming forces of nature. Time is also beneficial for survival to know, for example, in what season to plant or to harvest, or at which full moon to migrate to the summer highlands. The sense of time I am referring to is not measured by clocks and calendars; it is measured qualitatively by our own progress. Empowerment, discipline, and organization are the prime tools to work with. Patience through time is the lubrication that enables those behaviors to keep flowing. The greater our growth toward positive karma, the easier is it to be patient with the process.

Not Aligning with This Law

One of the most powerful aspects of the Law of Karma is the lesson it provides in creating our own reality. What we generate through feelings, thoughts, and actions is exactly what comes back to us. In order to take advantage of this principle, we must feel as if we have the freedom and ability to create a good life. Without that sense of empowerment, we don't feel as if we can create it. The assumption of the lack of personal power can cause us to get stuck in fear. Fear, in turn, can cause us to withdraw our creative energies and not even attempt to generate what we want. Fear can also impel us to try to control everything in our environment, including people. Thus, the primary misuse of the Law of Karma occurs when we act to protect ourselves at all costs in order to avoid that which we fear. Instead of prioritizing self-discipline, we try to control other people and events. Behavioral patterns that lead to controlling others are fear-based.

Fear is an interesting emotion. It can be based on the illusion of separation, that somehow we are outside the Oneness, and the support offered to all living creatures excludes us. Feeling fear can in turn generate reasons to be afraid. Our actions can reflect our fears when we pull away from others and become defensive. We can restrict our actions, choices, and relationships in order to avoid what we fear. Fear often pertains to the loss of something precious. Some fears are valid; others are not. Some fears are ours; others are not. We can be inundated by fears in childhood. Children can internalize their fears in the same way they internalize how to tie their shoes, seeing the fearful perspective as "just the way it is." Some of these early fears could be ethnic or tribal fears passed from generation to generation. Some may be more specific to our parents and nuclear family. For example, if our parents are unhappily married, we could avoid a committed relationship as adults. We may fear that our marriage will be unhappy as well. If the fear is irrational, nothing we do that appears logical will be effective, because we are not addressing the underlying emotion. If the fear is of something real, we can overcome it by being persistent in our awareness and our actions. Some fears can be quite valid, such as the fear of being hungry or homeless. My father's greatest fear was of being "old, lonely, and broke." But he responded to these fears with responsibility and hard work. Because he was so friendly and gentle, the probability of his being alone was slim. Because he was so hard-working, the potential for him to have little or no money was unrealistic. There was nothing he could do about getting old. As noted in chapter 6, we can minimize the experience of aging through proper health maintenance of body, mind, and soul, thereby diminishing the fear of something disastrous. Fortunately for my father, none of his fears was realized.

Some fears we can pick up from the media. We might become so imprinted by the daily misery in the world that we fear fire, robbery, or rape. Certainly, any of these experiences are possible, but it is unrealistic to become so consumed with fear of them that we make decisions and alter our life in order to avoid them.

Step one in dealing with fears is defining what they are. Once they have been defined, we can question if they are ours, or if we picked them up from someone else. As we separate from others, the next question is whether our fears are realistic. If not, we need to let them go. If they are, the final question to ask is: Are they real in present time? Our fears might be appropriate for a child or young adult. Or they might be significant for someone in a different status or stage of life, none of which applies to us. With this clarity, we can design a strategy to help us feel more empowered.

Dealing with our fears is unavoidable. If we're not doing this work, we may attract whatever it is we fear. Sooner or later, the fears will knock on our door, and we will have no choice but to deal with them. Until that point we may attempt to deflect what we fear without developing the sense of security that comes from overcoming it. There are many such coping mechanisms, and they all have to do with power and control. One method is to give our power away to someone else, who then becomes an external authority figure. We strive to please this person and conform to his or her values, needs, or even lifestyle. If we can receive approving feedback and recognition, we assume we will be safe. This authority figure could be a parent, partner, employer, the government, or a political figure. When we do this, we give away the power to create ourselves and our lives. We give away our power by allowing others to define, validate, or justify who we are and what we are doing. We give away our power when we allow other people's ideas of reality to define us. This is the same strategy animals employ when confronted with a bigger, stronger animal—they lie down and roll over. In so doing they put themselves in such a vulnerable position that they are not perceived as a threat. They hope to be left alone or at least not harmed. This is an ineffectual strategy for two reasons. It deprives us of the ability to create our own life or even to avail ourselves of realistic, desirable opportunities. Even if we deny our power in order to appear nonthreatening, there is no guarantee that we will not be harmed or taken advantage of. Ultimately, this strategy restricts our choices and causes us to feel inhibited. By not claiming and owning our power, our life will reflect other people's choices, leading to our feeling unfulfilled.

Misuse of the Law of Karma can also happen when we attempt to usurp others' power from them. This could be the basic domineering pattern of intimidating others so that they conform to our choices or needs. We might threaten someone physically or be verbally and emotionally abusive in order to manipulate them to be and do what we want. We might perceive life as a series of situations in which someone is in control and everyone else is not. Under these conditions, most people would prefer to be the one at the top, the one who gets to define the common reality and everyone else's role in it. But this is not the nature of reality. The karma generated by being a bully is to be bullied by others. At best, others will either dislike us or keep their distance. The desire to avoid being controlled can create a whole new series of problems.

Another abuse of the Law of Karma is codependency. Codependency is a pattern of relating in which other people's needs are consistently put before our own. This could be the result of projecting our needs or issues onto someone else or a way of avoiding responsibility for them by focusing our time and energy on helping someone to achieve their goals or desires. The cost of our actions could be doing something that is less than meaningful and satisfying to us.

Codependency can also be a form of control. Rather than browbeating or coercing others into submission, we might insinuate ourselves into their lives and their decision-making processes. This is an attempt to take responsibility for them, depriving them of that right, thereby avoiding taking responsibility for our own issues. Being codependent can also involve manipulating someone else to deal with our problems, while avoiding working to resolve them ourselves.

To be fair, we could be well-intentioned in offering help to others. We could attempt to offer assistance to someone in need but go too far. In this case, we lack the healthy limits and boundaries that should exist between us and others and as such, we exemplify "wrong action." This strategy allows us to avoid doing our personal work, while appearing as "the good guy" who helps out everybody else. We wind up depriving ourselves, as well as the other person, the opportunity to confront our own demons and to grow and become empowered through the process. In this way, we resist looking at the very issues that keep us in a fear-based state. The only people we should ever take responsibility for in an ongoing way are our children or other truly dependent people, such as elderly parents. Even then, the responsibility is limited both in scope and time. As a parent, our job is help our children grow roots and wings. When it's time for them to fly, we must cut the cord and send them forth with love. The lesson here is that instead of controlling others, we should look within self. Whatever we resist persists. Through resistance, we engage and support the very things we fear the most.

Another way we might misuse the Law of Karma is through guilt. In a legal context, being guilty means breaking the law. In our context, however, guilt is used to cover up something that might feel awkward or uncomfortable. We could feel guilty ourselves or manipulate someone else to feel guilty. Either case is an example of avoidance. Feeling guilty could be a way to avoid feeling something painful or dealing with something we find difficult. For example, we could feel guilty that our best friend has lost his job, while we just got a promotion. Our guilt could be covering up our own fears of job loss and poverty, or the fear that our friend won't like us because we are more successful than he is.

Similarly, we might feel guilty about our bounty. We may have wealth, or be talented, or have good health, or have other qualities that surpass those of most people. These qualities are parts of who we are because we have earned them. They are examples of good karma, blessings we have earned from past feelings, thoughts, and actions. They are not blind luck but the Law of Karma at work. If others want to be as we are, they are free to amass the same things we have by working as diligently and conscientiously as we have done to create them. The challenge to those of us who have earned these blessings is to continue on our path of right intention and right action. This will enable us to maintain what we have and even add to it. If we take our good karma for granted, however, we could squander in this life what we have worked so hard for in past lives. Beneficial qualities will not follow us into the next life unless we continue to nurture and develop them.

We could also feel guilty when we don't fulfill someone else's expectations. We might decide to become an artist rather than the physician or attorney our parents wanted us to be. In my case, my parents' programming was to lead me to an acceptable profession. Attorney, physician, or professor would have been just fine. Unfortunately, I fell in love with astrology when I was a twenty-year-old college student, and the die for my professional life was cast. Similarly, we might decide not to have children, preventing our parents from fulfilling their dream of being grandparents. We could also speak out about something important to us, rather than going along with someone else's choice or idea. This might cause a friend or partner to have second thoughts or lose some excitement over an anticipated experience. It's a hard choice either way: if we don't speak out, we're giving away our power; if we do speak out, we feel guilty. By owning our opinion, we establish our position in the situation, take responsibility for who we are, and challenge others to take another look at their intentions. They may decide to pursue their plans anyway, without our encouragement or participation. Or, upon further review, they might decide to alter them.

Another aspect of guilt goes back to the idea of doing something wrong. We may not be breaking a law; we may simply be doing something that we know is wrong, immoral, or unethical. Rather than changing our behavior, we persist in the habit, preferring guilt to facing the change we need to make.

The Law of Karma insists that we do things in a thoughtful, methodical way. This can run counter to the Law of Creativity, which supports our being spontaneous and courageous in trying new activities. One of the challenges we must respond to in applying universal principles to our daily lives is that of integrating seemingly incongruous rules into our behavior. One way of responding to this particular challenge is through trial and error. We will likely find that too much spontaneity can limit responsibility, and too much conscientiousness can limit creativity. By working consciously to integrate the qualities of both of these laws, they can function effectively in our life.

The Law of Karma is the one law that requires that we work with it throughout our entire life, because what we choose to do today and how we choose to do it affects us both now and in the future. Since everything we feel, think, and do becomes part of our karmic ledger, failing to access this law with consciousness can create debits in the ledger that will inevitably need to be paid off.

Spiritual Opportunity

Do unto others as you would have them do unto you. This sounds so simple. If everyone followed the Golden Rule, we would all create positive karma for ourselves, and the world would be a better, safer, happier place.

Because all of the universal principles are interconnected, if we pay conscious attention and willingly embrace the other principles, we will find that we accrue beneficial equity in the universal bank of karma. The more consistent and conscientious we are in this process, the more we can participate in the creation of our reality. This enables us to develop single-pointed concentration and greater clarity of mind. The immediate payoff of such mental discipline is the ability to remain focused on the choices and decisions we make and to ensure that they are aligned with our values and priorities. The more clarity we have about our intentions, the greater the potential for fulfillment and happiness. If our goals are oriented only toward material security and satisfaction, we may feel as if something is missing. If our goals are oriented toward eternal fulfillment, the security we achieve can be profound. The goals that we seek to achieve and the consistency with which we pursue them will determine our degree of satisfaction and fulfillment in this lifetime and beyond.

Yogananda said, "An evil action against society is a crime; an evil action against the welfare of the soul is a sin." If we are too identified with the material plane and all of its sense pleasures, we become confused and lose our connection to Divine Oneness. It is not a vengeful God who punishes us for turning away from the development of or identification with our own higher being. We are judge, jury, and executioner of our own destiny. But when we are uncentered, acting from a point of self-interest and prioritizing material gratification, we limit the karmic compensation of our life. Prioritizing personal responsibility enables us to work within the context of the universal laws and to realize the karmic benefits accordingly.

The Question of Free Will

The ultimate benefit of embracing the Law of Karma is freedom. The more conscious we are of what we are doing and why, the fewer obstructions we create for ourselves. The *I Ching* reminds us, "All life is conditioned and unfree. The only way we can even approximate freedom is to consciously choose how we will be limited." For example, if we pay attention to our exercise and diet, we might limit what we do and what we eat. We follow a daily routine that prioritizes a healthful lifestyle. We put certain limits on ourselves now and thereby maximize our opportunity for a longer, healthy life. Conversely, we might allow ourselves the freedom to do whatever we like and eat whatever we choose. In the long run, our health and well-being will then be limited. The key factors in making this decision are personal responsibility and self-discipline. By challenging ourselves to be conscious and self-aware in the moment, we function within a context of realistic limits.

Notice the connection between the Law of Karma and the law opposite to it on the wheel, the Law of the Eternal Present. By practicing being present, we create the quality of our life in the future. We accept what we can do and acknowledge what we cannot. In the twelve-step programs, the familiar motto is the serenity prayer: "God, grant me the serenity to accept the things I cannot change, the courage to change the things I can, and the wisdom to know the difference."

The choices we make, based on our realistic limits and boundaries, will determine the degree and quality of future karma. The limits in this sense mean the confines within which we choose to live. In addition to lifestyle matters, these could include the amount of time, energy, resources, interest, or motivation that we have in relationship to a certain person or part of our life. Boundaries are like the proverbial line drawn in the sand. They are our way of telling others how much we are willing to put up with from them.

This brings up the question of how much choice any of us really has in determining our experience in life. Freedom pertains to the application of willpower. There is a legitimate debate about the degree to which human beings have free will—or if such a thing exists at all. We seem defined and limited by so many external factors, from our childhood experiences, to the need to satisfy our physical and emotional drives and desires, to the need to pay "the cost of living." This is a phrase that usually pertains to our regular financial obligations, but I am using it in this context to include the emotional, psychological, and social costs that face us simply by being alive on this planet. We were born to the circumstances of our situation and yet don't seem to have had any choice in that matter, relative to other choices that might have been available. We are constantly confronted by the "haves" of daily existence and are sometimes overwhelmed by our own limitations, as well as external limitations. Many of us are constrained by our economic realities and the existential dilemma of time and place. We certainly are limited in our choices of when, where, and how we will die. What kind of free will does any of this illustrate?

The French philosopher Thomas Kempis wrote "Man proposes but God disposes." We may think we are writing our life's script, but the reality is that we are only free to exercise our creativity in responding to the conditions pre-established by the universal laws. The big picture is that we live in a universe defined by specific parameters. It is a system that functions in a cogent, orderly manner, using consistent rules and regulations. Scientists try to define these factors by using logic and analysis. We can also divine them in more intuitive or mystical ways. These principles could pertain to physical laws of nature or to human experience. The more we become familiar with what they are and how to work with them, the more we can apply our will and actions to conform to the big picture. Such a construct, however, is merely a recipe, providing the ingredients for the creation of our life experience but not the final product.

Ultimately, there will be uncertainty, chaos, and the always-present mystery of life that is part of the mix. How we integrate all of these factors is up to us. Whatever our experience in life, it must be defined and perceived within the same framework that applies to everything. In this sense, we are all limited. But by applying and working with the Law of Karma, we can come to realize and accept that many of the conditions of our life have been predetermined—not by some external arbiter of the universe, such as a jealous and vengeful god, or by a screwball trickster spirit, or by random chance. The circumstances were determined by our own choices and actions in the past. Ultimately, this is good news. Regardless of our pain, suffering, or alienation, if we accept the fact that we are creating reality, then we choose to work with the forces available to alter our situation for the better.

The spiritual quality associated with this law is *initiation*. An initiate is one who has learned to control him- or herself in relationship to emotional, mental, and physical drives and manifestations. This self-control leads to personal power. The power is meant to be used for the benefit of others, not the control of them. The initiates of the ancient Greek mystery schools were said to have been the founders of the sciences and philosophy, the generators of arts and crafts. They and their work formed the connection between the Divine and the mundane. The initiate was one who had successfully passed a series of tests, the most serious and significant being a personal rebirth. In the Druidic mysteries of the British Isles, a person seeking initiation was sent out to sea in an open boat. As we might imagine, many people lost their lives in this ordeal. The ones who returned were said to be "reborn" and were worthy of being instructed in the most powerful truths that had been preserved since antiquity. The biblical story of Jonah and the whale describes a similar trial. The whale can be seen as a metaphor for the pain of ignorance which engulfs a soul upon being born into a body. But it can also relate to the compassion of Providence that ushers to safety whoever is lost. In either case, upon release from the captivity of ignorance and confusion, one is initiated into the glory and beauty of life.

The initiate, therefore, is one who seeks, perseveres, and attains a higher state of awareness, a more expanded perspective on life. In turn, this consciousness confers certain powers and abilities that enable one to live a more empowered, creative, and liberated existence.

There is a marvelous story about a boy born into a noble family in ancient Egypt. The high priests recognized him immediately as a very highly evolved being. They trained him at the most exalted level of spiritual instruction. At a very young age, he earned the right to be initiated into the highest rank of Egyptian mysticism. The initiation ritual involved his walking down the path of a labyrinth into the deepest recesses of a sacred cave. Part way down that path, he was met by two young priests who instructed him to disrobe. They then proceeded to anoint his body with sacred oil and told him to continue down the path. As he descended, he felt himself getting weaker and weaker. The light grew dimmer. He realized he was dying and that the young priests had poisoned him. Apparently, they were jealous of his brilliance, ability, and youth. They were afraid that he would ascend beyond them in terms of recognition and spiritual and personal power. So they decided to kill him. With his last breath, he cursed them and their ancestors for generations to come.

In his next life, this initiate was born to an illiterate peasant who lived in a tiny cabin in the mountains. The peasant's wife had become pregnant late in life. Prior to her pregnancy, they were very happy and enjoyed each other immensely. Unfortunately, the wife died in childbirth. The man was bereft. The only thing in his life that he had loved, the only person that he felt comfortable with, was dead. He blamed the baby. He wrapped the boy in a blanket, walked to a nearby monastery, and left him at the gate. The monks found him, barely alive, and took him in. They raised him as a servant. His life consisted of nothing but hard work and doing the bidding of the monks. There was no warmth, no love, no appreciation. But the boy was still the same being that he had been in Egypt. He just had very different circumstances, and no opportunities presented to him. As he grew up, he learned how to do his chores quickly, leaving time to teach himself how to read. Eventually, he studied herbs. He enjoyed walking high in the mountains, collecting herbs to dry and use medicinally. After a while, people started coming to the monastery to ask the young man to treat them for various ailments. Soon, his reputation spread throughout the land. He was recognized as a brilliant healer, the same recognition that had come to him as a spiritual initiate in Egypt.

One day as he was hiking in the mountains, gathering wild herbs, he heard a noise behind him. Two young monks jumped out from behind some rocks and pushed him over the edge of the cliff. He had turned and had seen them just before the attack. He realized that these were the same beings who had poisoned him in his last life. But this time, instead of cursing them—and thereby creating the karma of an unpleasant lifetime—he smiled and blessed them, even as he fell to his death.

The Law of Karma asks the questions: What do we want, and what are we willing to do to achieve it? If our goals are motivated by self-interest and personal gratification, we may achieve those aims, but at what price? What will we be sacrificing in the long run? On the other hand, if our goals involve the development of the radiant self, seeking to become an embodiment of the Divine, and affirming the sanctity of our being and of life itself, gratification may be delayed. We will, of necessity, have to work through our own karmic choices and with the universal laws but eventually, we will be liberated in consciousness. Instead of identifying with our own limited material existence, we will awaken to the sacredness of life and to our own birthright as a divine being, a child of the light. We will become initiated.

An initiate is one who has attained a mystical awareness. By successfully passing through a series of tests, the initiate is given access to profound spiritual teachings. By mastering these lessons, he or she is given access to power. Three of these tests are reflected in the Laws of the Eternal Present, of Service, and of Eternal Life. If we are able to focus in the moment, being present to our immediate experience, and are careful to consistently express ourselves from the center of our being, we pass one test. If we dedicate our lives in some way to serving, intending to improve the quality or nature of life for other beings, we pass another test. If we are able to understand that death is like the end of a sentence and that after the period, a new one begins, we have passed another test. Responding with consciousness and clarity to these principles enables us to conquer our lower nature of physical desires and attachments and to start relating to life from the perspective of our higher being. For example, by consciously undergoing a significant personal transformation, we can move beyond the fundamental duality of life, which is death and rebirth. We can experientially understand that duality dissolves into the eternal unity.

Living within the context of these laws is an initiation in and of itself. Beyond that, we can be offered the opportunity to learn and have access to sacred information about the nature of life. With this understanding comes the ability to work with the elements of life in ways that are not only creative but that can also have profound influences on other people. Through the magnetism of our clarity, we can function as leaders, teachers, and healers who can guide others to a similar place of peace and power. This effect could arise spontaneously. Or we could deliberately choose to be a teacher, healer, counselor, or minister, and work with individuals in ways that enable them to work through and overcome their karmic conditions. We could function as an organizer of groups, seeking to affect the experience of large numbers of people simultaneously. If we function in a spiritual context as a minister or in a political context as community organizer, labor leader, or politician, we can integrate our awareness and personal development within a context that offers practical guidance and support to others. We could choose to be a physician, dedicated to helping the people in a third-world country or an urban ghetto in the United States. Whatever our choice or the specifics of the scenario, the effect of our words and actions will stimulate others to emulate our choices. Those affected could be motivated to work on themselves to overcome their karmic patterns and attachments, so that they might taste the power, love, and liberation available to them. When we serve as a conduit of consciousness, we offer this opportunity to others. As a mystic or an initiate, we chose a path guided by Spirit rather than by our own desires.

If we are in a position where we help others, it is imperative that we continue on our own path, as our primary responsibility is to continue our own growth and evolutionary development. We can always attain more clarity, more consciousness, more liberation. There is an allegorical story about a man climbing a tall mountain. As he climbs, his vision remains steadfast on the peak—achieving this destination is the goal of this life, and the mountain symbolizes his path. The peak represents the point of Oneness. As he ascends, his mind resides resolutely on that goal in single-pointed focus. The higher he climbs, the more enlightened he becomes. As he approaches his destination he hears a noise behind him. At first, it's very quiet, like a subtle humming. Gradually, it becomes louder, almost to the point of distraction and discomfort. Eventually, he turns around to see what is making this noise. A large crowd of people are following him up the mountain. This is the critical point of initiation. He could be tempted to assume that they are following him, that he is their goal and destination, rather than that they simply on the same path as he and pursuing the same goal of enlightenment. If he gives in to this temptation, he turns fully around to welcome them and assumes the role of their leader. But if he abandons his original goal, all further growth stops, or is at least restricted. In turn, that which he will have to offer his followers is limited to whatever he has already achieved. But if, upon noting the people, he turns right back to his path and continues his ascent, he will not only continue his own development but will inevitably lead the people to the same glorious peak of realization.

The Bottom Line

To blame and rail against external forces, such as our parents, the government, or even God, as the cause of our suffering is an affirmation that continues our suffering or frustration. It leaves us feeling victimized and unempowered. Our existence becomes based in fear, and our experiences are limited accordingly. If we can change our thinking and accept our lot as a result of our own past choices and decisions, we simultaneously liberate ourselves from the past and empower ourselves to create a different future.

The way to eliminate fear from our life is through responsibility and faith. (Faith will be addressed in chapter 12.) Responsibility is the prodigal child of the Law of Karma. By directing our attention to what we are doing, at all times in every way, we learn about personal responsibility. Everything that emanates from our being—whether a feeling, thought, or action—is a blueprint for manifestation and will have an equal and similar effect. To take responsibility is to discipline ourselves—mind, body, and soul—so that we are aware and in control of what we are doing. In so doing, we gain control, both of the conditions of our own life experience and the way we impact the world.

Affirmation: "I welcome the divine light of being into my life by purifying all my past karma and re-creating my identity in a context of sacredness."

> *Do not overlook negative actions merely because they are small; however small a spark may be, it can burn down a haystack as big as a mountain. Do not overlook tiny good actions, thinking they are of no benefit, even tiny drops of water in the end will fill a huge vessel.*
>
> —Buddha

Chapter 11: The Law of Impermanence

> *Everything in our experience is subject to impermanence. Recognizing this truth is fundamental to developing a spiritual perspective.*
>
> —Chagdud Tulku in *Gates of Buddhist Practice*

Both my college degrees are in the field of humanities. One of the requirements for receiving my master's degree was to be familiar with certain "master works." This involved choosing five creations that were written, composed, painted, choreographed, designed, or built in any historical time period and in any cultural context. The challenge was to weave together these various strands of human creation, regardless of the medium or cultural origin, and be able to analyze and describe how they reflect the nature of the human experience. One of the pieces I chose was a chapter from a book by the German philosopher Oswald Spengler. The book was titled *The Decline of the West*, and the chapter I chose was "The Soul of the City." One of the reasons I was drawn to this book is that it was published in Nazi Germany in 1926 and clearly posited the idea that Western civilization had already reached its highest level of development and was beginning its long, slow decline. Considering that Germany at that time was extolling the virtues of "the super race" and "the super man" in the form of blond-haired, blue-eyed descendents of the Aryan race, this book was heretical. After all, if the "super man" was creating "the super culture," then the best was yet to come. Yet Spengler wrote about a different reality—and somehow got away with it.

The theory expressed in "The Soul of the City" is that all the great cultures of the world have followed, and are following, the same path. They begin as nomadic tribes of hunter-gatherers ("nomadic fellah," in Spengler's terminology) and gradually develop a more sedentary lifestyle by cultivating agriculture and animal husbandry. Eventually, commerce takes hold among different clan groups that live in a similar area. Crops are traded for animals, and animal products are traded for produce. As time goes by, survival becomes easier and the population increases. Work can be completed with time left over to do other things, and culture starts to emerge. In the beginning, culture is usually oriented toward some type of spiritual ritual or experience that is depicted through the arts. Painting and music, including both singing and dancing, are expressed as an offering to the ineffable. These forms, too, evolve, and people start making things that have decorative as well as spiritual value. Certain people choose a lifestyle that enables them to concentrate most of their time and energy on their creativity, using their creations as trade items in exchange for items that are necessary for physical sustenance. These craftspeople and artisans tend to gather and live in small areas, preferring safety and convenience to the wide-open area of the plain, the forest, or the farm. These more contained areas become villages, which in turn become towns. The crafts created in these areas become more extensive. The pottery of one town is seen as desirable and attractive to those in another town, who may offer their beadwork in exchange. Basketry, textiles, shoes, even tools are invented and created in the newly discovered "free time." What might have started as a useful tool or a pretty trinket becomes a valued trade item. More and more people flock to the towns. They, in turn, might bring with them a certain skill or trade item that will provide barter for their survival.

Eventually, one clan group begins to stand out from the others. It may simply be larger and have more people in it, or it may be more organized in producing objects that others deem important and valuable. Or the group may be more effective at creating a religious context or governmental hierarchy. Perhaps they are more aggressive and consciously seek to impose their values and way of life on other groups. Whatever the combination of variables, more power begins to concentrate in the leadership of this clan, and the town that has been its center starts to grow. People from other clans are drawn to this expanding area for protection and security, as well as the creativity. The lure may be the arts, the ideas, and the sophistication, or simply that survival there is based more on refined skills than on hard physical labor.

The town eventually becomes a city. Its influence on the surrounding countryside becomes more extensive. Not only do the people of the city have influence on the aesthetics and values of those still living in the more rural areas, but they also exert profound economic and political influence. People are drawn to this city like a magnet, dazzled by the energy, the power, the excitement, the variety, and the freedom. No longer are they bound by the annual cycle of seasons. No longer are they at the mercy of the weather. They can create their reality in a sustainable and interesting way by using the power of their minds and the dexterity of their hands.

With more people comes more economic and political power, until eventually this city begins to establish dominion over a larger and larger area of land. Spengler calls this "the world city." Every major civilization that has been discovered to date has been centered around such a world city. Every empire that has ever conquered other clans or countries has had a world city that has created the economic foundation and military prowess, as well as an intellectual framework and cultural center from which that empire grew to power. Ancient Greece had Athens. The Roman Empire had Rome. The Aztec Empire had Mexico City. The European empires from the Renaissance to the mid-twentieth century were centered around London, Paris, Lisbon, and Madrid. Today, the world cities are focused more in the United States: New York, Chicago, Los Angeles, San Francisco.

At the peak of their prominence, these empires seemed inviolate. It was inconceivable that any group that had so much power and extended it in so many geographical areas—economically, militarily, theologically, and politically—could be stopped, let alone conquered. To those living under the hegemony of such a dominant culture, it seemed as if it would continue forever.

Spengler points out, however, that despite the impressive power at their peak, none of these world cities and their surrounding empire maintained their dominance. Even more significant is that none was destroyed externally. They were conquered from within, by their own excesses. The drive and moral fiber, the clarity of goal and direction that were present in the beginning, the spark of the village that caused it to grow to a town, then a city, were replaced over time with lethargy, greed, and corruption. Eventually, the world city fell into disrepair and ruin. The empire had outgrown its ability to sustain its own center and to control the areas and peoples that it had conquered. The power and sophistication, which had been so viable and visible, disintegrated. Without the attractions and ease of city life, people returned to the countryside. As the city became less economically dominant, the goods and services produced within it became less valuable, of poorer quality, and eventually ceased to exist. People had to once again rely on the land for their survival. The city was reduced to a town and sometimes back to a village. Rather than being a cultural center, it became merely a center for trading commodities. Ultimately, the clan group returned to its primal condition of hunters and gatherers, the nomadic fellah that were at the beginning and end of the cycle.

Different people can be attracted to various parts of this cycle of civilization. One person might want to live in the country and grow his own food, while another prefers the stimulation of the city. And even though this cycle far exceeds the lifetime of one person, or even the collective memory of several generations, it is a mistake to become attached to any part of that cycle or to assume that it will always be as it is. Regardless of how big, how powerful, how dominant one group of people is, and regardless of how advanced they are in terms of inventing and producing technology, history teaches us that eventually they will crumble and be replaced by a new world city. The new urban center will come to power on a new surge of energy, drive, and creativity.

The metaphor of the rise and decline of the world city is a reflection of the individual experience of everything that exists, human or otherwise. As a newborn child, we are in a very dependent state of being. Our whole focus is on survival. As we grow, we become socialized, interacting with extended family, friends, and neighbors. We reach adulthood, perhaps marry, have our own children, and accept responsibilities. Regardless of our degree of success and happiness, however, we and whatever we possess or have done eventually will pass from this plane of consciousness. Nothing ever remains the same. Everything is in a state of continuous change. If something seems unchanging to us, it is a misperception that causes us to experience it that way. We might like to imagine that something or someone we like or love will remain as is. This assumption provides a sense of security and well-being. In reality, this is a false sense of security. This might provide a way of feeling good, safer, or more secure, but real security comes from understanding and working with the universal Law of Impermanence. True liberation comes from the acceptance of this principle.

Astrological Correlation

The sign associated with this law is Aquarius. The nature of the Aquarian experience is to challenge the status quo, to be continually involved in the process of pushing the limits of reality. The progressive, the avant-garde, and the cutting edge is where Aquarius lives. This can manifest both in a metaphysical understanding of life and in social relations. In some respects, Aquarius is idealistic to the point of being utopian. This sign is conscious of and prioritizes the reality of the oneness of the human family. Aquarius espouses the idea that the greatest good for the greatest number of people is the best political philosophy, yet Aquarius is also one of most independent of the twelve signs. The Aquarian challenge is to bridge the gap between championing social causes and the need for complete personal freedom.

The off-center Aquarius will either deal with only one of those points of awareness or will vacillate between the two. In this state, the changes would be sudden, extreme, and rebellious. This is the Aquarian who is perceived as being cold, aloof, and detached, with an imperious attitude toward others that smacks of being the-know-it-all. This type of Aquarian expression embraces change but often in the form of change for the sake of change. Its shifts tend to be born of frustration or boredom and are actually more reactionary (working against the status quo) than they are designed to create or present a new concept of being.

The centered Aquarius, however, is open to being both a source of inspiration for some and inspired by others. The resulting changes will tend to be oriented toward personal liberation in a social context that supports the freedom of the entire human family. The centered Aquarian knows who to relate to, why, and for how long. After a period of social activity, he can retreat to the privacy of his own reality, followed in turn by returning to his social interests in harmonious ways.

Aquarius is comfortable with change. It embraces the idea of impermanence as an opportunity for awakening to new consciousness. Thus, Aquarians can be innovative and experimental, even as they scoff at tradition and convention. After all, why remain attached to something that is going to eventually change? The shift could be imminent or take years to transpire, but change it will nonetheless. Change is life, and life is change.

Aquarius has an affinity with the planet Uranus. Uranus was discovered in 1781, a time when revolutionary ideas and actions were taking hold in the Western world that affected the political and economic forces of the culture. Politically, democratic revolutions took place in the United States and France. The people began to take power and create a reality that was more egalitarian and less hierarchical. Economically, this period marked the beginning of the Industrial Revolution. Inventions were devised that would make life easier and more secure. All of the prime concepts of that period (revolution emanating from and benefitting the masses, and innovational change that challenged and advanced the preexisting reality) are Aquarian.

What the revolutions of this time also brought about, however, was alienation. Prior to the Industrial Revolution, families lived in multigenerational extended families. They subsisted by farming and living off the land or as artisans or craftsmen. What they lacked in creature comforts and material security was compensated for by the closeness of the family. With the revolutions of the late eighteenth century, however, people had to leave the land and their families in order to work in the factories and keep up with the challenges and opportunities of the day. The price they paid for increased material comfort and possessions was alienation. Originally, it was the men who left the family to live in cities and work, as opposed to being independent farmers or craftsmen. Then the women went, and finally, the children. In my family, my grandfather went to work in a factory when he was nine years old in order to help support his family. Even though he continued to go to school, at least part-time, he no doubt suffered from the loss of his childhood and adolescence. Where he did benefit, however, was in understanding the industry that his employer supported. When he turned eighteen, he borrowed some money, opened his own factory, and proceeded to become quite successful until the Great Depression forced the closure of most factories.

Currently, most people of all ages and genders have become alienated from the natural environment, their families, and eventually, themselves. Ultimately, the environment itself has suffered. Some think that we are no longer directly and obviously dependent on nature for survival and have thus been exploiting the material resources of the planet. By no longer directly relating to the environment on a daily basis, we have become either unaware of or uncaring about the damage to the environment.

Even when the Aquarian relates to life in a centered way, integrating collective concern with personal liberation, one must still work to overcome a sense of alienation. This sense could come from relating to life in too idealistic or conceptual a manner or by being so far ahead of the wave of change that the Aquarian winds up being misunderstood or related to as a cranky eccentric. The process of weaving together the threads of humanitarianism with individuation and facilitating social and consciousness change is the ongoing challenge to the Aquarian.

How to Align with This Law

In chapter 7 of the *Tao Te Ching*, Lao Tzu writes: "Heaven and earth last forever. Why do heaven and earth last forever? They are unborn, so ever living. The sage stays behind, thus he is ahead. He is detached, thus at one with all. Through selfless action, he attains fulfillment." The ultimate goal of consciousness development is the ability to perceive and function within a context of life that is whole. Life is a continuum. No beginning, no end. This has been established through the Law of Eternal Life. By extension, the Law of Eternal Life applies to all phenomena. A life begins and then it ends. Thoughts arise and then decline. Relationships begin and then end. If you observe the flow of water through a riverbed, it becomes clear that the river is always changing. The molecules of water move from point to point, never to return. If the temperature drops below 32 degrees Fahrenheit, the water will become ice and cease to flow. As the temperature rises, the ice melts back to its primal form. As the temperature continues to rise, eventually the water evaporates and becomes vapor or steam. If you live along that river long enough, you could experience all three forms of this element. Yet regardless of the changes, its inherent qualities remain. This is true of all material manifestation, because beyond the form of a thing is its inherent essence. The deeper you look into the core of matter, the more you realize that ultimately, all matter is the same, all an expression of the Law of Creation. Eventually, this law meets the Law of Eternal Life, and whatever has been created passes on to a different state of being in a new act of creation. One important way to access the Law of Impermanence is to develop the willingness to allow everything to be exactly what it is: temporary.

There's a story about a Buddhist lama who speaks about enlightenment. His students implore him to teach them how to attain this state. He tells them to meditate on impermanence. "Night turns into day; day turns into night. The seasons change. Once you were young; now you are grown; soon you will be old; then you will pass away. Our body is constantly changing; our environment is constantly changing. There is nothing more important on the journey to enlightenment than to understand the nature of impermanence."

His point is that to meditate on impermanence is to realize that everything we are surrounded by—or think, feel, want, or are—is impermanent. The benefit of becoming aware of this truth is that it provides perspective on that which is *not* impermanent: Divine Oneness.

The mind is continuously changing. One thought after another flows through the mind. One of the techniques of Buddhist meditation is to find the space between thought. We don't try to stop the thoughts; we attempt to notice when one has passed and another has not yet arrived. One way to do this is by noticing the breath. The breath, too, is always changing. We breathe in and breathe out, breathe in and breathe out. The breath is like the mind. Thoughts come and go, as do the breaths. We allow ourselves to breathe in a steady, rhythmic manner. We don't breathe in and hold on to that breath, or breathe out and hold it out. We simply notice the breathing. In a similar fashion, we notice the thoughts flowing in and out. We don't hold on to any specific thought, nor do we attempt to block all thought from our mind. We just notice and in the process, find that precious space between thought. This is the place where we can make the mystical connection to Source.

Expect the Unexpected

One way of accessing the reality of this law is to be open to unexpected changes. We might have a clearly defined goal, a specific intention that is in alignment with the Law of Karma, but it's important to be open to what might spontaneously arise during the course of carrying out that plan. If we are only focused on the goal, our ability to adapt to changing circumstances is limited; consequently, the outcome of the experience will also be limited. It will be less than it could have been had we been open to changing course based on changing circumstances.

An example of how the unexpected can lead to enlightenment is a method used by Zen masters. As a group of people are sitting in meditation, especially on a retreat, the master will walk among them. Suddenly, he might strike one of the meditators. The idea is that the unexpected blow on the hand, arm, back, or head can awaken the aspirant to a new state of consciousness. One might assume that a long period of focus on the empty mind (a Buddhist precept) can awaken the consciousness, which it can, but so, too, can something totally startling.

Spontaneity can also provide access to the Principle of Impermanence. If everything is always changing, then periodically things will occur that were unforeseen. Beyond the methodical cycles and rules prioritized by the Law of Karma, unpredictable phenomena pop up and challenge us to think and act in unconventional and previously unexplored ways. We need to be able to react quickly to these changes and the challenges that they bring. In so doing, we become part of the progressive life experience. Being open in this way enables us to be inventive and innovative in our thoughts, behaviors, and goals. We can adopt new methods of problem-solving and new activities in which to become involved.

Embrace the Unique

Becoming aware of the unique is another way to access this law. Even though everything is in constant flux, each aspect of every change is unique unto itself. Our life is a good example of something that is a continuum of change. We might be so active that we generate numerous changes daily, or we may prefer a life of quiet contemplation that is more predictable. In the former scenario, our changes are more obvious; in the latter, more subtle. These changes are mirrors of who we are. Each shift of circumstance is unique, as we ourselves are unique. Tuning into our uniqueness and becoming aware of what we do—how, why, and with whom we do it—are all parts of our individuated self. In turn, the never-ending changes of our inimitable self reflect the eternal and inimitable changes generated by the Oneness of life.

When we are open to uniqueness, we perceive life in a mystical way, becoming more tuned in to the wonder of everything. Every moment, every person, every experience, every day is unique. Being aware of the uniqueness of any experience enables us to also be open and accepting of how distinct we are. We can allow ourselves to explore and express our individuality without judgment, because we realize that in our singularity we reflect and participate in a natural state of being. Allowing our uniqueness to flow connects us with the continuum of eternally changing life.

Innovation

One element of Spengler's world city is its ability to produce new technologies that enable people to become more efficient and productive. The historical event in our time that generated the most widespread and significant technological breakthroughs was the Industrial Revolution that began in the mid-eighteenth century. During this period, changes were instituted that have continued to affect people, both individually and collectively. This shift so accelerated social change that new social behaviors and institutions have continued to evolve.

Inventions begin as experiments. Not all the inventions—mechanical, scientific, or social—that originated during the Industrial Revolution have prevailed. Some have become obsolete. The important thing is that the concept of innovation was born and became widely accepted as a desirable thing to do. One way to personalize this concept is to define new activities or behaviors as experiments. In a sense, life on the physical plane itself is an invention or experiment. Paleontologists have discovered entire species of life, both animals and plants, that have become extinct. They might have been eliminated by stronger or better-adapted species or simply by changing climatological conditions. One might presume from this that these manifestations of divine creativity were a mistake—failed experiments. But as George Bernard Shaw wrote, "God makes mistakes." Mistakes and failures are natural parts of the continuum of life. Life is always changing, reinventing, refining, and perfecting itself and adapting to the state of impermanence that is its inherent nature. This is a fundamental precept of the Law of Creativity. To become an active, conscious part of this process, it is useful to frame the creation of our life experience as an experiment. If something doesn't work out, at worst you're in the company of God. At best, you can use the experience as an opportunity to learn more about your unique potential and see yourself in the context of the ever-changing reality of life.

As individuals, committing to the experimental life enables us to be more open to inspiration. Inspiration can be surprising. It can lead us into unexpected places, into doing things that we have never done before. Think of being inspired as being "divinely guided." This is different from just having a good idea. An inspiration takes us into uncharted territory, providing an opportunity to wake up to parts of ourselves and to elements of life of which we were previously unaware. Being detached and open to experiment allows us to take risks and to make whatever investments are necessary to embody and take action on our inspiration.

Inspiration and invention are similar in that they stimulate the new. The difference is that inspiration can take us into whole new areas of awareness or experience. It can stimulate and vitalize the soul. Invention is more in the realm of the mental. It is a conscious and deliberate way to manifest either something new or to improve upon something already existing. The former is theoretical; the latter, more practical.

Democracy

An example of an experiment that affects a collective body of people is the form of government called democracy. Never before in the known history of humanity has a large, diverse group of people living in an industrial society sought to live within the context of a democratically elected government. There are numerous examples of indigenous tribes practicing democracy that have done so successfully for hundreds of years. But those societies were ethnically homogenous and lived in small areas and within a relatively simple and materially sustainable context. The democratic revolutions that began in the late eighteenth century are different. Some countries seeking to become democracies were composed of ethnically diverse groups of people, some of whom didn't even speak the same language. These countries' citizens came from different backgrounds and held different values and expectations about life. They were also engaged in different ways of surviving. For the most part, these democratic societies, particularly in the United States and Western Europe, became industrialized. This gave everyone in that country a common focus: generating prosperity and security. They didn't have to rely solely on the land to provide material sustenance. These societies represent the stage of development that distinguishes the "world city," in Spengler's terms.

Democracy was a brand new concept, a whole new way of living. It liberated people from relying for their livelihood on the vagaries of nature, the weather, the crops, the flocks, and the herds. Instead, democracy engendered dependence on the vicissitudes of the employer and the marketplace. In return, citizens were free to choose their leaders. One irony in this freedom is that—at least at the inception of the United States—the only people who were given that freedom were white males who owned property. Much of the economic supremacy generated in the United States was actually based on slave labor and European wealth. Freedom, democracy, and industrial power were limited. Experiments require the flexibility to change conditions once the reality of experience meets the philosophical theory. Thomas Jefferson suggested that in order for a democracy to survive and thrive, it would need a revolution every seventy-five years. Without this, the probability of corruption developing among the political leaders would limit the people's freedom in choosing leaders.

It took almost one hundred years before nonwhite men were allowed to vote, even longer for women of any color. And the experiment continues. There always seems a push/pull of forces that are trying to define exactly on what the United States is based and who is in charge. Is it the movers and shakers of the economic elite—the people who are at the top of the food chain and responsible for hiring other people, who in turn do the actual work of manufacturing? Or is it the people themselves, the ones who do the work? What is the appropriate balance between these two demographics, in terms of making policy decisions that affect the welfare and well-being of all the people? The answer is that the experiment is ongoing. It may, in the long run, not work at all, and one of the groups may seize all the power. Whether that would be good or bad is not the issue. The point is that the experiment would be over; democracy would have run its course. The concept of a popular government of, by, and for the people is a new paradigm. There is always the danger that it could revert back to the power of the few who rule over the citizenry. On the other hand, as long as the groups keep dialoguing, interacting, and trying new and different formulas, the ebb and flow of the experiment will survive.

Detachment

One of the most important qualities that we can develop to enhance our openness to inspiration is detachment. The Law of Karma reminds us of the importance of having a clearly defined goal. Being conscious of our intention and being conscientious in carrying it out enables us to generate the quality of life we desire. Seemingly in contrast, detachment requires that we be focused on the process of what we are doing without expectations. Expectations are not the same as goals. Goals are what we want to achieve. Expectations are our assumptions about what will happen on the journey toward those goals. When we have expectations, we tend to try to control a situation. It's as if our fulfillment comes from something happening in a certain way, rather than from doing it from a place of joy or curiosity, or for the simple satisfaction of doing it. When we act from joy, the divine quality of the Law of Abundance, we bring that law into our lives. When we detach from outcome, we are less controlling and more creative. If we cannot act with detachment, but instead try to bring about a certain end in a certain way, we prioritize expediency and efficiency over creative satisfaction. There probably will be situations in which both the quality of our actions and the results of those actions will be satisfying. But when we focus more on intention and methodology than on outcome, we are more likely to remain in a creative mind space and manifest a higher-quality experience for all concerned.

Not Aligning with This Law

The undergraduate college professor I discussed in chapter 9 who left such a strong mark on me, Ernest Becker, was as inspiring as he was quirky. He was the professor who wanted us to think for ourselves; to delve into the internal wellspring of creativity. Failing to do that, he theorized, would put us under the dominion of the "societal demonic." This is a term he coined that pertains to the shoulds and shouldn'ts that "they" expect us to follow without question. These are the rules and regulations that tend to keep individuals and society locked up in static, predictable patterns. The societal demonic limits our potential to explore, innovate, and experiment. By challenging us to respond to his lectures creatively, Becker attempted to liberate us from those limitations, or at least to realize that there were exciting places that our minds and lives could go that had never been explored. Failure to accept the Law of Impermanence threatens to keep us under the dominion of this very societal demonic.

When we attempt to define something that is as vast and complex as the nature of life, we run the risk of perceiving it as more limited than it really is. In so doing, we restrict our ability to create conscious connection to Oneness. Rather than being open in the here and now to the continuous flow of life energy, we limit our awareness of what life is. Such restriction prevents full access to the Law of Impermanence, because we end up attempting to relate to something as static when it is not. Our definition or conception might provide a sense of security, but it is false. We may want to define life as something we understand and can control, when in fact we can do neither. By attempting to control, we believe that permanence can be accomplished.

Developing detachment is useful, but it can also be a trap. We might cultivate an attitude of detachment to the point of not caring about ourselves or other people. We could become aloof and indifferent, believing that we are superior to others. This isn't detachment at all—narcissism and self-absorption, maybe, but not detachment. Detachment is not lack of caring but rather, lack of attachment to outcome.

Sometimes aloofness can be a behavioral pose through which we attempt to establish our unique identity. We project an attitude of "I don't care about what you think, what you believe, what you say, or what your reaction is to my behavior, appearance, or lifestyle." This really is a form of rebellion, a reaction against the status quo and conventions of behavior. With this attitude, we are more interested in "proving" our uniqueness to others rather than developing it ourselves. Because the social theater in which this scenario is being played out is variable, we have to alter our role in order to impress each different audience. This can lead to a lot of change for change's sake. Such changes are typically not authentic; they merely keep us in reaction mode. Although it may seem as if we are expressing our uniqueness, we are actually allowing the societal demonic to define reality and then seeking to separate ourselves from it. If, on the other hand, we are centered and truly in touch with who we are, we can define and validate our own reality. We can express our uniqueness in a harmonious rather than confrontational way.

I remember a client of mine from many years ago. She was still in high school, but her parents thought it would be useful for her to have an astrological reading. She came into my office in the teenage mode of the day: spiked hair dyed purple and pink, with several earrings in each ear and one in her nose. Her clothing was vintage yet coquettish. She obviously had a lot invested in making others take note of her personal style. When I looked at her chart, I realized that the image she was projecting did not match her real energy. So the first thing I said in the reading was in the form of a question: "You're actually a pretty conservative person, aren't you?" Her eyes got very big, her mouth dropped to her knees, and she just nodded in agreement.

For someone her age, the persona this girl had created through her appearance could be a normal experiment on the road to self-discovery. If the pattern persisted into adulthood, or if a relatively conservative adult suddenly starts acting out in extreme behaviors, one can conclude that the "prove it" game has replaced real individuation. Trying so hard to convince others who we are doesn't leave time or energy to discover who we *really* are, nor does it incline us to validate our own uniqueness. When we rebel from either our own previous patterns or from societal norms and expectations, our focus is more on what and where we have been than on where we are going. Instead of moving forward in an ever-changing creative process, we live our life by looking in the rearview mirror. This can prevent us from clearly seeing our options for moving forward.

Another potential problem with detachment is that it can be symptomatic of alienation. We may feel so different from everybody that we just don't care about anything or anybody, including ourselves. We feel so separate from the world around us that we don't connect with anybody or anything in a meaningful way. This could be due to uncontrollable changes happening around us at a fast pace, with seemingly little or no input from us. We then feel overwhelmed by a sense of insignificance and lack of empowerment. It could also be a result of not engaging in life; we sit on the sidelines, watching things take place while neglecting to jump in and join the flow ourselves.

Another potential misuse of this principle comes from confusing impermanence with chaos. As the universe continually unfolds and re-creates itself, it does so within clearly structured parameters. One of the realizations of the Enlightenment or Age of Reason (from the mid-seventeenth to the end of the eighteenth centuries) was that there is an underlying order within which change takes place. In other words, there are definable rules that control when and how things change. One key to working with the Law of Impermanence is integrating change within structure. Like a parent who defines the family rules and values, we must allow for alterations within preexisting patterns. When there is little or no room for change, stagnation and decay result. Without any rules or a clear and consistent enforcement of them, change becomes haphazard, and time and energy will tend to be wasted.

The Law of Impermanence

Rules not only provide a sense of structure, they also provide a sense of direction. Productivity results from a clearly defined intention that is supported by the freedom to change and grow. Insisting on rules without freedom or freedom without rules dooms us to boredom and resentment toward authority..

The radical changes that have ensued since the beginning of the Industrial Revolution are a reflection of the Principle of Impermanence. Life has changed more since that time than in the previous 2,500 years. But change without direction or healthy priorities undermines the fabric of reality and the quality of life for many beings on this planet. We misuse this law when we fail to commit ourselves to something meaningful, even if it takes a long time to accomplish. We are left in a state of constant change that is born of restlessness, boredom, or frustration. We continuously trade one set of variables for another. The stimulation provided by the change is relatively short-lived, leaving us, once again, discouraged and with our lives in chaos. This is played out by people who constantly change jobs, partners, or living situations. Often this pattern is accompanied by feelings of victimization, as if the external variables (the boss, the sex life, the neighbors) left us no choice but to leave. This pattern indicates that we are avoiding our own responsibility for the changes. Ultimately, this type of change leaves us dissatisfied and unfulfilled.

The Law of Survival provides the impetus to develop patience as a key tool in creating a viable, sustainable life. It can be challenging to be patient in a world of constant change. Since all the laws are always in play, and aligning ourselves with them provides clarity and support for our journey of consciousness development, these laws are not in conflict. Invoking patience in the face of continuous change enables us to be deliberate and thoughtful in our decision-making process. It helps us to respond effectively to a world of continuous change in a way that enables us to create a degree of material safety and comfort. Conflict might ensue, however, if our patience is actually an attempt to slow the changes around us so that they conform to a more enduring rhythm or to a life where nothing changes at all.

If we realize that parts of our life are unacceptable and that we feel stuck, we need to be open to changing them. It is important to remember that when deciding to change a situation, we must always start with ourselves Spend some time on the internal architecture. How did we get involved in the current situation in the first place? Did we create it or just go with the flow? Using this type of self-inquiry, it will become clear which personal internal changes we need to go through before any decisions can be made and before the external change can manifest.

There are two primary paths available to us as we approach change; either or both can be useful in improving our condition. One is to experiment with new possibilities. If we want a new career, we could take a part-time job in the field that appeals to us. With new experience, we would have more data and clarity about the viability of that direction and whether it is worthy of our commitment. We need to be open to the possibility that the experiment may not work out as we had hoped. We may have to take several part-time jobs, eliminating the ones that don't fit, until we find the right one that does. As long as we are configuring this process as an exercise or a process, we realize that there is no failure. If a job doesn't meet our needs, we move on to explore another option. In the process, we also get clearer about our uniqueness, more refined in our thinking, and more likely to make effective, accurate choices for ourselves in the future.

The other avenue of positive change is being open to inspiration. Inspiration is a true child of the Law of Impermanence. When feeling inspired, we should act on it as soon as possible. There is an excitement that accompanies inspiration, but if we wait to act on it, the excitement soon fades. If we feel a sense of exhilaration about a new idea or prospect, this could be sign that we are on the right track and that the change will be a good one. If we don't feel inspired, we could either be more methodical and logical in planning a change or wait patiently for inspiration to strike.

Spiritual Opportunity

By becoming aware of the Principle of Impermanence and accepting the inevitable changes it brings, we get in touch with the greater continuum of life. As we strive for individuation and the development of our uniqueness, we realize that every person, every act, every experience is also unique. This enables us to feel part of the entire human spectrum of experience, to overcome any feelings of alienation, and to become ourselves, creating a viable reality. One of the primary tenets of Buddhism is that while everything in life is separate from every other part, all parts are connected. The analogy often used is of a chain of flower petals. Each petal is distinctly and uniquely different from the others, but they are joined by a thread that has been woven through each, connecting them all to a greater whole.

The ability to manage the balancing act required by this principle is found when we tap into the spiritual quality associated with this law: *wisdom*. Wisdom involves integration. It can be defined as merging the left and right hemispheres of the brain—the logical meeting the intuitive; the linear combining with the creative.

Accessing wisdom also involves interfacing the realm of impermanence with that which lies beyond it: Divine Oneness. In doing so, we become aware of functioning in both arenas and take responsibility for our thoughts, feelings, and actions in both realms, simultaneously and continuously. This challenge is one of integrating the Law of Impermanence with the Law of the Eternal Present. The latter teaches us that our personal experience in the present provide a powerful and compelling connection to the Divine. The Law of Impermanence offers a bigger picture and the opportunity to adopt an objective overview that connects a limitless series of moments into a continuous flow of change. This flow affects and involves everybody and everything. By understanding how these laws are integrated we can connect our personal experience of the moment to the collective consciousness. We develop the ability to flow with life. We create change where we can, or adapt to the preexisting reality if we can't. We remain detached from expectations and outcomes, even if we are the prime mover of a situation. At all times we do the best we can, hoping for the best but accepting the results of our efforts. We learn from our mistakes and move on.

On the wheel of these twelve universal laws, the one opposing the Law of Impermanence is the Law of Love. Love is the prime quality through which we can connect with that which is changeless. The integration of these two principles can come about by first grounding our consciousness in love. This is an eternal quality that is always available to us, regardless of the nature, quality, or rate of change we are experiencing. Knowing that we are connected to life through love connects us to the security of our relationship to the internal divine. From that realization, we can use change as a vehicle for improving our lives without the fear that the changes will lead to loss and instability

In the awareness of the One, we are an agent of the Divine. We realize that we are a limitless manifestation of creation, that the presence of the Divine Being is with us at all times because it *is* us at all times. In this state of mind we always work for the greatest good for the greatest number of living beings. We give to others what it is we have to offer and assume that what we would like or need in return is on its way, according to the same principle.

We develop the perception that everything in manifest form is part of Oneness. Understanding this concept prevents us from falling into the trap of alienation or narcissism, thinking that who we are and where we are in our process is the ultimate or the end, when it is merely part of the transitional flow. This attitude involves accepting change both within and outside of us.

Within, there needs to be constant exploration, experimentation, and expression of all the various parts of ourselves. Any of those parts that are hard to accept need to be integrated and included, not repressed and rejected. The challenge is to transform that lower expression into something more acceptable to us (see "The Law of Eternal Life"). All facets of ourselves are useful, even if merely to act as compost for desirable manifestations later on.

Similarly, we can see all others as reflections or extensions of ourselves. As we strive to integrate all our disparate parts, transmuting and transforming as we go, we can become more compassionate and humanitarian by realizing that everyone else is challenged to do the same. Whether they are actually engaged in this process is not the point, although their inattentiveness to this process may limit our relating to them. Cultivating an inclusive attitude helps us to perceive life as a flow of vibrating, pulsating energy.

Healthy detachment can help us to be inclusive in our attitudes and behavioral patterns. When we aren't trying to control something in order to affect a certain result, we are free to realize how all things play their role in life. We can literally feel the flow of Spirit, the will of God, manifesting through our body, mind, and soul. We can feel included with that vibration and tune in to the eternal creativity and change that is life. In this state of awareness, we know that there is no separation. Life and all its manifestations are a cohesive creation.

The Bottom Line

I love airports. As a child my family moved every few years, so I often felt like an outsider. I developed a sensitivity to being "the new kid," the one who was different. I became familiar with not knowing anyone or knowing what was or was not cool and acceptable. The kids who had been at a school had some sort of predatory right to determine who was and who wasn't cool. But no one lives at an airport. No one has territorial rights there—that's why I like these public spaces. I can't feel like an outsider when there is no one who is an insider. Airports reduce us all to the common denominator of being human. We are all going here or coming from there. But no one is there for very long. The airport is a metaphor for life: we are all just passing through.

The ultimate gift of the Law of Impermanence is liberation. We liberate our mind from our cultural context and the societal shoulds and shouldn'ts (the societal demonic). We liberate our psyche from family programming. We liberate ourselves even from karmic attachments to people, objects, or events. Eventually, our liberation enables us to function within as well as beyond the material plane altogether. We start identifying more as a cosmic citizen, a denizen of the Divine. We understand and accept that the being that we are is eternal, yet it is here in its current form for a relatively short time.

The realization of liberation facilitates a quickening of our evolutionary journey. We are free to identify with the creation and process of change, rather than with the changes themselves. Identifying with the primal cause enables us to be involved in the process of creating the person we want to be, the life we want to live, and the state of consciousness within which we perceive and experience life.

Affirmation: "I accept the permanence of change and the uniqueness of each moment and manifestation within the eternal sea of Oneness."

> *Humility, lack of hypocrisy, harmlessness, forgivingness, uprightness, service, purity of mind and body, steadfastness, self-control;*
>
> *Indifference to sense objects, absence of egotism, understanding of the pain inherent in mortal life: birth, illness, old age and death;*
>
> *Nonattachment, nonidentification of the Self with such as one's children, wife and home requires constant equal-mindedness in desirable and undesirable circumstances;*
>
> *Unswerving devotion to Spirit.*
>
> —Bhagavad-Gita, XIII: 7–11

Chapter 12: The Law of Transcendence

The great Tao flows everywhere, both to the left and to the right.
The ten thousand things depend upon it; it holds nothing back.
It fulfills its purpose silently and makes no claim.

It nourishes the ten thousand things,
And yet is not their lord.
It has no aim; it is very small.

The ten thousand things return to it,
Yet it is not their lord,
It is very great.

It does not show greatness,
And is therefore truly great.

—*Tao Te Ching*, verse 34

My five children are an important part of my life. Two live in the same area as I do, but the other three live far away. It's a rare event when we are all in the same place at the same time. At a July 4 gathering a couple of years ago, the entire clan came to our house for a barbecue. Late in the afternoon I went into my vegetable garden in the backyard to water the plants. The garden is quite small, a bed each of tomatoes, peppers, lettuce, and corn, and I usually water it several times a week in the summer. Although this was a routine practice, somehow this time, I felt a deep internal glow as I watered. It started in my belly, then quickly rose to my heart. The expression "feeling the Oneness" came to mind as I looked around me and felt absolutely connected to everything I saw. Each plant was alive with radiant light. Each leaf seemed to wave at me in a gesture of welcoming embrace. The air circulated through me, and everything else, organic or otherwise, that I saw connected us in a divine dance of interactive forms and colors. Across my mind came the words: "Practice being in the presence of God."

I blinked my eyes a few times to clear my vision from this apparent hallucination. But each time I opened them the vision was the same. I went into logical mode and questioned why this was happening. I love my garden, but it's such a regular part of my life that just being in it wasn't going to throw me into an altered state of consciousness. Certainly my heart was more open than usual, due to my children and grandchildren all being present and having a good reunion. Perhaps this was the catalyst. But in the end, once I turned off the analytical mind, I felt that although this was an unusual experience for me, it wasn't bizarre, unique, or hallucinogenic. I realized that, in fact, this state of awareness is available to me and everyone else at all times. It is a state that completely subsumes ordinary daily events and enables one to become aware of a much larger, all-inclusive understanding of what life really is. This is the state of transcendence.

In the consciousness of duality, there appear to be three fundamental ingredients. First is the person who observes that which is outside the self. Second is what is being observed. Third is the act of observation. In the state of transcendent awareness, the three merge into one. We see duality as illusion because we realize that all that exists is Oneness. The trick is to be able to see through the fracturing of the One into infinite forms and to perceive reality as it is. Life is just the Oneness all along.

When in this state of awareness, all the other universal laws and their divine qualities come into play. In the presence of the *light* we are at *peace*. We realize how all things are *included* in a spirit of *compassion* and *love*. It becomes evident that all things *serve* and are *being served* in a seamless flow of *harmonious*, eternal renewal and *transformation*. At that moment in the garden, I felt deep *joy* and vowed to be more conscious and take more *responsibility* for my intentions and actions in order to access this state again and allow *wisdom* to permeate my being.

I would like to report that I have remained in that state ever since. Unfortunately, I haven't. Since that day I have consciously tried to evoke this mode of perception. It does recur on occasion, usually lasting somewhere between a split-second and a few minutes. Sometimes it happens in my meditation, sometimes while in my garden or playing music, or sometimes while just walking down the street. One thing that triggers it is the affirmation "Practice being in the presence of God." This statement lifts me out of my normal self-defined and self-oriented sense of what life is into a much more inclusive state. It allows me to identify myself not just as a person who has this or does that or whose children or friends are so-and-so, but as a being who is part of a never-ending chain of life force. I am a being who has the potential to be aware of and live in an energy field in a way that is immediately uplifting. This enables me to realize the contributions I can make when aligned with this force of Oneness by just being who I am. I can see and feel how I am connected to the One and how the seemingly insignificant abilities or talents that I have are, in fact, no accident and not unimportant. They are as vital to life as each cell of a plant is to its growth and continued existence.   Spiritual masters from all traditions have discussed, written, and lectured about this transcendent state. Some call it self-realization; others define it as God consciousness, Christ consciousness, Nirvana, or enlightenment. It's similar to the variety of names by which people define the prime deity. It doesn't matter what name describes it. What does matter is that it is attainable by everyone. It is part of our birthright as human beings. What I experienced in the garden was not an accident and was not something available only to me or a chosen few. The challenge is in knowing how to experience it, not as an idea or concept to be debated and discussed but as an actual state of perception and being.

Astrological Correlation

The sign reflected by this principle is Pisces. As the last sign of the zodiac, Pisces provides the energy and orientation to help us integrate all the experiences of the previous eleven signs. It provides the perspective from which to perceive the entire life experience within the context of Oneness. As such, Pisces is an extremely ethereal sign whose intention is to transcend whatever earth-plane experiences we have had so that we feel the spiritual connection. The previous eleven signs have a clear sense of who they are; their spiritual challenge is to realize the Oneness of life. As the twelfth sign, Pisces begins life with a clear awareness of the Oneness, but its spiritual challenge is to realize that it has a self!

The selflessness of Pisces is both a benefit and a liability. The benefit occurs when one is centered. This enables Pisces to look beyond their own personal needs and be of service to others. Helping others becomes a higher priority than personal gain. By extension, this enables the Pisces to focus on spiritual growth and consciousness development, rather than achieving on the material plain.

The off-center Pisces can be so confused about self that their choices and behaviors become self-undermining, even to a point of self-destruction. Feeling overwhelmed by the information brought to them by their intuitive openness, they may be drawn to self-medication through drugs or alcohol as a way of coping with emotional challenges or psychological confusion. This manifestation of selflessness is actually ego loss in an unhealthy sense. As defined in chapter 5, the ego is the bridge that connects our eternal spiritual being with our temporary material form. Without the ego, we lose track of what our physical needs are, what our relationships and responsibilities to others are, and as a result, we wind up being ineffectual in growing spiritually.

The totem that represents Pisces is two fish swimming in opposite directions. I refer to the two primary expressions as the downstream Pisces and the upstream Pisces. The downstream Pisces flows with the current of the river of life and eventually merges with the ocean of being through the development of Christ consciousness. This Pisces is independent and loves to travel in order to understand life from a cross-cultural perspective. Pisceans are inherently compassionate and can function effectively and fulfillingly as artists and healers.

The upstream Pisces flows against the current, essentially fighting the flow of life energy. These people tend to be dependent and lacking in both self-awareness and self-love. They might martyr themselves on the cross of idealism and strive to achieve things that are unrealistic and clearly beyond their means or ability. Hence, feelings of disappointment or disillusionment can result from their efforts. They might also be so strongly influenced by powerful forces in their lives, be they powerful authority figures or cultural trends, that they strive to emulate others rather than being themselves.

Pisces is the sign of surrender. It is so open that it is quite comfortable accepting any form of energy that passes by or through its force field. It is so comfortable being in the transcendent state that it can find it difficult to pay attention and be grounded in the material world.

Piscean individuals need quality time alone every day. Their psychic sensitivity is so strong that they can literally absorb other peoples' energy. So they need time to wring out their psychic sponge in order to perceive where they stop and where others begin. With this clarity they can be remarkable healers, due to their ability to understand and empathize with others.

How to Align with This Law

The Principle of Transcendence provides the ultimate tool that enables us to integrate self with Self. The vital point is to be aware that we are a part of that which is greater than we are: an inextricable part of the whole. The transcendent state is subtle. It prefers to tease and tickle rather than pound us into submission. Paramahansa Yogananda suggests adopting an open and receptive state of mind in order to entice this gentle awareness to enter our point of perception. In one song he says, "Door of my heart, open wide I keep for Thee. Will Thou come, will Thou come? Just for once come to me."

It's been said that a person who makes friends with stray cats will have a good life. Why? Because cats can be skittish and often on the defensive. Their ability to survive resides in their quick reflexes and their wariness of anything new or unknown. Making friends with such an animal requires patience. One must slowly strive to overcome their natural tendency to bolt and run. It's the same with transcendence—not in the sense that it is trying to get away from us but in the sense that its subtlety requires a deftness and sensitivity in order to perceive and work with it. To be friends with the cat we must become like the cat: wary yet gentle, intuitive yet alert. In seeking the Divine we must act as divine.

Being in the presence of God means feeling the support, the love and devotion that the Divine is providing all the time, every moment. So one way to activate this law is to strive to be as devoted to the awareness of the Presence as it is to us. We don't have to actually do anything in a physical sense. The doing is more in our awareness and in our devotion to the process of evoking and remaining in it. We can express our devotion by feeling and showing our love for those closest to us: partner, children, family, and friends. We can also access the state of devotion by working in service for a cause that is oriented to relieving pain and suffering in people or animals. The goal is to make the world a better place, and we contribute whatever gifts we have to offer. Our motivation is the realization that the object of our devotion is as much a manifestation of the Divine as we are, and as such is as worthy of unconditional love as we are. By feeling that devotion and the unconditional love implied, we can access transcendence.

If we put the universal laws on a wheel, the law opposite transcendence is that of service. In astrology, opposite signs tend toward similar experiences but come from different points of view. The Laws of Service and Transcendence are similar in that they both hold the capacity for adaptability. They don't try to control an experience as much as they seek to gain knowledge and expand their consciousness through it. The Principle of Service prioritizes actions that support physical activity. It provides its qualities of analysis, organization, and efficiency to enable things to flow in

The Law of Transcendence

healthy ways. So, too, the Law of Transcendence prioritizes service, because it is through serving others that we can remain humble and overcome our ego-identification. Seeking neither recognition nor control allows us the freedom to prioritize union with Oneness. The Principle of Transcendence prioritizes service over and above material concerns and activities. It offers the energy and perspective that enables others to clear their psyche from self-oriented activities and actualize their potential for spiritual communion.

The transcendent state is ubiquitous. It is everywhere, yet nowhere. It is so obvious that it's easy to overlook. Transcendence expands the Principle of Impermanence (being aware of our ever-changing immediate reality within the context of the eternal Oneness) by enabling us to tune into the big picture rather than to the constant changes taking place within it. The Law of Transcendence is supported by the Law of the Eternal Present, as the latter enables us to focus on our personal emotional experience in the immediate present. From this awareness it is a small step to transcend personal experience and realize our presence in the One.

In working to access the transcendent principle, it is important that we not overlook the obvious. Being conscious implies the need to tune in to everything we are experiencing at any given time. This requires an open mind that seeks to absorb every nuance of sight, sound, smell, vibration, and feeling transpiring simultaneously, both within and without. The key is a receptive mind or an open point of attention. This may not work while driving, operating heavy equipment, or changing the baby's diaper, so time must be set aside to allow one to focus in this way. During that time, we should strive to look, feel, and see beyond the material present, within which all things are defined. This means we seek the interconnection among all things, not just an understanding of what each of those things is and how they can be useful or dangerous to our comfort or survival.

Some Christians refer to "the silent hand of God acting behind all manifestation." I've taken this to mean that there is more going on than the obvious. Beyond the immediate human drama, life is being played out on a much grander scale. For example, we might feel intense sadness over someone's personal tragedy. We could get caught up in an apparent injustice to that individual. As we've learned from the Law of Karma, however, what is happening to us in the present is a result of what we did in the past. The Law of Love, however, suggests that the silent hand of God is offering us devotion, love, and compassion at all times. The way out of our mess is always available. We can always reach out to the Divine for support and encouragement.

Things are not always what they seem. If we perceive something only in terms of what it appears to be or in terms of its relationship to us, we could overlook its connection to Oneness. For example, we may be drawn to a person for certain reasons without seeing the totality of who he or she is. We could then become overwhelmed, disappointed, or blindsided by the ensuing relationship. If, however, we are able to relate to that person in objective terms, we will be more realistic about who he is and better able to determine how to relate to him. The idea is not to become hard-hearted but rather to seek awareness of a person in a larger context. A similar thing is asked of us with regard to current events that create misery and suffering. By relating to them in a transcendent context we can hold them in a broad and more complex view and perhaps then realize how, on some level, they make sense.

There's an interesting parable told by many spiritual teachers. It pertains to an old couple who were very poor. Their only form of wealth and comfort was a milking cow. One day a tree limb broke off and killed the cow. The old couple was filled with grief and anger. How could a just and loving God take such a valuable asset? As the old man vented his feelings, he was filled with the realization that it actually was time for his wife to die, but God took the cow instead.

In human terms we can assume that God demonstrated compassion for the couple when he substituted the cow for the wife. Similarly, we can flow with the Principle of Transcendence when we relate to others with compassion. A simple definition of compassion is suffering with another. When we practice this, we are connected with those whose suffering is similar to our own. Rather than feeling sorry for ourselves or judging those who are in pain, we identify with them through shared suffering. We seek to support others by providing them with whatever assistance or service we have to offer. In so doing, we karmically attract to us those who can provide healing support for our own situation.

Meditation

In terms of specific techniques, the best and most effective one that will enable us to tap into transcendence is meditation—formal, sitting meditation. There are many varieties to choose from but the best are the ancient techniques that were given to humanity hundreds—if not thousands—of years ago. Any form of yoga or Buddhist meditation would qualify as such. In his book *The Holy Science*, Swami Sri Yukteswar calculates that the Golden Age of India, during which it received all the spiritual teachings that are still available, ended around 6700 BC. No one actually knows the source or origin of this wisdom. Did it come from enlightened humans? From light beings who incarnated to share this knowledge with humans? From extraterrestrial beings? All we know is that the information is timeless and that it connects us to the Divine. Accessing some of those teachings in the form of the meditation techniques they gave us is a surefire way to transcend our limited earth-plane and body-dominated consciousness. In this way, we can eventually merge in consciousness with Spirit.

Mysticism and Transcendence

Mystics throughout history have offered different tools to access the transcendent state. The *I Ching*, an ancient Chinese book of divination, comes from the Taoist tradition. It is estimated to be approximately five thousand years old, although it was refined to its current form by Confucius about 2,500 years ago. It provides a way of using words, images, and concepts to access and understand nonlinear reality. It is useful in divining the nature of the energy available at whatever moment one chooses to consult it. As such, the *I Ching* offers a connection between the ego and the higher Self, helping one to transcend the immediate awareness of a situation and perceive it in a more inclusive context. This tool is a practical yet mystical method for integrating the transcendent with the mundane. It's a system that connects the personal, familial, political, and spiritual aspects of life. It enables the seeker to be aware of the current set of conditions as well as the larger context, and it shows a path that helps to resolve internal or interactive conflicts.

The Old Testament prophet Ezekiel was a mystic. He saw God in the form of "the wheel in the middle of the sky." He spoke of his vision as a being with four heads—the ox, the lion, the eagle, and the human, which are associated with the four "fixed" signs of the zodiac: Taurus, Leo, Scorpio, and Aquarius. As fixed signs, one attribute they share is strength of will. The Bible instructs that God created heaven and earth through exercise of will. With this understanding, we can see that Ezekiel's vision was a way of perceiving the Divine, which reminded us that through will, activated with clarity of intention, profound things can be created. His story illustrates that the human and the Divine are one. The only thing that separates us is our lack of awareness of that connection. We seem to have a veil of illusion drawn over our eyes, preventing us from seeing truth.

Another effective way to activate the Principle of Transcendence is through sacred sexuality. As I've pointed out previously (chapter 2, "The Law of Survival" and chapter 8, "The Law of Eternal Life"), Tantra yoga is a technique that utilizes intimate physical contact between two people as a vehicle for transcending the physical plane and accessing Divine Oneness. Similarly, as mentioned in chapter 6, "The Law of Service," in ancient times when the great goddess was revered as the prime deity, women could devote themselves to the goddess by residing in her temple. One of their tasks was to act as surrogates of the goddess by offering their bodies to men who came to worship her. These women were called vestal virgins or sacred prostitutes. Here, too, sexuality was used as a vehicle for transcending the limitations of the material plane.

The Arts

Another viable way to access transcendence is through music. Playing an instrument, singing, or simply listening to music provides access to transcendent energy. Dancing offers another way to access transcendence. For example, Sufi dancing is a way to use the body to transcend physical awareness. Dancing of any kind can feel good to the body, so that eventually the body/mind ceases to notice that our attention is slowly withdrawn from the physical and moves into an identification with something much greater than *maya*.

Visual arts also play a role in accessing a transcendent awareness. Through them, the artist can perceive the physical plane as being more mutable than it appears, as shapes and colors are manipulated into an intuited or felt presentation. Such an act of expression taps into the flow of creative energy that is always present. By relying on the eyes rather than the ears, the material plane emerges as being what it truly is—the manifestation of properties that all exist in a relative and changeable framework.

Plant Allies

Another very effective way to access this law, utilized by cultures around the world and throughout human history, involves the utilization of psychotropic plants. In modern history some of those plants have been synthesized into what are commonly called psychedelic drugs. Both Terence McKenna, psychedelic philosopher, author, and colleague of Timothy Leary, and author/anthropologist Rianne Eisler have theorized that primates in northern Africa ingested psilocybin mushrooms. This enabled them to access altered states of consciousness. It also inspired evolutionary advances such as raising their young to reproductive age and creating a conscious connection to the environment (spiritual and physical) and to each other. In recent times, these tools have been ignored, misused, or misunderstood. When used properly, however, they have proven effective as consciousness-expanding substances.

When used indiscriminately, these plants and drugs can create nightmarish, psychotic states that have led, in some cases, to mental imbalance or death. Their history also suggests that they have held prominent places as healing agents and ritual catalysts in a variety of cultures. Chinese healers recorded use of these substances as far back as 3,500 years ago. The Persian *Zend Avesta* discusses the use of *haoma*, and literature in India refers to the use of *soma*. Ritual participants who ingested these substances were overcome with rapture and the awareness that "half of them was on earth, the other half in heaven" (*Rig Veda*). Some authorities consider the use of soma to have had a significant influence on the development of the Hindu philosophy and religion.

In Central America, various pre-Columbian cultures, such as the Aztecs, Toltecs, and Mayans, as well as contemporary Indian groups, such as the Huichols and the Yaquis, have used mind-altering substances as a regular, normal part of their spiritual life. Peyote, psilocybin mushrooms, and morning glory seeds are among the well-known substances used. In South America the most popular psychotropic substances are San Pedro cactus and ayahuasca. These are used in puberty rituals as well as for healing and visionary and telepathic purposes.

Although modern scientific studies of the effects of these substances have been few, research has been done on alkaloids, such as LSD and mescaline, in both natural and synthesized states. Some research dates back to 1897 in Germany. Although this research is over a century old, fear, political pressure, and irresponsible use of both the organics and the synthetics have caused the substances to be banned in laboratories as well as in clinical applications since the mid-1970s. Some of the research that had already been done, however, has shown that the chemicals found in extremely high amounts in these plants also exist naturally in the human brain. The most exciting and significant elements of this discovery are twofold: first, ingesting these substances in safe, controlled, therapeutic environments can be beneficial for the exploration of one's own psyche. This can lead to greater emotional health, psychological clarity, and spiritual transcendence. Second, and even more exciting, is the realization that whatever these substances can catalyze in terms of consciousness change can also be achieved without the substances. It's as if the psychotropics and psychedelics take us to the finish line and say, "This is where you want to be. Now go back to where you were and figure out how to get here without the crutch." The potential to tap into rarified and previously unexplored states of consciousness is part of our birthright as human beings. Actualizing this potential puts us in sync with the Principle of Transcendence.

The one single activity that all the above suggestions offer and require is surrender. Surrender asks that we let go of our need to maintain constant awareness of our body and its needs or desires, that we give up our need to control a situation or be attached to outcome. Transcendence asks that we surrender the natural human desire for logical understanding of our perceptions, that we be willing to accept things as they come to us. In so doing, we need to let go of the projections usually rooted in fear-based reactions to experiences we've had in the past. By relinquishing these qualities and habits we put ourselves in the flow of being, where we are connected to, supported by, and enlightened by all that is.

The most important factor in accessing this law is making it a priority. The Buddhists remind us that having a body is a blessing simply because it affords the greatest opportunity to alter our consciousness away from the gross physical and toward the more subtle transcendent.

Not Aligning with This Law

There are several reasons why being aware of this law and its attendant state of consciousness is difficult. One is the instinctual sense of attachment to the body. The Law of Survival, with its instinctive concern for physical-plane security and comfort, can seem to work against us as we strive to function in a state of consciousness that persists past the existence of our body. It is true that while incarnate, we must give the body a lot of attention. After all, it is the vehicle that allows us to be here and to be who we are—or at least to be who we *think* we are. We tune in to what the body needs—everything from the necessities of food, clothing, and shelter to the luxuries of sensual gratification. Much time, effort, and resources are given over to pursuing the satisfaction of those needs. To some, this point of attention can occupy most of our mental time. Even if we set aside some time and energy to pursue the nonphysical elements of life, is it enough? Or does the body continuously pull us back to its needs? The body and the ego-self can operate in a conspiratorial tandem to keep our attention on them to the exclusion of everything else. This plot is merely our own habit of prioritizing the physical to the exclusion, or at least to the minimization, of the ethereal.

To overcome this habit it is necessary to devote some of our time to establishing a time and place that is safe and sanctuarial enough to allow us to tune in to those realities not limited to the material plane. It's also important to remember, however, that the transcendent state includes physical existence. Eliminating or overlooking the material can also prevent us from being in the transcendent state. Transcendence equates with Oneness. This is not the Oneness that includes everything *but* the physical, but the Oneness that *is* everything. To exclude awareness of any part prevents the perception of the whole. One of the challenges to activating this law is that of unifying the apparent duality that our mind creates between the material and the nonmaterial. To focus on one to the exclusion of the other creates an imbalance and ultimately a misuse of this law.

By including the material in our awareness of the One, we become centered. From this perspective we can actually see through the illusion of the physical plane. The Hindus refer to the world of form as *maya*, which means illusion. This doesn't connote hallucination or imagination. Rather, it connotes the ephemeral—brief and transient. The Law of Impermanence teaches us that everything in life, including that which exists in form, is changing. The Law of Transcendence connects us to that which is eternal. The more we identify with our body and give it preeminence in our priorities and choices, the more likely we are to assume that form is real, and everything not embodied is illusion. In fact the opposite is true. The more emphasis we place on the material, to the exclusion of the transcendent, the more confused, disappointed, and disillusioned we will become. Less meaning will accrue in our lives, and our actions and accomplishments will have less significance. This is because of the instability of the material world which is, after all, the plane of impermanence. If we take *maya* into account in our lives, then we must take responsibility for our feelings, thoughts, and actions. To

The Law of Transcendence

include *maya* and look beyond it, or to see it as part of a much greater whole, is to live in consciousness with the Law of Transcendence.

One significant problem that can manifest with this law is simply not taking advantage of it. Material success, recognition, and acquisitions have their place and can certainly create comfort, but in time they fade. We are then left pondering if the sole meaning of life is to grow up, work, and die. Even if we're conscientious and strive to implement the other eleven laws impeccably, if we don't take advantage of this one, the results of all our good intentions may feel hollow.

Undervaluing the mystical experience of transcendence can result from living within an intellectual context that defines reality in terms of logical analysis. The "scientific method" has enabled us to make amazing, wonderful, seemingly miraculous discoveries in areas ranging from food production and health care to astronomy and archeology. But those breakthroughs have come at the price of spiritual alienation. We are taught that the universe is a mechanical construct, within which everything functions according strictly defined laws. Anything that cannot be understood in a logical framework is illusory, and it is cast aside as meaningless at best, superstitious at worst. The intuitive arts, such as astrology, poetry, and art, are demeaned. The entire history of Western mysticism remains shrouded by an inner circle of adepts who zealously guard the truths and insights of that tradition. One reason is because they have learned from centuries of harassment that secular leaders have responded to mystics and their rituals and teachings with persecution. Although people may feel more comfortable or secure in their bodies and on the earth plane, we may be farther from transcendent consciousness than humanity has ever been.

Another reason it is difficult to align with the Law of Transcendence is that we are living in a culture whose values are firmly rooted in youth, beauty, luxury, and consumerism. Anything that cannot be commodified or that cannot provide sensual gratification is seen as boring and useless. What conventional culture offers as an antidote or balance to the extremes and limits of its materialism is ... more physical gratification. It comes highly touted and glossily advertised as being what the "in" people, the pretty people, the happy people, and the successful people do: consume substances that alter awareness. Alcohol, tobacco, sugar, and pharmaceutical drugs, or any drugs that are taken in a casual or party-type atmosphere are displayed as wonderful and desirable things that make life worth living. They create the aura that "it doesn't get any better than this."

Even within the so-called counter-culture, which condones or espouses drug use outside a therapeutic or ritual context, the value of consciousness-altering substances is demeaned. Instead, they replace the potential of a meaningful transcendent experience with what is essentially a cheap thrill. This is more counter-consciousness than counter-culture. The saddest part of this picture is that the people who participate in it often don't know what a real transcendent experience is. If we have never had a truly transcendent experience, we have nothing to compare to the temporary buzz of sugar, alcohol, pills, or street drugs. These substances are escape mechanisms that provide the illusion of transcendence. Misuse of this law can come from misunderstanding what a transcendent experience is.

Substance Abuse

Pharmaceutical drugs can also be misused, although they do, of course, alleviate pain and suffering in mind as well as in body. They have been highly successful in improving the quality of and extending the lives of millions of people. To claim that it is only through drugs that healing can take place, however, is short-sighted. These substances are often overprescribed to the point that they create new health problems, even as they may alleviate others. There are more people addicted to prescription drugs than to street drugs. Some people have been so overly medicated that they have become immune to their benefits. Sometimes a person takes so many pharmaceutical drugs that the side effects of one creates a problem that has to be alleviated by another, which in turn could create other undesirable side effects, leading to more prescriptions. Sadly, our culture has traditionally limited the definition of healing to that which can be affected by drugs. In recent years this belief system has been changing, and healing systems such as acupuncture and naturopathy are becoming more popular. But why the preeminence of drugs in the first place?

In the late nineteenth century, many forms of healing were employed by a variety of healers. Herbology, osteopathy, and naturopathy were quite popular and considered as effective as allopathy. Allopathy is a system that seeks to heal a disease by introducing a substance, such as a drug, to the body that is different from the disease. During that time John D. Rockefeller commissioned a study that would determine which of all existing and known forms of healing was the best. When his panel returned with its results, the conclusions were predictable: allopathy was deemed the best form of healing. The drugs upon which allopathy depends would have to be manufactured, and therefore, money could be made through their sale. Rockefeller was able to utilize his immense wealth to discredit the other forms of healing to the point that today they are marginalized, if not illegal. Do allopathic drugs have their place in the medicine cabinet? Of course. But not exclusively.

One of the disastrous side effects of the drug and alcohol monopoly is that it has created the illusion that only something that exists outside of us can enhance our life and make us feel good. The reality is that whatever we rely on that is external to us will eventually fade in significance. As a young person we might have marveled at the effects of drinking a few beers or smoking a joint or popping a pill. These experiences may have brought new feelings and perhaps even realizations. We may have felt "high" and perceived things, people, and even ourselves in a different manner. This would seem to be a compelling reason to repeat the experience. Ingest the substance. Notice the perceptual changes. The buzz becomes the reality.

Before the rise of allopathic medicine, when herbs were considered acceptable substances for healing, one of the texts used to teach about them was *Culpepper's Herbal* by Nicholas Culpepper, who lived in the seventeenth century. In addition to being an herbalist, Culpepper was also an astrologer. He knew which herbs and plants corresponded with which planets and signs. In his discussion of cannabis (today called marijuana), Culpepper assigned it to the rulership of Saturn. Excluding those people who use marijuana to ease their physical suffering, as it has been prescribed for centuries, I'm sure that most people who smoke marijuana for pleasure assume that it is bringing an expansion to their awareness and an alteration to their state of mind. Saturn, however, represents limitation. This isn't necessarily bad, as limits can be useful in defining a goal and working diligently over time to achieve it. According to Culpepper, however, cannabis is not an expansive experience but rather a contractive one. It can provide a personal perspective of something but not necessarily one that can be physically manifested or shared with others. So, here again, we see that relying upon an external substance develops the habit of looking outside ourselves for something that only exists internally.

Another aspect of drugs is their side effects, thus limiting the experience or benefit from the drugs. Continuing our consumption indefinitely will inevitably lead to dependency and addiction, without enhancing or improving the quality of our life. It can also lead to confusing illusion with reality and to settling for the illusion rather than seeing it as the fantasy that it is.

One of the side effects of substances is that they perpetrate the dualistic experience. We ingest and feel great. After a while the substance leaves our body, and we don't feel so great anymore. What goes up must come down. This creates a cycle that can be a form of self-destruction. True transcendence, however, is an experience that just keeps expanding. As we learned in the Law of Expansion, there is always more. One of the beautiful qualities of life is that self-destruction is not required!

Dealing with life in a conscious way is hard. Trying to do the right thing, being a good person, wanting to make a sincere contribution while keeping body and soul together for oneself and one's family is not easy. Peak and valley experiences only make it harder, and they result from any type of addiction. Love, sex, romance, food, shopping, drama, and crisis are all similar paths. Each serves to create a semblance of momentary happiness—respite from the pain of our apparent reality. In the end, they don't deliver the goods.

They do not really allow us an ever-deepening sense of satisfaction that our feelings, thoughts, and actions are creating a sustainable state of contentment. The universe does not want us to suffer. It has provided everything we need to take care of ourselves and to be happy as well. It offers avenues for developing our consciousness so that we can perceive reality as it exists, far beyond the limitations of our physical plane. So, by definition, any sort of material crutch tends to keep us locked onto this plane; the tools of transcendence help us to surpass it.

Another misuse of this law comes from indulgence in fantasy. If this is a deliberate manifestation of the imagination, done in a creative context or simply something to be enjoyed, such as a movie, play, or book, no problem. Even if the fantasy is something acted out consciously in a person's life or between people, this could be beneficial. In fact, fantasy can engender a type of transcendence. But if we lose track of where our fantasy world stops and the collective consensus reality begins, it becomes another self-destructive illusion that prevents true transcendence from taking place. Remember that transcendence is a normal, natural manifestation of life. It is not a denial of anything, nor does it remove us from anywhere. It is simply the awareness of the complex interaction of all that is experienced as Oneness. Attempting to escape into a fantasy world can limit our awareness, and hence, our ability to perceive the interconnected wholeness.

Indulging in fantasy can also be the result of mental illness. The Law of Impermanence teaches about the importance of the uniqueness of each person. But if the expression of our uniqueness takes us completely beyond the realm of our agreed-upon consensus reality, it can be limiting and self-destructive. This type of experience can lead to psychosis. It can be drug-induced or a manifestation of an imbalance of brain chemistry or other type of physical malfunction of the brain. One of my clients was a bright young man who periodically drifted into psychosis. He also had the habit of chronically using drugs, such as methamphetamine. He was arrested and later released, but during his incarceration he was, of course, unable to use drugs. During that time, his psychosis cleared up and has not returned.

Mental illness is different from being lost in a fog of confusion, a state often characterized as being "spaced out." Sometimes the latter comes from simply being ungrounded. If we overlook our material responsibilities, to ourselves as well as to others, if we allow ourselves to drift along in our own idealized reality, of which we are the only member, or if we abuse or overlook the needs of a healthy body, we are too unconscious to take advantage of this law. Some mental illness can develop as a result of feeling that we have no control over our life. Depression, for example, can result from a perceived, chronic lack of control over one's life.

Self-Sacrifice

Another example of the misuse of transcendence comes through something called the Golden Chain. This is a state wherein one is so attached to an activity or state of being that is self-defined as spiritual that it becomes a form of prideful ego-identification, rather than an exercise that leads to transcendence. For example, we might be extremely committed to our daily spiritual practice. We wouldn't miss it for anything. We are so dedicated that we eschew most other experiences in life. Our goal is the radiant golden light, and we frequently remind others of that goal. Even though we may truly be committed to this end, the chain of our self-imposed restrictions actually limits rather than liberates us.

An example of the Golden Chain is prioritizing service to others to such a degree that we martyr ourselves to the ideal of service. Self-effacing humility can be beneficial in seeking to transcend ego-identification, but if we become too identified with service and attached to the idea of it, we are likely to be ego-identified with the image of our service and not really transcending anything. Extending service as far as self-sacrifice, seeing ourselves as the savior of others, is a misuse of this law.

Martyrdom can also lead to misuse of this principle by impelling us to sacrifice ourselves for others in some way. We could give so much time, energy, or material goods to a person or a cause—more than we can realistically afford—that we actually create a deficit or hardship for ourselves. An immediate rush of fulfillment could follow any martyr-like action. But unless we have attained total enlightenment, this sense of satisfaction will soon fade. Sometimes an act that appears to be selfless can actually represent a desire for approval and recognition from others. After the initial complements, others forget us or perhaps were never interested in our efforts in the first place, and they go away. We are left feeling empty and bereft. What we had has been given away, and there is nothing of lasting value that has come to compensate for the loss.

Another ineffective application of the Principle of Transcendence occurs when we adopt the role of the savior. We may be well-intended in our actions, but they are, nonetheless, misplaced. Trying to help, fix, or save someone else has two major problems. One is that it can subtly leave us more concerned with others' problems than our own. In this sense, the savior pattern is one of denial. The second problem is that we may be taking on someone else's issues without being asked. Rather than being appreciated with abundant recognition, we are then perceived as nosy and invasive. Striving to save someone else can also be a form of disrespect. We assume that someone can't solve his own problems without our help and intervention.

Misuse of this law can also come from people who try to prevent others from accessing it, such as those who espouse a dogmatic religious philosophy and seek to establish the basis of life in fear rather than in love. An example of this is how certain powerful men in the early Christian Church wrote about women in general and sexuality in particular. Rather than seeing them in their spiritual aspect, women and sex were defined as dirty and unworthy. Saint Augustine was particularly harsh. In his "Letter 243," he wrote: "What is the difference whether it is in a wife or a mother, it is still Eve the temptress that we must beware of in any woman." In the "Enchiridion," Augustine blames original sin for all of humanity's problems, and Eve, specifically, for perpetrating that sin. Martin Luther follows in Augustine's philosophical footsteps. In *A History of God*, Karen Armstrong wrote, "Luther was a rabid anti-Semite and a misogynist who was convulsed with a loathing and horror of sexuality."

Sex can be used as a drug and a form of addiction. It can be used as a way of escaping from conditions of life that are unpleasant or painful. But to assume that sexuality per se, let alone half the human race, is the cause of all misery is in itself an illusion. It overlooks the possibility that the body can be a vehicle for sharing love and accessing a blissful state of transcendent consciousness.

Spiritual Opportunity

The spiritual quality associated with this law is *faith*. One mustn't confuse faith with wishing and hoping, which is akin to closing our eyes, holding our nose, and jumping. Faith is not blind. Real faith is based in knowing and trust. We know without doubt that we are part of the whole because we have had actual, personal experiences that validate that. It might have been a one-time experience, or something that persisted over time, or something that continues on an ongoing basis. Sometimes it is a matter of simply paying attention and noticing when the "silent hand of God" is opening doors and providing us with opportunities for happiness and fulfillment. In faith, we are confident that as a limitless manifestation of the Divine, we are always being supported by the Creator, just as a child is supported by its parent. Nothing will be denied to us, provided that we ask properly and proceed to act in accordance with divine law. The universe never says no. It will give us whatever we want or at least provide the opportunity to create it for ourselves. Whether what we want is healthy, or ultimately brings peace and joy, or brings us closer to Source, that's another matter. The universe is quite willing to allow us to make all the mistakes we need and then, when we turn back in the direction of the light, it will be there to help us in every way.

One potential problem in keeping the faith is the rational mind, which continually questions a situation and in so, doing opens the door to doubts. Having faith means transcending these doubts by addressing the situation in a nonrational way, a way that is more

The Law of Transcendence

feeling or intuitive and that enables us to *feel* the connection to Source. The challenge is to quiet the rational mind and realize that knowing without doubt is a good definition of faith.

Yogananda tells the story of a person dying and meeting God. When God inquires about the person's experience on earth, the response is filled with recrimination about all the pain and suffering, much of it as a result of loneliness and having to carry his burdens all by himself. So God manifests a beautiful beach with two sets of footprints walking along side by side. The person is informed that one set of footprints was his; the other was God's. God narrates this person's life story as they walk along together in the path of the footprints. Suddenly, one set of footprints disappears, and the person asks why. "That was when you went through a particularly hard time," God answers. "Aha! I knew it," the person says. "When things were going fine, you were right there with me, but when things got hard you left me alone." "No," God says, "You don't understand. That one set of prints was mine. That was when I was carrying you."

We are never alone. We never have obstacles that are insurmountable. We never lack the tools needed to respond to and overcome what is on our path. Knowing this is true faith. With faith as the foundation for our life, we can be more positive and joyful in creating it. Without faith, our lives tend to be more fear-based. Living a fear-based life can prevent us from being aware of all our options and taking advantage of the ones most beneficial to us. Fear, in turn, can cause us to strive to control a situation, rather than surrender to it.

One of the challenges of faith, once we have it, is keeping it. The more faith we have, the greater the challenges to maintaining it. It may seem as if the current problem is much greater than the one before. The next situation is even worse. Having faith is like being pregnant. We can't just be a little pregnant, and we can't have a little faith. We are either pregnant or we're not, and we either have faith or we don't.

Think of faith-challenging problems as lessons on the path to being within the transcendent Oneness. Each time we are confronted with something seemingly impossible, we need to remind ourselves that everything worked out before, so why won't it now? Even if the difficulty continues to mount and lasts for a long time, we must realize that it is merely our karma at work. We are being given another chance to do something different this time, to pay off the karmic debt and move on in both consciousness and life experience.

In a mystical state of consciousness, we surrender to the flow of life experience. We do not judge, control, or project our expectations onto people or situations. We strive to become aware of the ebb and flow of life. We notice as new energy comes into being and notice when it passes. We perceive life from a single-pointed consciousness, wherein all phenomena are emanating from the same source, connected to all things, and supported by abundance, providence, and love.

In return for this surrender, the mystic receives guidance from the center of his spiritual being. I call this an inner directive. It combines clarity of intuition (the divine quality of the Law of the Eternal Present) and faith with a clearly defined direction for the proper course of action. With this clarity, combined with patience, the seeker finds right action that will, in turn, lead to a successful and fulfilling conclusion.

It is in this sense that this principle teaches the value of humility—not false modesty, whereby we disavow compliments even if they are warranted, and we know it. Humility is a type of perspective. We realize that whatever we have accomplished, whomever we have served or helped, however much we identify with Spirit, there is always more. Humility comes from realizing that all that we are and have are gifts from Spirit. Being humble simply means knowing that our actions always take place in the context of a reality so immense that our perceptual and cognitive abilities are overwhelmed. Knowing this and cultivating humility enables us to be in a state of mind and being that is always open to the recognition of and welcoming of the divine spark that resides in all of us.

The Bottom Line

"Every man, whose heart is no longer shaken by any doubt, knows with certainty that there is no being save only One ... In his divine majesty the me and we, the thou, are not found, for in the One there can be no distinction." Thus does the Sufi Gulshan-Raz define the ultimate mystical state. It is a condition experienced by every true seeker who has ever had the motivation and patience to pursue this state of consciousness.

What provides the motivation to embark on this journey? It may be the pain of alienation or feelings of hopelessness or depression so strong that we are willing to do anything to overcome it. It could be a glimpse into the totality of being that occurs during an altered state of consciousness. It could be a spontaneous spiritual experience. It could be tapping into a universal desire that exists in the heart and soul of all people, a longing to develop our consciousness so that we become aware of our inclusion in Divine Oneness. We seek to access the state of being wherein every aspect of life is embraced as all-inclusive Spirit. In any case, this motivation, combined with the patience and persistence needed to pursue this goal, regardless of how long it takes, will enable us to experience life beyond the confusion of duality. We can begin to perceive all manifestation as existing simultaneously in the same unity.

If we achieve this state, an ensuing unshakable faith develops that we are a manifestation of the limitless Creator nourished and generated by a boundless supply of love. We come to realize, with every ounce and facet of our being, that we are all manifestations of divine love, light, and creativity and potentially limitless in the expression of those divine qualities. Embodying those qualities is our birthright. Feeling this is bliss. When we are ready to identify with the Oneness instead of our own ego-defined individuality, when we have successfully and consciously integrated all the other laws, we are able to step into a state of consciousness in which we feel ecstatic. This quality of bliss is not a metaphor; it is an actual state of being, available to all who prioritize it and are willing to do the work necessary to achieve it.

My client Sherry was on vacation in Reno, Nevada. One evening while walking through town, she noticed the sunset. It was strikingly beautiful and provided an awesome display of color that created an uplifting feeling. Wanting to share this experience with someone, she ran into the first store she saw. She noticed a young woman standing idly behind the counter. Flushed with enthusiasm, Sherry exhorted this person to come outside and partake of the moment, which she did. After several minutes the colors faded and the clerk went back inside, thanking Sherry for her thoughtfulness. Feeling full and happy Sherry went on her way.

There is a small magazine called the *Daily Word*, published by the Unitarian Church, whose purpose is to provide an uplifting thought, prayer, or story each day of the year for the reader. Sherry was a subscriber to this publication. Years after that day in Reno, she read a story in the magazine that amazed her. It was written by a woman who described the depression she experienced when going through her divorce. She had relocated to Reno and taken a job in order to expedite and pay for the painful divorce. One day she felt she could go on no longer and thoughts of suicide permeated her consciousness. In the depths of her despair, she was suddenly exhorted by a stranger who had come in to the store and insisted she join her outside to view the sunset. Once there, she was overwhelmed by the beauty and power of the spectacle. It filled her with hope, eradicated her thoughts of self-destruction, and literally brought the light back into her life. From that point on, she felt as if her life was worth living. She didn't know who that stranger was but she felt she owed her a debt to at least say thank you.

Sherry was deeply touched by this story, not only because it had been her own enthusiasm that had prodded the woman to come outside, but because she felt as if she had been personally chosen to deliver the message. Maybe she was just in the right place at the right time. She was paying attention, and because of this, she had derived such tremendous fulfillment from the sunset that she felt impelled to follow her intuition to seek out someone else to observe it. The later discovery that her act had been a pivotal event for this woman was quite meaningful.

The Law of Transcendence

Sherry and the woman had shared a transcendent experience. Sharing any positive experience enhances its significance, but when the experience is inherently spiritual the positivity is exponentially expanded. In the moment of sharing the Oneness with another person, our separateness fades. What remains is the perception and awareness that the two of us are actually one. Duality has been replaced by unity. It also validates that we are part of the whole. We are inseparable parts of all that is. Each of us is simply one pair of eyes and ears, arms, and legs of endless divine manifestation. The veil of illusion that causes us to feel trapped in the limited material plane, separate from all other forms and aspects of manifestation, is lifted, and we awaken to the divine light that is what life is.

Over the past two thousand years, mystics have sought communion with the Divine and with the realization of their birthright by retreating to monasteries, ashrams, hermitages, and caves. In solitary spiritual practice, perhaps under the guidance of a more advanced teacher, they have sought divine consciousness. In the contemporary world it is important that the monks come down from the mountains. It is imperative that they share what they know, even as they continue on their journey to know. The veil of illusion that separates different states of consciousness and dimensions of reality is thinning. What used to be considered reality is giving way to the realization that this "reality" is only a possibility that is perceived from one level of awareness. Expanded consciousness leads to expanded possibilities of how humanity could create life on this planet.

The Bhagavad-Gita teaches us about the nature and benefits of yoga, but its meaning can be interpreted on many levels. One describes the state of a kingdom after the old king has died. Two sides are vying with each other for the throne. On one side is the king's younger brother and his followers. On the other side are the king's children and their followers. One of the most famous passages of the Bhagavad-Gita involves the king's youngest son, Arjuna. He is sitting in his chariot awaiting the start of the battle, but he is conflicted. As a member of the warrior caste, he knows that it is his duty to be part of the battle. But as a thoughtful person, he is concerned that by fighting and perhaps killing his relatives and teachers, he would be creating very negative karma for himself.

In those times, the nobility were well armed and armored and rode in the back of a chariot. The chariot was driven by an unarmed and unprotected slave. As Arjuna soliloquizes about his conundrum, his chariot driver overhears him. Unbeknownst to Arjuna but known by the reader, the charioteer is not a slave at all but Lord Krishna, the embodiment of Divine Spirit. At one point in the soliloquy Krishna interrupts Arjuna to remind him that as a member of the warrior caste, it is first and foremost his duty, as well as his karma, to act in accordance with his position in life. If a battle presents itself, he must fight. Arjuna likes this advice as it relieves him of his problem. But on the other hand, he wonders if he really wants to take the word of a slave. So he questions the slave (Krishna) about who he is and by what power he can make that statement. Krishna responds by essentially saying, "Trust me. I have friends in high places." But the royal Arjuna is not satisfied with this reply and commands the slave to reveal his sources. So to prove his point and validate his authority, Krishna removes the veil of illusion from Arjuna, who instantly becomes aware of the true nature of life. He perceives the endless flow of energy as sound and color that has no perceptible shape or context. The enormity of this experience overwhelms Arjuna and, now realizing who he has been talking to, he begs Krishna to restore the veil. Arjuna was thrust into the mystical realm of Oneness with no preparation or warning of what to expect or how to function and navigate within a framework that has no concrete parameters. This is no easy task and typically cannot be borne for long without destroying our normal ego framework.

One of the benefits of doing our inner work is that it prepares us for such a moment when we are confronted with a "veil-less" reality. Instead of reacting with fear and feeling overwhelmed, we might be able to feel comfortable, knowing that what we are experiencing is total consciousness. There are no limits to perception, other than the fear that keeps us in the limited framework of the logical mind, wherein everything is defined, has a cognitive and practical purpose, and can be controlled in a way that enables us to feel safe and secure.

The Law of Transcendence

When we surrender to the flow of eternal Oneness, our well-being comes from knowing that we are inextricably connected to all that is. There is no separation, no hierarchy, and no limit to the light and love that we can experience.

Throughout history human beings have displayed violence toward each other. Political and military conflicts have been part of the human condition. During the past few hundred years, the drive for economic power and freedom has merely exacerbated the misery. Recently, the accelerated exploitation of our environment, and with it the possibility of losing the earth as a viable habitat for humanity, is challenging everyone to move past their attachments and addictions. We have arrived at a point in human history where the shift to the mystical vision, to the ability to live within the consciousness of the One, is incumbent for our survival as a species. For those of us committed to this journey, the evolution of our consciousness will enable us to perceive and enter new realms of being, regardless of the political, economic, and moral will of the nations of the world. In the process of this undertaking, we can also make significant contributions, whatever our unique gifts and tools may be, to awakening others to the possibilities of a new, enlightened reality.

Affirmation: "I am the radiant Oneness flowing lovingly, creatively, and receptively through all being in the seen and unseen, in the known and unknown."

> *There was something formlessly fashioned,*
> *That existed before heaven and earth;*
> *Without sound, without substance,*
> *Dependent on nothing, unchanging, all pervading, unfailing,*
> *One may think of it as the mother of all things under heaven.*
> *Its true name we do not know.*
> *Way is the by-name that we give it.*
> —Tao Te Ching

Chapter 13: The Universe Wants Us to Be Happy

> *When the kings had died, a pauper, barefooted and hungry, came and sat on the throne. "God," he whispered, "the eyes of man cannot bear to look directly at the sun, for they are blinded. How then, Omnipotent, can they look directly at you? Have pity, Lord; temper your strength, turn down your splendor so that I, who am poor and afflicted, may see you!" Then listen, old man! God became a piece of bread, a cup of cool water, a warm tunic, a hut, and in front of the hut, a woman giving suck to an infant. "Thank you, Lord," he whispered. "You humbled yourself for my sake. You became bread, water, a warm tunic, and my wife and son in order that I may see you. And I did see you. I bow down and worship your beloved many-faced face!"*
>
> —Nikos Kazantzakis, *The Last Temptation of Christ*

As a young person I became aware of the pain and suffering that appears to be a universal part of the human experience. It seemed as if the various ethnic groups, nations, and religions were always fighting for survival and domination. Even within the United States, there were factions vying for supremacy and leaving a legacy of anguish in their wake. The haves and the have-nots were forever at odds. This perspective didn't change once I became an adult. Is this the true nature of life? Are we condemned to a world that is fractured with alienation? Why are we here anyway?

As noted in chapter 1, the prevailing theory among contemporary cosmologists is that the earth began as an amorphous cloud of dust and gasses. Some philosophers and metaphysicians expand on this theory, stipulating that the original beings who inhabited this planet were just as formless. As the earth condensed and solidified, so did the beings. The molecules of the planet and its inhabitants slowed down and became denser.

Modern quantum physics theorizes that reality is whatever humans perceive it to be. Although the material world appears solid, it is actually a flow of energy that is continuously changing form. This quantum universe constantly pulsates and creates new manifestations of light and substance. Some take hold, grow, and develop. Most don't.

From this perspective it is not too great a leap to understand that what we perceive and define as reality is arbitrary, a by-product of the collective consciousness and its resultant consensus reality. Most people perceive material reality more or less in the same way. To change this perception requires a shift of collective consciousness. This is an expanded twist on the concept that in order to change the world, you have to change yourself. As we change and develop our own consciousness, we become a part of the process of collective consciousness change. In addition, we are free to move to a different "reality" where the collective consciousness is more in line with our evolving perceptions. Ultimately, this shift brings us farther and farther into mystical alignment with Divine Oneness.

The principles defined and discussed in this book are designed to help you develop your potential for perceiving and operating within mystical reality and to thereby relate more fully and successfully to life. Aligning with these laws can enable you to move beyond relating to Divine Source as being external; they empower all of us to remember and feel that Spirit is internal. It is who we are. Pain and suffering may be universal, but they are not the only option. It is certainly not the point of life.

Yogananda said, "This world, existing in God's suggestion of a relativity of time and space, is merely a condensed thought of God. The wonder I behold is that everything in this universe God has created out of nothing but his own dream, his own ideations."

In *Doors of Perception*, Aldous Huxley defined the human brain as a reducing chamber, in as much as it enables us to limit the vast lumber of phenomena that are constantly bombarding our senses. These limits provide us the opportunity to be more in control of our environment, but they simultaneously limit our consciousness. Our challenge as mystics, and as people of consciousness, is to expand this chamber and to allow more perceptions and levels of realization into our point of awareness. Remaining in touch with the consensus reality of the collective consciousness at the same time ensures our continued material-plane security, even as we aspire to greater awareness.

Recent research in astronomy and physics has led to a theory, based on mathematical calculations, that has altered the scientific understanding and definition of reality. According to the research, we live in a multidimensional universe. Accordingly, some scientists have posited that there could be as many as twelve totally different dimensions, perhaps more. They call these dimensions "branes," which is short for membranes. The idea is that each brane is self-contained. All of the physical laws that we know to exist in our dimension also exist in and enclose each of the twelve branes. However, since they are all self-contained, there is no physical awareness of or interaction with other branes. There could be one or more passing right through your living room as you are reading this book, but it would be invisible to you, as you would be to the beings living in that brane. It is in this sense that we could assume that other branes are as real as our own and that the beings who reside there have a focus and a function as do we. It is possible that the molecules in other branes move faster and are less dense than those in our own. But it is also possible that however physically self-contained each brane may be, they are all permeable to consciousness. Someday, therefore, we might be able to communicate with beings in other branes, as they might with us.

By extension, it is possible that in at least one of those branes, the beings who live there love us, take care of us, guide us, and exist to provide direction for our healing and growth. Perhaps they are our ancestors. Perhaps they are our guardian angels. Perhaps beings from others branes are the so-called aliens who have understood and learned how to work with the laws of time and space so that they can pass between branes at will. They could be periodically spotted in spaceships (which would actually be "dimension" ships) as they pass from their brane to ours. Perhaps the brane that a person enters upon leaving the body and the earth plane is determined by his karma, his degree of consciousness development, and his personal advancement. Ultimately, the beings of the more evolved branes—however we might characterize or define them—could serve to help us grow so that we will eventually wake up and realize the true nature of who we are: unlimited manifestations of the Divine Source of creation.

It is possible that from the beginning of human consciousness, our ancestors were in touch with these beings. Perhaps the original amorphous entities that hovered around this planet were able to freely move between dimensions. Indigenous people still practicing their traditional culture today often make contact with the ancestors and, perhaps, beings from other branes, through ceremonial ritual. They use ceremonial art and dance as tools to maintain connection with their departed loved ones and wise ones who are, in turn, conduits to beings of still more expanded consciousness.

As noted in chapter 1, "The Law of Creativity," the initial state of the primitive human mind was totally coincident with Oneness. The first beings on or around this planet were ethereal; that is, they actually had no bodies at all. They existed as pure consciousness and were able to create with thought alone. In this state they were free to create whatever they chose. They existed within "the ideations" of God and, as such, flowed with the same limitless creative potential. This freedom to create is one quality that has remained as everything else has changed. As noted above, as the earth became more dense, so did the beings that inhabited it, while maintaining the free will that was used previously to remain in divine creativity. Eventually, some of these beings became totally corporeal, identifying more with their body and its potential than with their mind and its potential. Now, even though most, if not all, of the potential to create limitlessly with the mind and will alone has been lost, we still have the ability to exercise our free will. The questions remain: in what way and to what end?

Early humans, and indigenous people to this day, did not experience any sense of separateness between themselves and the world around them. Everything was perceived or felt to be part of the same living organism, and people were considered to be part of the natural environment. People were born, lived, and died without any sense of individuation. Through time, as cultures and people became more individuated, the intimate connection to the Divine became fractured and, in most cases, lost. The stories and myths that evolved could have been attempts to maintain a sense of connection to Oneness as the day-to-day human experience moved farther from it.

For example, in the West, the story about the origin of human life that is best known is the biblical story of Adam and Eve in the Garden of Eden. The Garden of Eden was a magical place in which everything was provided to the original couple so that they might live in peace and harmony with each other and their environment. This couple lived there in divine consciousness, not differentiating the spiritual from the earthbound, as both of these realms offered the experience of joyful interconnection. There was no self-awareness or sense of individuation; hence, no sense of duality. Adam and Eve's potential to create was as open and limitless as original Source because they perceived that there was, and is, no separation from that Source. This is a similar state maintained by the "ancient ones" spoken of in cultures throughout the world. The "fall" was a result of Adam and Eve's becoming more identified with material desires and sensual gratification. They voluntarily left the consciousness of unity, pursuing the physical. They weren't evicted by a vengeful and angry father-God. Although there are strict principles that govern our universe, it is the exercise of our free will that determines our experience. If we act in accordance with those rules, the result is harmony with life. If we act in ways that are counter to those laws, any pain we experience after those acts is a direct result of our choice to act apart from the principles and not because a vengeful deity wants us to suffer. The laws are there to help us achieve the enlightenment of Christ consciousness. Not following them restricts us to mundane consciousness.

In this sense, therefore, we are still in the Garden. We never left. The potential to be present within a context of consciousness that integrates the physical with the nonphysical as one continuous energy flow remains available to all of us. Yet the consciousness and priorities of most human beings are such that we no longer perceive life in terms of Unity and in terms of the abundance that exists for us to cultivate, sustain, enjoy, and share. When we allow ourselves to become completely absorbed in our temporary body and its physical desires, we lose track of our eternal spiritual being and the quest for reintegration with Source. If, however, our intention is be a conscious caretaker of the beauty and resources of the earth (including our own bodies) in a way that prioritizes the greatest good for the planet and its inhabitants, we have greater potential to experience material sustenance and satisfaction, and spiritual growth and consciousness development is ours.

The story of humanity's evolution from the spiritual to the physical is universal. The Hindu account of the symbolic first man and woman is called the Srimad Bhagavata. In this story, the original people were Svayambhuva Manu ("man born of the Creator") and his wife, Shatarupa ("having a hundred images or forms"). The offspring of this couple intermarried with Prajapatis, who were perfect celestial beings who took physical forms to become the progenitors of mankind. These beings maintained their divine consciousness (or "Eden") and returned to Spirit or the heavenly realms after a blissful sojourn on earth. They maintained the awareness of their eternal and inseparable connection to oneness. Feelings of joy and fulfillment were part of that connection. The "fallen beings" were the ones who prioritized physical attachments and material desires and thus became enveloped in endless cycles of reincarnation. Their perceptions and consciousness eventually alienated them from Oneness. Even though people had "left the garden," it wasn't necessarily a choice made in consciousness of its ramifications. In time, they found themselves feeling (as most people do today) as if they were outside the divine realm. The quest for material gratification left them (and us) with psychological trauma, emotional fear, and feelings of spiritual abandonment.

The story of the Srimad Bhagavata describes what could well have been an actual human experience prior to the beginning of human culture. The price we are paying for our tools and the ability to successfully (if dangerously) manipulate our environment is spiritual alienation. This separation, accelerated with the advent of agriculture and animal husbandry, is discussed in chapter 11.

Once people fully shifted away from the nomadic life, they lost conscious contact with the beings of other realms and with their own ability to move freely between different stages of consciousness. As their true spiritual nature faded from their experience, they no longer perceived themselves as being "in the garden." They saw life as a duality; that is, they perceived themselves as being separate from each other, and most felt separate from the Divine as well.

It is doubtless that there were and still are people who have sought or been selectively brought into mystical initiation. These people were able to be conduits that connected others to transcendent states of consciousness and to the beings that reside in them (could they be brane beings?). Most contemporary cultures, however, have devalued the experience and knowledge of the mystic or the shaman. Uninitiated people tend to compensate for their alienation by projecting their unowned and unconscious spiritual potential onto images of deities, whom they conceive of as being more powerful than they are. These images may have led to the development of myths and stories that taught our ancestors important concepts about the nature of life. These projections often led to the creation of external beings who had to be propitiated in order to earn their favors and, in particular, the means of physical survival itself. There is, after all, no sense in becoming attached to the material plane and all of its properties if there is no way to maintain those attachments. So, in the face of overwhelming odds, challenging environments, predators, invaders, and the ever-present need to eat, humans developed and refined rituals and ceremonies that created and connected them to beings greater than themselves—beings who could help provide the means of defense and survival as well as the meaning of life itself.

Thus were born the gods and goddesses recognized by the so-called pagan cultures. One might ask if these deities were created by the human mind out of necessity, or if they were actually projections of their unowned and long-forgotten inherent power and spiritual connectedness. Or, did these deities or higher beings actually exist in an unbroken continuum with the initial creation? If so, the myths and pagan rituals might have represented a way to reconnect with those who did not choose to identify with the physical plane and who remained inseparably connected to Oneness.

Mythic stories evolved over time about the origins of the deities, about the way in which the indigenous cultures developed, and about what humans had to do to stay in their god's good graces. Some pagan cultures still seek to make direct and personal contact with the beings of their immediate environment, the nature spirits. These cultures seem to yearn to remain connected to aspects of the ancient human experience that now remain only in mythic form, having come from the deepest recesses of human history.

Another theory about the origin of the deities was posited in the twelfth century AD by the Persian sheik Sohravardi, who wrote of a place called Na-koja-abad. This roughly translates as "No-where," and it is the equivalent to the Buddhists referral to God as "No-thing." It doesn't mean nonexistence; it simply means that it cannot be defined in a limited, linear sense. Na-koja-abad is not a place like New York or Europe. Its existence can only be discerned in a visionary state. We must use our imaginative consciousness or cognitive imagination to become aware of it. For this reason Na-koja-abad, and places like it, has been spoken of as an "imaginal" realm. Perhaps these realms are similar to branes. Beings inhabit them, as humans live on earth, but with one significant difference.

They are not identified with the physical properties of their realm but rather have remained connected in consciousness to the Creator.

When we use our visionary, mystical potential to arrive in an imaginal realm, we find it to be a place of initiation, and to do so we must leave the world of sensory experience. Part of the initiation involves bathing in a mystical spring through which we find the meaning of true reality. Emerging from the spring, we have the ability to re-access Oneness with Creator. The beings we connect with on our journey to the imaginal can be thought of as spirit guides. In this sense, the pagan gods and goddesses may be renderings of these guides. Thus, in the context of the universal Law of Eternal Life, when a person chooses to become initiated, leaving one state of consciousness for another, or when a soul leaves its body at the end of an earth incarnation, it could ascend to one of the imaginal realms.

As discussed in chapter 2, "The Law of Survival," the female was originally, from the dawn of humanity, perceived as the source of life and family. By extension, this led to the female being perceived as the prime deity. Humans are born from women and therefore our roots, individually as well as collectively, trace back to the female. When a woman experiences physical pain and risks death through childbirth, she also acts as a direct channel for the creative power of the Divine. With the birth of the child she can also experience the power of love that is the prime mover of all creation. With the rise of agriculture, the male ascended to power. He was bigger and stronger, more capable of seizing and defining a plot of arable soil as his own, and defending it while the crops grew and the harvest was stored. The physical prowess previously necessary for hunting started to be used in a different way. Men began to assume the role of "source," as in source of survival. With the means of physical survival at hand, men could remain around the home, rather than spending days looking for game. Women were no longer valued as the sustainers of the home and the bearers of children and hence, the actual source of life in human form. Instead, they began to be seen as possessions and as a form of wealth, capable of contributing sons to help the father maintain the family plot but not having intrinsic value beyond that. The more women, the more children. The more children, the more land. The more land, the more power. This pattern continues to this day.

This shift also parallels the pattern of development of human consciousness. Originally the female-oriented society supported a matriarchal cosmology that resulted from an intuitive perception of reality and a sense of Oneness within a benevolent, nurturing, interconnected reality and social order. The relationship of the matriarchal culture to the Divine might have been through conscious contact with beings in the imaginal realm, in which case there would have been great value placed on the ability to perceive reality through intuition and receptivity, qualities that tend to be more highly developed in women. The prime deity was conceived as the great goddess. As time went by, and agriculture developed, the needs and realities of the human experience changed. Logic, the linear perspective and the ability to physically control elements of the material plane, became more highly valued than the ability to tune in to and communicate with beings in other realms. Society became more male-dominated and became supported cosmologically by a patriarchal and warlike deity. The prime deity became defined as the Heavenly Father.

It is important to realize that this shift from goddess to God wasn't something that was just foisted on women through the sheer dominance and force of the male body and mind. Both men and women were complicit in it. Men are more able to control the physical world, and women can benefit from that control by being protected from hostile elements. For those who descended from beings who valued the material over the spiritual, this was a natural extension of that decision.

The challenge that humanity confronts today is that of understanding the consciousness that led to, allowed, and supported male dominance and of moving beyond it. It is time for consciousness to collectively evolve again, as this is the only way that we can retrieve our divine birthrights. The prime Source is sexless. As soon as it is assigned a gender, it ceases to be the One and becomes merely a reflection of the duality.

As stated in "The Law of Both/And," chapter 3, our world is involved in a constant struggle between tribes, cultures, and religions. We have responded to our alienation from Oneness with war as well as exploitation of other people and our environment. Ultimately, this led to a fear-based proclivity to champion the dominant "alpha male" who became the embodiment of the wrathful God. At the same time, we have developed a highly sophisticated rational mind that has, in true God-like fashion, created an endless series of intellectual and material concepts and comforts. We have also used our creative intellect to generate more sophisticated ways of killing each other. Yet we also have the ability and potential to develop the consciousness of who we are and who we could be. This can be both individually and collectively in order to recover the awareness of the divine reality in which we live. We can do this while still consciously choosing the quality and nature of the physical and social elements of our reality.

The ancient awareness has, in fact, survived, although it is veiled to most. Through mystical teachings in all cultures throughout history, the potential to connect with those in the imaginal realms, and hence to experience the internal divine, has remained an option. In one form or another, we can be consciously involved in the process of a personal transformation that opens the door of our individual consciousness to reintegrate with Divine Oneness. Despite the density of today's consumeristic, materialistic culture, these teachings have remained available, if often underground. In the West, the teachings have typically been hidden by dogmatic rituals established by organized religions. Some of the practices that are still available to us are yoga, and the rituals of ancient Egypt or Western paganism (the "real" old-time religion). Some people tune in to the mystical by following enlightened masters such as Jesus; there are those who suggest that Jesus's real mission and message was to share the tools and techniques of the transformation of consciousness from the mundane to the Divine. Others posit that Jesus was an adept in the mystical school of the Sacred Feminine. In any case, Jesus's true mission of reestablishing our consciousness in the Divine has been misinterpreted by people who either lacked his consciousness or deliberately used his magnetism and the universal appeal of a divinely inspired person for their own political and financial gain.

Our challenge in the twenty-first century is to utilize the universal Law of Both/And to develop our consciousness beyond duality, so that we may rediscover our unity. We can use the teachings of any or all the great masters, gurus, saints, and bodhisattvas as tools and vehicles of transformation. Humanity had defined the prime deity as female and created a culture that supported that premise. It has also defined the prime deity as male and created a culture that supported that premise. History suggests that neither is the way. We have the opportunity as well as the responsibility to move human consciousness along by learning where we have been, defining where we want to go, and working with the universal laws available to us to help us get there.

Understanding the nature of the laws defined and described in this book can be useful to anyone who has a sincere desire to be an agent of consciousness evolution. We are at a unique point in human history. Ordinary people can access and utilize these ancient mystical principles to further both their own evolutionary development of consciousness and to help maintain the viability of human life. Ultimately, the proper, consistent, conscious employment of these laws will enable us to rediscover the Divine within. Like the masters, we too can experience life as Oneness.

One aspect of this process can best be realized by employing the universal Law of the Eternal Present, which enables us to remain in the eternal Oneness of the "garden" as we are simultaneously aware of our immediate needs, feelings, and relationships. As we evolve into a more realized state, the perception and experience of duality dissolves. So all that is left is the One. This process involves watching the interplay between Oneness and duality until eventually, only Oneness remains. This is the dance of the eternal and the relative—the eternal being the embodiment of light; relativity existing in a realm of shadows.

Physical attachments have fostered spiritual alienation, yet the human body is not a bad thing. Its desires should be seen in their proper perspective. Its highest use is as a vehicle for achieving realization. Using the body judiciously can be a wonderful asset in our quest. The Buddha believed that the only way to experience enlightenment is in an embodied state. In addition, our feelings are not things to be avoided or overlooked. By turning within, we can re-access Source and our place in the divine order.

The Bhagavad-Gita refers to the days and nights of Brahman. Brahman is the totality, the fundamental spark of being. It is said that Brahman creates God. The days and nights refer to an eternal dance of alternating periods of cosmic inertia and activity. At the dawn of Brahman's day, all creation is reborn and emerges from the state of nonmanifestation. At the dusk, heralding Brahman's night, all creation sinks into the sleep of nonmanifestation" (VIII: 3, 17–18).

This is very similar to another modern theory of physics (the first is branes). The concept is that prior to the big bang, which created the physical universe as we know it, all matter existed in the form of a single dot. The density of that dot is beyond comprehension. The dot was all there was: it contained everything that would become galaxies, solar systems, planets, and the life inhabiting them. It was the center of life and being, but it was unmanifested, similar to Brahman's night. The big bang began Brahman's day. At this moment, the dot expanded to an infinite number of forms. All form had been the dot and hence, everything that physically exists now is the center of being. It is the manifestation and the manifestor. All things contain within them everything that is, just as everything that is reflects and contains all manifestation. The universe is a hologram. That's who and where we are now—seemingly fractured in the forms of duality, when in fact we are all still at the center.

On the scale of human consciousness, this mirrors the alternating point of focus between unity and relativity, between impermanence and permanence. The goal is to be simultaneously aware of the pulse of life as it creates and flows through all manifestation (permanence), while also paying attention to the responsibilities we have chosen to accept and the desires that brought us back into physical form in the first place (impermanence). This, of course, implies that desires are not restricted to physical manifestation. Our soul is eternal. Even when discarnate, the experiences and choices made by a soul during incarnation are known by that being. The challenge is working to satisfy the desires while simultaneously remaining mindful of our eternal or spiritual being.

Through such integration, we arrive at a true union with Source. We become aware of who we are and where we are from. As we feel and embrace that connection, we begin to feel genuine, unconditional love, the essence of life itself. We experience it surrounding and filling us, and we know that that is the basis of life. Love is the ever-flowing fountain that feeds, sustains, and guides us. Feeling that connection, the universal Law of Love seems to be the law most essential in enabling us to realize our nature and birthright as human beings. Love is the highest priority. It is the point and purpose of life. The point is not material productivity, not propitiation of an external god, not personal gratification or recognition. Through the melding of opposites, the real purpose of the whole experience of life becomes obvious. We are not here simply to enjoy ourselves by gathering and hoarding the most stuff. We are part of a never-ending chain in which the primal juice of life, love, is to be experienced to the greatest degree possible. It must also be shared with others in ways that put their needs and feelings into high focus. Quantum physicists put forward the idea that life is a continuum of creativity. The metaphysicians theorize that what motivates creation at the most fundamental and the most exalted levels is love.

From the place of heart-centered consciousness, we can relate to our fellow beings with humility, as in the universal Law of Service. When we are truly connected to Source we feel self-contained. From this place it is easy to serve as we put others' interests before our own. We function as conscious co-creators with the Divine by being accommodating and adaptable to the requirements of any time and place, and feel uplifted by performing tasks that make others' lives more functional or healthy. What makes our efforts to serve viable is that we don't sacrifice ourselves or our own needs and interests in order to be helpful to others.

Continuing along the wheel of laws, invoking the universal Law of Harmony, we realize that changes in our personal consciousness, as with any shift in the collective consciousness, can be done in a graceful way, with congeniality and consideration of others. Striving for harmony can help create the balance necessary to continue surviving in our physical environment. We further ourselves on the path to Oneness by living a balanced life, in which we successfully integrate the physical with the spiritual and the emotional with the mental. We also need to pay attention in our acts of service in relationship to others, to ensure that what we do for them is balanced by what we do for ourselves. It follows that we allow others to also do for us in a healthy way. By extension, when we care for life, life takes care of us.

The deepest and most primal fear that plagues people is death which is, in turn, based on our attachments—to our bodies, our families, our status, our possessions, our memories, our self-concept, and our experiences. Since our stay here on earth is very short, to attach to anything that is derived from and remains in the physical plane does not ultimately lead to happiness. Attachment to the impermanent realm of the physical can be overcome by developing a deep understanding and intuitive connection to the Law of Eternal Life. This state of consciousness provides a sense of security and well-being that elements of the physical plane cannot provide. When we realize the security that comes from understanding our place in the universal scheme, we can relax. Fear is gone, worry abandoned, insecurity seen for the illusion that it is.

In this state of peace we can become aware of the wealth that is available to us through the Law of Abundance. We can experientially remember that we are still in the Garden. Everything we need is right here. We may need to work at learning how to access it and to be patient with the process. Yogananda taught that God is shy. The Source of life does not impose itself upon us—it waits patiently for us to open up, with clear and persistent intention, before it reveals itself. With patience, we wait for Spirit. The Principle of Abundance teaches us to be optimistic in anticipation and grateful in response to the experience of self-realization or Christ consciousness. This creates a joyful attitude through which to experience and express ourselves.

When we pursue a mystical connection to Source, our level of consciousness, our consideration of others, our integrity, and the clarity with which we identify our goals are all important factors. These will all play a part in determining the results of our experience. The Law of Karma is the ultimate expression of empowerment and freedom. The degree of personal responsibility that we willingly take on and discharge will determine our success in achieving our goals. What we put into our experience determines what we get out of it. This eliminates the need for external projections. We are not innocent victims waiting to be saved by some larger-than-life being. We are free to change whatever we don't like about ourselves and our circumstances, because we are the ones who created our reality in the first place.

The Law of Impermanence compliments the Law of Karma. It teaches that nothing lasts forever. If we don't like our circumstances, we can just wait around for them to change—and they will. But if we don't take an active interest in and responsibility for what we've done and are doing, it could get worse. If, however, we are willing to accept personal responsibility for our condition and apply the laws consciously and consistently, we can work toward creating a better life. We work with the Law of Impermanence to change what we don't like about our lives—internal or external, social or emotional, physical or spiritual—and thereby generate a more desirable, fulfilling reality.

The Law of Transcendence offers us our reward for following the previous eleven tenets. It holds the ultimate potential of the mystical state: that of moving beyond the ego-identified self into the divine identification with Self. It enables us to transcend the personal love that might be felt for our partner and family into the divine love felt for all manifestations. It enables us to realize that the power, the creativity, the joy, and the unconditional love of the universe is available at all times. We can then share these qualities with others or simply allow them to percolate within ourselves. Whatever we do when we access these qualities, our perceptions of life are forever altered. We see all people as our brothers and sisters by tuning in to the spark of light in their eyes and relating to them accordingly.

We feel the eternal flow of the life force permeating through and beyond all manifestation. Our perception of reality surpasses the impermanent realm of the material. We are uplifted and inspired by the fundamental light of being as it brings joy and oneness into our own lives. Ultimately, we perceive life itself as the eternal flow of interconnected oneness. There is nothing else.

The universal laws together comprise a template for how to live our lives as conscious, seeking beings. They exist as reminders to each of us that the universe truly is an integrated whole. Each individual manifestation carries within it the seed of this whole. The seed is light, and as light beings, we are cocreators of heaven and earth. This process is ongoing. We can ask ourselves, what form and quality of life do we want to manifest and live within? These can, in turn, become the bylaws of life by which we—and ultimately, all people—relate and by which all nations establish their rules.

The universe wants us to be happy. We have been created in love with the purpose of reintegrating with Oneness through this love. The joy and bliss that we experience when we effectively and successfully work with these laws is part of our birthright and what the ultimate purpose of life is. The laws help us seek greater awareness of life and the truth of being. They each stand on their own, yet also work cumulatively and synergistically. As we become more comfortable with understanding and applying them, they can become rules to live by that continually enhance the quality of our lives.

One day, as I was reading a newspaper, my three-year-old grandson was playing nearby with toy cars. He moved the cars around the base of my chair and then in and around each of its legs. Suddenly, he looked up at me and asked, "Grandpa, are we people, or are we God?" Hiding my surprise at his precociousness, I spontaneously responded, "I think that we are God." He said, "I think so, too" and continued playing with his cars.

> Affirmation: "In Divine Light in the Center of Life
> I express gratitude and prayers of thanksgiving
> For all my blessings.

In Divine Light in the Center of Life
I call upon and acknowledge all beings whose consciousness is greater than mine
To guide me to the realization of my own Divinity.

In Divine Light in the Center of Life
I sing Praise for the Oneness
To whom all praise is due."

The enlightened mind is the true nature of our minds. It is the utmost peaceful, joyful, omniscient state of the mind, free from the self-limiting conditions of dualistic discriminations and emotional afflictions. It is the ultimate nature of the mind of every being. The fully enlightened mind sees things openly, without the usual duality of a subject and an object or the usual discriminations of liking happy experiences and disliking painful one. Since everything is realized "as one," the vista of perception opens up without limits. Space is boundless, time is timeless, and the restrictions of the past, present, and future are recognized as mere designations imposed by the conceptual mind.

—Tulku Thondup, *Boundless Healing*

Bibliography

Armstrong, Karen. *A History of God*. New York: Ballantine Books, 1993.

Bethards, Betty. *The Dream Book*. Inner Light Foundation, 2001.

The Holy Bible, King James Version. Wichita, KS: Heirloom Bible Publishing.

Bonder, Rabbi Milton. *The Kabbalah of Money*. Boston: Shambala, 1996.

Buddha. *The Teaching of Buddha*. Tokyo, Japan: Buddhist Promoting Foundation, 1996.

Cahill, Thomas. *The Gifts of the Jews*. New York: Anchor Books, 1998.

Campbell, Joseph. *The Power of Myth*. New York: Doubleday, 1988.

Chaseling, Wilbur. *Yulengor, Nomads of Arnhem Land*. London: Epworth Press, 1957.

Durant, Will. *Our Oriental Heritage*. New York: Simon and Schuster, 1954.

Eisler, Rianne. *The Chalice and the Blade*. San Francisco: Harper and Row, 1988.

Grant, Michael. *Myths of the Greeks and Romans*. New York: Mentor Books, 1962.

Grof, Stanislav. *The Adventure of Self-Discovery*. State University of New York Press, 1988.

Hall, Manley Palmer. *The Secret Teachings of All Ages*. Los Angeles: Philosophical Research Society, 1971.

Hamilton, Edith. *Mythology*. New York: Mentor Books, 1940.

Hill, Napoleon. *Think and Grow Rich*. Hollywood: Wilshire Book Co, 1966.

Hitchcock, Susan Tyler and Esposito, John L. *The Geography of Religion*. National Geographic, 2007.

Howard, David. *Sacred Journey*. New York: Taschen, 2007.

Isaacs, Jennifer. *Australian Dreaming, 40,000 Years of Aboriginal History*. Sydney: Landsdowne Press, 1980.

King, Serge. *Kahuna Healing*. Wheaton, IL: Theosophical Publishing House, 1983.

The Koran. London: Penguin Books, 1999.

Lao Tzu. *Tao Te Ching*. London: Penguin Books, 1970.

Martin, Joel and Romanowski, Patricia. *We Don't Die*. New York: Berkley Books, 1988.

Moody, Raymond. *Reflections on Life after Life*. New York: Bantam Books, 1977.

Newton, Michael, *Journey of Souls,* St. Paul, Minnesota, Llewellyn Publications, 1995.

Patanjali. *How to Know God, The Aphorisms of Patanjali*. New York: Mentor Books, 1953.

Ram Dass. *Remember, Be Here Now*. New York: Crown Publishing Group, 1978.

Roob, Alexander. *Alchemy and Mysticism*. Taschen Books, 2001.

Smith, Sir William. *Smaller Classical Dictionary*. New York: Dutton, 1958.

Talbot, Michael. *The Holographic Universe*. Harper Perennial, 1992.

Tolle, Eckhart. *The Power of Now*. Novato, CA: New World Library, 2004.

Trinklein & Huffer. *Modern Space Science*. New York: Holt, Rinehart, Winston, 1961.

Tulku, Chagdud. *Gates of Buddhist Practice*. Junction City, CA: Padma Publishing, 2001.

Welch, Thomas. *Taoism*. Boston: Beacon Press, 1975.

Wolf, Fred Alan. *Taking the Quantum Leap*. New York: Harper & Row, 1989.

Yogananda, Paramahansa. *The Autobiography of a Yogi*. Los Angeles: Self-Realization Fellowship.

Yogananda, Paramahansa. *The Bhagavad-Gita*. Los Angeles: Self-Realization Fellowship.

Paramahansa, Yogananda. *Man's Eternal Quest*. Los Angeles: Self-Realization Fellowship.

Paramahansa, Yogananda. *Sayings of Yogananda*. Los Angeles: Self-Realization Fellowship.

Paramahansa Yogananda. *The Second Coming of Christ*. Los Angeles: Self-Realization Fellowship.

Paramahansa, Yogananda. *Whispers From Eternity.* Los Angeles: Self-Realization Fellowship.

CPSIA information can be obtained at www.ICGtesting.com
Printed in the USA
LVOW130935030313

322423LV00001B/129/P